RAND

National Defense Re

T0154937

CHARACTERIZING THE FUTURE DEFENSE WORKFORCE

DINA G. LEVY

HARRY J. THIE

ALBERT A. ROBBERT

SCOTT NAFTEL

CHARLES CANNON

RUDY EHRENBERG

MATTHEW GERSHWIN

Prepared for the
Office of the Secretary of Defense

The research described in this report was sponsored by the Office of the Secretary of Defense (OSD). The research was conducted in RAND's National Defense Research Institute, a federally funded research and development center supported by the OSD, the Joint Staff, the unified commands, and the defense agencies under Contract DASW01-01-C-0004.

Library of Congress Cataloging-in-Publication Data

Characterizing the future defense workforce / Dina G. Levy ... [et al.].
    p. cm.
    "MR-1304."
    Includes bibliographical references.
    ISBN 0-8330-2965-7
    1. United States—Armed Forces—Occupational specialties. 2. United States—Armed Forces—Civilian employees—Classification. I. Levy, Dina G.

    UB337 .C43 2001
    355.3'0973—dc21

                        2001020494

RAND is a nonprofit institution that helps improve policy and decisionmaking through research and analysis. RAND® is a registered trademark. RAND's publications do not necessarily reflect the opinions or policies of its research sponsors.

Published 2001 by RAND
1700 Main Street, P.O. Box 2138, Santa Monica, CA 90407-2138
1200 South Hayes Street, Arlington, VA 22202-5050
RAND URL: http://www.rand.org/
To order RAND documents or to obtain additional information,
contact Distribution Services: Telephone: (310) 451-7002;
Fax: (310) 451-6915; Internet: order@rand.org

The Director for Manpower and Personnel, J1, the Joint Staff, has had a long-standing interest in the types of service personnel who will be needed in the future and whether they will be different from past personnel. As a result, the research reported here has been sponsored by three successive incumbents in that office. The Deputy Assistant Secretary of Defense for Civilian Personnel Policy also became interested in how change in the defense environment might affect the defense civil service workforce and became an additional sponsor of the research. In response to these interests, RAND developed a study that addressed both military and civilian workforces.

This report provides our assessment of the change in levels of work (generalized work activities and work context) and worker characteristics (knowledge, skills, and abilities) that will be needed in the environment visualized in the Joint Staff's *Joint Vision 2010* (JCS, 1995). Study findings should be of interest to military personnel managers, analysts, and policymakers. In particular, those involved in occupational analysis and management, training, and education will find the detailed data included in appendices of interest. The appendices also contain details about our conceptual approach, which should be of more interest to the analytical community.

This research was conducted for the Under Secretary of Defense for Personnel and Readiness and for the Joint Staff within the Forces and Resources Policy Center of RAND's National Defense Research Institute (NDRI). NDRI is a federally funded research and development center sponsored by the Office of the Secretary of Defense, the Joint Staff, the unified commands, and the defense agencies.

CONTENTS

FIGURES

During the early 1990s, the Department of Defense (DoD) began to change its focus from the Cold War to pursue more diverse missions. Questions arose about how future changes in military missions, organizations, and technology would affect the nature of military work and the characteristics of the military and civilian members of the DoD workforce.

To address these questions, RAND undertook an occupational-level analysis of the effects of the future environment on the characteristics of DoD work and workers. The occupational framework chosen for this analysis is the Department of Labor's Occupational Information Network (O*NET). Each occupation is rated on 232 dimensions spread across five domains: generalized work activities, work context, knowledge, skills, and abilities. To make the O*NET framework more relevant to the DoD workforce and to reduce the number of occupational groupings to a manageable level, RAND transformed O*NET's 1,122 occupations, through a series of crosswalks and cluster analyses, to 46 occupational clusters.

To contrast the characteristics of future work and workers against those of the past (as represented in the available O*NET database), RAND sought to obtain new rating scores on O*NET occupational dimensions, predicated on a general description of the future DoD environment. For a characterization of the future environment, we used *Joint Vision 2010* (JCS, 1995), a projection developed by the Joint Staff, and other related information. New rating scores were assigned by several groups of occupational analysts—some who work in military occupational analysis and some who participated in developing the original O*NET ratings. RAND then analyzed the differences between future and past scores to determine the dimensions in which significant change is expected. We highlighted changes within occupational clusters and those that occur more generally across military and civilian workforces.

On the whole, we find that despite the many changes anticipated in DoD processes as a result of the revolutions in military and business affairs, relatively small subsets of work and worker characteristics are expected to change. We predict no significant changes in worker abilities, a finding that implies that given existing selection and training processes, and given the workforce shaping and development tools available to DoD human resources managers, current and prospective workforces should be able to adapt to the expected changes. The changes anticipated in the remaining characteristics of work and workers separate into four broad themes: an enhanced service orientation, more advanced technical knowledge and skills, better problem-solving skills, and an increase in the need to stay current. We found evidence that these themes are consistent with ongoing change in the broader U.S. work environment outside of DoD.

ACKNOWLEDGMENTS

We wish to thank the many people who assisted us at important times in our research. Anita Lancaster and John Fowlkes of the Defense Manpower Data Center (DMDC) were the source of particularly useful information. George Nebeling of ASM Research, Inc. (a firm providing occupational data support to DMDC), provided invaluable assistance. They helped immeasurably by giving us access to DMDC's occupational databases and classification system crosswalks.

The Department of Labor (DoL), in the process of researching and implementing a new occupational system for the United States, allowed us to use its research and databases for our project. Kristen Fiske of the DoL O*NET project was particularly helpful. Jay Tartell of the Air Force Occupational Measurement Squadron, Dr. Jim Mitchell of the Institute for Job and Occupational Analysis, Dr. Don Drewes of North Carolina State University, and a large number of occupational analysts in their respective organizations generously contributed their time and talents toward generating a complete set of occupational ratings.

We thank Dr. Diane Disney and Dr. Larry Lacy in the Office of the Deputy Assistant Secretary of Defense for Civilian Personnel Policy for their support of this research and their feedback at all stages of the project. Similarly, we are grateful to BrigGen Pat Adams for his support. RAND colleagues Eric Derghazarian and Laura Zakaras contributed to the research. The project also benefited from thoughtful reviews by Roger Brown and Larry Hanser.

ACRONYMS

AB	Abilities
AFOMS	Air Force Occupational Measurement Squadron
AFSC	Air Force Specialty Code
DoD	Department of Defense
DMDC	Defense Manpower Data Center
DoL	Department of Labor
DOT	Dictionary of Occupational Titles
ETA	Employment and Training Administration, U.S. Department of Labor
GWA	Generalized Work Activities
HR	Human Resources
IJOA	Institute for Job and Occupational Analysis
JCS	Joint Chiefs of Staff
KN	Knowledge
MOC	Military Occupational Codes
MOS	Military Occupational Specialty
MOTD	Military Occupational Training Database

NCES	National Center for Education Statistics, U.S. Department of Education
NCSU	North Carolina State University
NDRI	National Defense Research Institute
ODB	Occupational Data Base
O*NET	Occupational Information Network
OOTW	Operations Other Than War
OPM	U.S. Office of Personnel Management
OSD	Office of the Secretary of Defense
SK	Skills
WC	Work Context

Chapter One

INTRODUCTION

BACKGROUND

During the early 1990s, the Department of Defense (DoD) began to change its focus from the Cold War to multiple contingencies of various sizes and scope. Even as the military services got smaller, they were increasingly asked to pursue more diverse missions. Questions arose about how current and future changes would affect the nature of military work and the characteristics of successful workers. Would the future warrior need to be significantly different from his Cold War counterpart?

Following publication of *Joint Vision 2010* (JCS, 1995), RAND was asked by the Director for Manpower and Personnel (J1) on the Joint Staff how the concepts elaborated there and in the succeeding implementation documents would affect both future military work and future personnel in the Army, Navy, Air Force, and Marine Corps. Shortly thereafter, the Deputy Assistant Secretary of Defense for Civilian Personnel Policy asked similar questions about the defense civil service workforce. Both were interested in learning about the specific ways that work and workers in existing occupations would need to change given the anticipated changes in future defense missions, organization, and technology outlined in *Joint Vision 2010*.

SCOPE

The scope of this workforce planning project was large. We were asked to provide answers for a workforce of 1.4 million active military and 800,000 defense civilians representing thousands of occupations described in at least seven defense occupational classification systems. Although we did not study the reserve components directly, changes projected for military work context and activities and for military personnel characteristics and attributes will affect them as well.

Sponsor direction limited the scope of the project in several ways. First, the sponsors wanted to understand the effect of *Joint Vision 2010* on the defense workforce, not the potential effects of multiple possible futures. This limited our focus to a single scenario for a period of time about 10 years distant. Second, we were not asked to address how the force structure might change in terms of the numbers of civilian or military workers. We were asked to focus on how characteristics of occupations and workers might change—an equally challenging but different task. Finally, the use of new tools and techniques in occupational analysis enabled us to condense existing data and collect new data more efficiently than was previously possible.

THREE KEY QUESTIONS

We identified the following three key questions whose answers would facilitate workforce planning for the year 2010:

- What changes in military missions, organizations, and technology are anticipated by 2010?

- To what extent will changes in military missions, organizations, and technology affect defense work context and activities?

- How will changes in work affect the desired characteristics of workers?

To answer each of these questions, our general strategy was to characterize both the past and the future state of affairs in each case and to compare the two to determine change. The focus of this study is on change, in detail, for work and the workforce under a *Joint Vision 2010* scenario compared to a Cold War environment.

APPROACH

Characterizing the Past and Future Contexts

We drew on a number of sources for our analysis. *Joint Vision 2010* (JCS, 1995) and its companion implementation plan provided assumptions about the future context. Other documents, such as the *Defense Planning Guidance* (Cohen, 1997), were used as supplements to help answer the first key question: What changes in military missions, organizations, and technology are anticipated by 2010? The past defense context was derived from comparable documents for earlier periods. Characterizations of the past and future environments derived from these sources are summarized in Table 1.1. This material provided the answer to the first of our three key questions and became the basis for answering the next two questions.

Characterizing Expected Changes in Work and Workers

In developing our approach to answering the second and third questions about changes in work and workers, we sought to avoid broad characterizations of the workforce that other studies have used and instead to identify a detailed and comprehensive model of work and workers for a wide range of occupations. We found these desired characteristics in the Occupational Information Network (O*NET), commissioned by the Department of Labor (DoL).

O*NET is a comprehensive system for collecting, organizing, describing, and disseminating data on job characteristics and worker attributes. It is both a classification and a description system. O*NET replaces DoL's *Dictionary of Occupational Titles* (DOT) and also provides a new conceptual framework that reflects the advanced technologies, adaptable workplace structures, and wide-ranging skills required by today's changing workplace. It contains information on work content and the context in which work is done as well as on the knowledge, skills, and abilities of workers (the domains of the database).[1]

---

[1]O*NET is sponsored by DoL's Employment and Training Administration with regional support provided by five Occupational Analysis Field Centers and four Assessment Research and Development Program Centers.

Table 1.1

Comparison of Past and Future Missions, Organization, and Technology

Past Missions	Future Missions
Single mission	Multiple missions
Primary focus on countering the other superpower	Multiple adversaries and global concerns
One vital interest	Multiple vital, nonvital, and humanitarian interests
One primary threat	Multiple threats and concerns (military and nonmilitary)
One primary location—Europe	Multiple locations worldwide
Objective of destruction	Objective of containment or peaceful resolution
Simple doctrine	Multiple doctrines
Preparation for warfighting	Preparation for peacekeeping and operations other than war (OOTW)
Secondary emphasis on other missions	Multiple and diverse missions
Clear distinction between friends and foes	Multiple allies and adversaries—and constantly changing
In-house support structure	Oversight of outsourced support
	Adoption of efficiency and effectiveness practices found in the private sector

Past Organization	Future Organization
OSD, JCS, and services	Same
Clearly defined roles for military and civilian, enlisted and officer	Overlapping roles
Clear historical allies	New, different, changing allies
Centralized planning and centralized execution	Centralized planning and decentralized execution
Hierarchical organization and rigid processes	Less hierarchical organization and fluid, flexible processes

Table 1.1 (continued)

Past Organization	Future Organization
	Increasing importance and role of unified commands
	More decentralized operations and support
Limited employment/deployment scenarios	Multiple scenarios and locations
Greater linkage between organizations and technology	Accelerates
Procedures and conditions clearer and more fixed	Procedures and conditions murkier, more flexible and changing
Clearer distinction between military and civilian	Less distinction; more civilians on or near the battlefield

Past Technology	Future Technology
More technology and greater effect have made the world a smaller place	Continues
Able to anticipate technological advances	Advances more difficult to anticipate
Wide range of technological diversity relative to potential adversaries	Greater parity in technology
Emphasis on nuclear weapons and military firepower	Many different instruments for resolving conflict (economics, etc.)
Weapons require increasing skill	Accelerates
Focus on weapons	Focus on management and support
	Increased reliance on information technology for precision engagement
	Increased reliance on information technology for focused logistics

We entered into an agreement with DoL to use O*NET materials as the basis of our occupational model, which gave us access to their research and to a database of occupational information.[2] Because the O*NET database provided both past data and a good framework, we chose to make use of the O*NET model and data-collection materials in our effort to collect data about the future.

Fifty-two occupational analysts provided ratings for the future. Eleven of them were graduate students in occupational analysis at North Carolina State University (NCSU), some of whom had participated in parts of the O*NET project. Thirty-five analysts from the Air Force Occupational Measurement Squadron (AFOMS)—17 civilian and 18 military personnel—also provided ratings. Finally, six civilian analysts from the Institute for Job and Occupational Analysis (IJOA) participated in the project. Twenty-five percent of the raters had prior experience working with O*NET.

We chose to use job analysts, as opposed to job incumbents or supervisors, as raters for a number of reasons. First, the information in the O*NET database was provided by occupational analysts, and given our intention to compare ratings of the future with ratings from the O*NET database, it seemed most sensible to use the same types of raters. Second, as noted in the *O*NET Final Technical Report* (1997), job analysts are commonly considered to be more objective in their consideration of job requirements, to have a broader perspective when evaluating those requirements, and to be more experienced in completing questionnaires covering multiple occupations. Given this perspective and our emphasis on changes across many occupations, job analysts emerged as the preferred choice over other potential raters with more specialized knowledge of a single occupation. Finally, several studies cited in the *O*NET Final Technical Report* have found high agreement between ratings obtained from analysts, incumbents, and supervisors.

The resulting dataset of past and future occupational ratings is large and comprehensive. Each combination of 232 O*NET occupational

---

[2]At the time we conducted our research, the O*NET database consisted of occupational ratings rendered by occupational analysts. DoL plans to release a richer database in the future, incorporating ratings by incumbents of the various occupations.

dimensions and 46 DoD occupational clusters was rated by between six and nine analysts, yielding over 80,000 independent data points and 10,672 mean change scores (differences between past ratings and mean future ratings on a specific dimension in a specific occupation).

It is important to note that earlier efforts to characterize the nature of work and workers needed in the future have consisted mainly of loosely framed general statements of expert opinion about future trends. Our approach results in a much larger collection of detailed judgments organized along a common set of comprehensive dimensions. This new approach has a number of advantages. First, analysts are forced to quantify their opinions, increasing their degree of precision and permitting reliable statistical analysis of the data. Second, the use of a common set of rating scales enables comparison across analysts. Finally, analysts must dissect their general opinions about the future and think about the implications for very specific characteristics of work and workers, occupation by occupation. This enhanced level of detail allows for explicit differentiation between aspects of work and workers that are different in subtle ways or that would not normally be separated in the analyst's mind. For these reasons, the data presented in this report comprise the most detailed and comprehensive collection of opinions about future defense work and workers reported to date.

Workforce Shaping and Development

Of course, once needed changes in work and workers are identified, DoD human resource (HR) managers might contemplate the kinds of shifts in workforce shaping and development tools needed to accommodate the expected changes. We therefore included a consideration of the ways in which tools such as classification, selection, promotion, training, education, compensation, acculturation, and retention might be used to bring about the changes identified in this study.

ORGANIZATION OF THE REPORT

Chapter Two provides the detailed methodology we used to answer the sponsors' questions and describes the characteristics of the data and our analysis. Chapter Three presents our findings regarding changes in selected occupational clusters and in selected characteristics of work and workers. This chapter also includes observations about the private sector trends in these characteristics. We offer our thoughts on workforce shaping and development in Chapter Four and conclusions and implications in Chapter Five. Several appendices provide additional detail about the analysis, in particular, details of our analysis for individual occupational clusters in each military service and in the defense civil service workforce.

Chapter Two

METHODOLOGY AND DATA CHARACTERISTICS

CHARACTERIZING PAST WORK AND WORKERS

As discussed in the introduction, comprehensive information on past work and workers was available to us through O*NET. We relied on O*NET's assessments to provide a reasonable baseline against which to compare expected future occupational requirements.

The O*NET Analyst Database

The O*NET Analyst Database contains quantitative ratings of the level, importance, and frequency of 232 work- and worker-related dimensions for 1,122 occupations. Occupational analysts and graduate students in industrial/organizational psychology participating in the O*NET Direct Rating Project provided the ratings captured in this database.

The work-related dimensions fall into two domains: generalized work activities (GWA) and work context (WC). Worker-related dimensions fall into three domains: knowledge (KN), skills (SK), and abilities (AB). These domains are described as follows (ETA, 1998):

- *Generalized work activities*: general types of job behaviors occurring on multiple jobs;

- *Work context*: physical and social factors that influence the nature of work, including interpersonal relationships, physical work conditions, and structural job characteristics;

- *Knowledge*: organized sets of principles and facts applying in general work settings;

- *Skills*: developed capacities to perform tasks, predicated, in part, on the individual's possession of relevant underlying abilities; and

- *Abilities*: enduring attributes of the individual that influence performance; regarded as traits in that they exhibit some degree of stability over relatively long periods of time.

Dimensions included within each domain are listed in Appendix A. Definitions of these dimensions can be found in O*NET materials. See, for example, the *O*NET 98 Data Dictionary* (ETA, 1998), available through the Internet at http://www.doleta.gov/programs/onet.

Although the general structure and content of the O*NET database were for the most part well suited to our purposes, changes and additions were necessary in several areas. First, the database was not structured along the lines of the defense workforce. To aid in our analysis, we restructured the data to reflect defense occupational classifications. Second, to make data collection manageable, we needed to reduce the number of ratings required for a comprehensive picture of the future defense workforce. The O*NET Direct Rating Project took place on a much larger scale than was permitted in this project. Finally, the O*NET database was missing data on purely military, combat-oriented occupations. We address each of these additions and changes in turn.

Importing O*NET Data into a Structure for the Defense Workforce

The effort to restructure past data and to allow analysis of the defense workforce required crosswalks through several occupational classification systems for military and civilian occupations. The objective was to place both military and civilian occupations in a common framework and to import available O*NET occupational ratings into this framework. We selected the Military Occupational Training Database (MOTD) as the common framework because crosswalks from the four services' military occupational classification structures were readily available.[1] The crosswalks are depicted in Figure 2.1.

For military occupations, ratings for the 232 dimensions in the O*NET database were assigned to corresponding military occupational codes (MOCs) for each service using an existing O*NET crosswalk.[2] In this step, 468 of the 1,122 O*NET occupations were matched to 5,300 MOCs.[3] Next, we used available crosswalks from the service MOCs to 141 occupations in the MOTD. In this second step, ratings were weighted according to the numbers of people in

RAND*MR1304-2.1-1100*

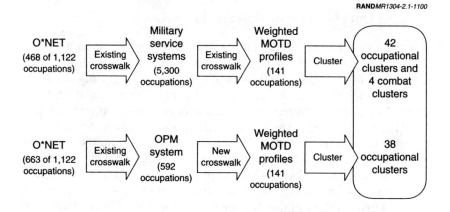

Figure 2.1—Crosswalks from the O*NET to Occupational Clusters for
Military and Civilian Occupations

---

[1]The MOTD is maintained by the Defense Manpower Data Center (DMDC) as part of the Occupational Data Base (ODB). The MOTD is the basis for a DoD publication called *Military Careers*, which was developed to help educators and youth learn about the many career opportunities the military has to offer. The MOTD contains descriptions of 141 aggregate enlisted and officer occupations that have common task, training, aptitude, and experience profiles. Crosswalks between various military and other occupational classification systems are part of the ODB.

[2]The MOCs are, for example, military occupational specialties (MOSs) or Air Force specialty codes (AFSCs).

[3]In the crosswalk from O*NET occupations to MOCs, for cases in which one O*NET occupation corresponded to multiple MOCs, the same O*NET rating was applied to all equivalent MOCs. The same procedure was followed in all cases where a crosswalk matched one occupation to many occupations.

each MOC and then combined to produce a single rating for an MOTD occupation.

An analogous route was followed in the case of civilian occupations, but the intermediate occupational categories used were taken from civil service occupational series established by the U.S. Office of Personnel Management (OPM). Here, 663 O*NET occupations corresponded to 592 civil service occupations found within DoD. In the second step of this transformation, we devised our own crosswalk to map the civil service occupations to the MOTD occupations.[4]

Making Data Collection Manageable

Even after restructuring the data as described above, the data-collection task was too large. We chose two of several options for reducing the scope of the task. First, we collected ratings on only the *level* scale for each dimension. Ratings of the level, importance, and frequency of dimensions tend to be highly correlated, and we were primarily interested in level, so we excluded the importance and frequency ratings from our analysis. Second, we conducted a cluster analysis to further reduce the number of occupational clusters to be evaluated. The cluster analysis produced 42 occupational clusters plus four clusters of combat specialties. All of these occupational clusters exist in the military services; 38 of them exist in the DoD civil service workforce. Appendix C contains a list of the 46 occupational clusters and the details of the cluster analysis.

Once the cluster analysis was completed, we created titles for the new occupational clusters based on the occupations they comprised and compiled new task lists from the MOTD and OPM database to reflect the occupations included in each cluster. The tasks chosen to represent occupations in the occupational cluster were based on the weighting of occupations in the cluster. That is, occupations with greater numbers of workers in them were given more weight in selecting tasks to describe the overall occupational cluster. The new

---

[4]These transformations underscore the multiplicity of job classification and description systems and of jobs themselves throughout DoD. We aggregated thousands of these jobs into 46 occupational clusters that met our analytical needs. We note that perhaps a concerted effort on the part of military and civilian managers could lead to a useful simplification of the multiple systems now in use.

occupational clusters, though broad, combined occupations that were highly similar in terms of their O*NET profiles.[5] Likewise, occupations falling in different occupational clusters exhibited little overlap in their O*NET profiles.

Appendices F through J contain listings of, respectively, the Army, Navy, Air Force, Marine Corps, and civil service occupations within each of the occupational clusters we created. Additionally, Appendix K contains a cross-reference index that can be used to determine the occupational cluster containing a given military or civil service occupation code.

CHARACTERIZING FUTURE WORK AND WORKERS

To generate ratings of future work and workers, analysts were given a general description of past and future work environments and asked to determine how differences between these environments might affect specific occupations.[6] Occupational clusters were assigned to analysts using a Latin square design. For each cluster to be rated, analysts were given a definition and list of tasks. Figure 2.2 shows the definition and task list for a sample cluster.[7]

Analysts used rating sheets like the one depicted in Figure 2.3 to record their ratings. This example was used to rate future levels for the 26 dimensions in the ability domain for the Administrative, Personnel, and Supply Specialists occupational cluster. The abilities dimensions are listed down the left column along with their past levels adapted from the O*NET Analyst Database. For each ability, analysts were instructed to assume that the past level was accurate and to judge whether the level of the ability would stay the same or

---

[5]Nevertheless, some analysts expressed concerns about combinations of occupations and of different positions (e.g., managerial compared to nonmanagerial) within those occupations.

[6]This material distinguished the Cold War environment that existed up to the late 1980s from the expected future environment described in *Joint Vision 2010*. Appendix A contains a summary of the changes in missions, organizations, and technology that were outlined in this material.

[7]Of course, as a result of the occupational clustering, analysts were able to predict change only at the level of the cluster, not at a more detailed level. So, in effect, occupations clustered together would be assumed to change in the same direction.

RAND*MR1304-2.2-1100*

ADMINISTRATIVE, PERSONNEL, AND SUPPLY SPECIALISTS

Definition

Administrative, Personnel, and Support Specialists record information, type reports, and maintain files to assist in the operation of organizations. They may specialize in personnel management, shipping and receiving, financial affairs, medical records, or other general administrative duties.

Task Statements

Administrative, Personnel, and Supply Specialists perform some or all of the following duties:

Type letters, reports, requisition (order) forms, and official documents

Organize and maintain information and files, including personnel records, budgetary files, and medical records

Enter and retrieve personnel and other information using computer terminals

Record details of financial transactions on accounting forms

Audit financial records

Provide information about personnel programs and career guidance to personnel

Assign personnel to jobs and schedule training and leave

Perform inventory and financial management procedures, including ordering, receiving, and storing supplies

Locate, catalog, move, and display stock

Figure 2.2—Definition and Task List for One Occupational Cluster

RAND*MR1304-2.3-1100*

ABILITIES				
Administrative, Personnel, and Supply Specialists	**Past Level**	**Future Level** *Whole Numbers*		
1 Oral Comprehension	3.7	0 ☐ Same	1 ☐ Change to:
2 Written Comprehension	3.7	0 ☐ Same	1 ☐ Change to:
3 Oral Expression	3.9	0 ☐ Same	1 ☐ Change to:
4 Written Expression	3.5	0 ☐ Same	1 ☐ Change to:
5 Fluency of Ideas	2.4	0 ☐ Same	1 ☐ Change to:
6 Originality	2.2	0 ☐ Same	1 ☐ Change to:
7 Problem Sensitivity	2.7	0 ☐ Same	1 ☐ Change to:
8 Deductive Reasoning	2.8	0 ☐ Same	1 ☐ Change to:
9 Inductive Reasoning	2.5	0 ☐ Same	1 ☐ Change to:
10 Information Ordering	3.1	0 ☐ Same	1 ☐ Change to:
11 Category Flexibility	2.6	0 ☐ Same	1 ☐ Change to:
12 Mathematical Reasoning	2.8	0 ☐ Same	1 ☐ Change to:
13 Number Facility	3.3	0 ☐ Same	1 ☐ Change to:
14 Memorization	2.9	0 ☐ Same	1 ☐ Change to:
15 Speed of Closure	2.4	0 ☐ Same	1 ☐ Change to:
16 Flexibility of Closure	1.7	0 ☐ Same	1 ☐ Change to:
17 Perceptual Speed	2.5	0 ☐ Same	1 ☐ Change to:
18 Spatial Orientation	1.7	0 ☐ Same	1 ☐ Change to:
19 Visualization	1.9	0 ☐ Same	1 ☐ Change to:
20 Selective Attention	2.2	0 ☐ Same	1 ☐ Change to:
21 Time Sharing	2.5	0 ☐ Same	1 ☐ Change to:
22 Arm-Hand Steadiness	1.8	0 ☐ Same	1 ☐ Change to:
23 Manual Dexterity	2.0	0 ☐ Same	1 ☐ Change to:
24 Finger Dexterity	2.0	0 ☐ Same	1 ☐ Change to:
25 Control Precision	1.5	0 ☐ Same	1 ☐ Change to:
26 Multilimb Coordination	1.3	0 ☐ Same	1 ☐ Change to:
27 Response Orientation	1.6	0 ☐ Same	1 ☐ Change to:

Figure 2.3—Sample Rating Sheet

change in the future. If an analyst judged that the level would change in the future, a whole number rating for the future would be entered in the column labeled "Future Level."

For the four occupational clusters that were uniquely military (Special Operations Forces, Combat Arms, Aircraft Launch and Recovery Specialists, and Ordnance Specialists), no ratings of the past were available from the O*NET Analyst Database. Hence, in those cases, analysts were asked to first designate a past level for each dimension, then to return to the top of the list and judge whether or not those past levels would need to change in the future, and if so, by how much.

As an aid to completing the rating sheets, analysts were given copies of O*NET rating scales for each dimension. Each rating scale is accompanied by a definition of the dimension to be rated, high-level and low-level descriptions of the scale, and concrete task anchors to help ensure that all analysts use the rating scale in a consistent manner. For generalized work activities, knowledge, skills, and abilities, all scales had a range of 1 to 7 with a "not relevant" option that was subsequently coded as a rating of zero. The scales for dimensions of work context were not uniform either in terms of their structure or in terms of the aspect of the dimension being rated. Some work context dimensions were rated on level, but others were rated on importance, frequency, seriousness, etc.

ANALYTICAL APPROACH

Once we had the complete dataset, we computed change scores (future rating minus past rating) for each combination of occupational cluster and O*NET dimension. We then determined the significance of the change scores. In selecting an appropriate test of significance, we noted first that the change scores were not normally distributed. This property precluded the use of a t-test. Second, because we found little inter-rater agreement in the data overall,[8] we

---

[8]Low variability in the data precluded the use of standard measures of inter-rater reliability—intraclass correlations. Instead, we used a measure of inter-rater agreement (kappa) that takes categories of data as inputs. In this case, change scores were split into two categories: "more," and "same or less." Even using this cruder measure, inter-rater agreement ranged from "poor" to "slight" for Abilities, Skills, and

opted to use a strict test, the Wilcoxon sign-rank test, which demands high inter-rater agreement in the subset of the data under consideration for it to reach statistical significance. Using the Wilcoxon test, for a given mean change score to be statistically significant at the p < .05 level, total or near-total agreement is required across the six to nine raters whose ratings contributed to the score.

CHARACTERISTICS OF THE DATA

Overall, our analysis shows what we generally expected: Approximately 70 percent of the over 80,000 ratings we collected predict no change in the dimensions of work or workers for the future; the average magnitude of change predicted for individual dimensions is typically very small and positive. We did have negative predicted change for some dimensions in some occupational clusters, but none of the negative change is statistically significant. However, much of the change that was assessed *is* significant across the entire defense workforce, for particular components of the workforce (military and civilian), for particular occupational clusters, and for particular domains and dimensions that characterize work and workers.

Generalized Work Activities, and from "poor" to "fair" for Knowledge and Work Context dimensions (Landis and Koch, 1977). Also, although the mean change scores provided by different groups of raters did not differ significantly, there were some subtler differences between groups of raters, which are discussed in Appendix B.

Chapter Three

EXPECTED CHANGES IN WORK AND WORKERS

In this chapter, we present our analysis of the data in two complementary ways. We look first within the occupational clusters to find those that show significant change in specific dimensions and, somewhat more broadly, in one or more of the five O*NET domains. Then, we pool the data across all occupational clusters to look for themes and patterns across workforces. In both cases, we present results for the defense workforce as a whole and for the civilian and military workforces separately.

CHANGES IN DIMENSIONS WITHIN OCCUPATIONAL CLUSTERS

The distribution of number of changed dimensions within each of our 46 occupational clusters is shown in Figure 3.1. More than half (54 percent) of all occupational clusters had change in five or fewer dimensions; indeed, over 20 percent of all occupational clusters had no changed dimensions at all. Only five occupational clusters had more than 20 dimensions changed.[1]

We also examined how the number of changed dimensions was distributed by size of occupational cluster. We characterized this change on two scales. We arbitrarily decided that 20 or fewer changed dimensions (out of a total of 232 dimensions) represented

---

[1]The results reported in the first section of this chapter are intended to be largely descriptive. Statistically significant patterns of results are considered beginning with the second section.

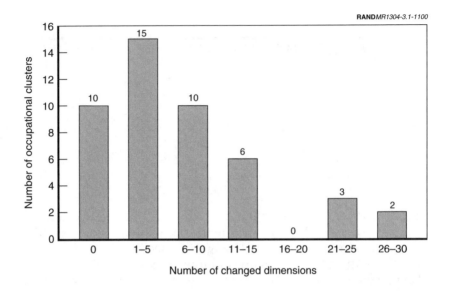

RAND*MR1304-3.1-1100*

**Figure 3.1—Distribution of Occupational Clusters by Number of
Changed Dimensions**

few changes on that scale. On a scale relating to sizes of the occupational clusters, those containing less than 3 percent of the overall
workforce were considered *small*. Figure 3.2 shows the results of that
comparison. Across the aggregate defense workforces, two large occupational clusters and three small occupational clusters have a
large number of changed dimensions. Another 10 occupational
clusters are characterized as large but have a small number of
changed dimensions. The remaining occupational clusters have
either few (25 occupational clusters) or no (10) changed dimensions.
(Table D.1 provides a listing of occupational clusters by military service and DoD civilian workforce, indicating where each would fall in
a distribution similar to that depicted in Figure 3.2.)

Detailed information on dimensional changes within occupational
clusters is likely to be most useful to human resource managers responsible for the development and use of various occupational

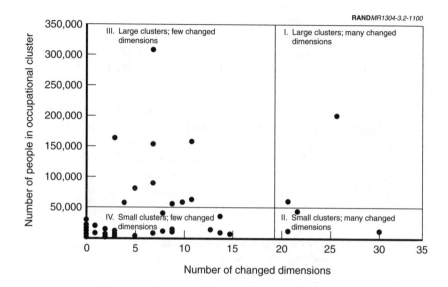

Figure 3.2—Distribution of Occupational Clusters by Size and Number of Changed Dimensions

groupings.[2] Accordingly, we have assembled detailed information that might be useful to these managers. As an example of the available information, Tables 3.1 and 3.2 present dimensional changes for the two occupational clusters identified in sector I of Figure 3.2 (large occupational clusters with more than 20 dimensional changes). (In Appendix E, we provide a complete listing of significant dimensional changes for all occupational clusters.)

Each table in this chapter and in Appendix E shows dimensions (and their associated domain) that have significantly *higher* levels in the future than they did in the past for the occupational cluster. Moreover, the tables also show the past relative level (upper quartile, middle two quartiles, or lower quartile) of the dimension compared to all other dimensions in the occupational cluster. For example, in the

_____

[2]Development and use of military and civilian personnel within DoD is often managed by career management teams, organized by occupational groupings similar to the occupational clusters in our analysis.

Aircraft, Automotive, and Electrical Maintenance Specialists cluster (Table 3.1), note that Computers and Electronics, a dimension in the knowledge domain, was in the middle quartile of all dimensions for this occupational cluster in the past but is projected to have a higher level in the future.

We present the data in quartiles because we believe that qualitatively different determinations of meaning of the data might be made by occupational managers depending on the past level of the dimension. For example, if a dimension required relatively high levels in the past and is projected to be higher in the future, the occupational manager is likely to be aware of the dimension and can probably

Table 3.1

Dimensions with Higher Future Levels—Aircraft, Automotive, and Electrical Maintenance Specialists

Domain	Dimension	Past Level (Quartile)
GW	Updating and using job-relevant knowledge	Upper
WC	Consequence of error	Upper
WC	Degree of automation	Upper
KN	Mechanical	Upper
KN	Engineering and technology	Upper
SK	Repairing	Upper
SK	Equipment maintenance	Upper
SK	Troubleshooting	Upper
SK	Problem identification	Upper
SK	Equipment selection	Upper
SK	Testing	Upper
SK	Reading comprehension	Upper
SK	Critical thinking	Upper
SK	Mathematics	Upper
SK	Information gathering	Upper
SK	Identification of key causes	Upper
WC	Responsible for others' health and safety	Middle
WC	Responsibility for outcomes and results	Middle
WC	Provide a service to others	Middle
KN	Computers and electronics	Middle
KN	Public safety and security	Middle
SK	Information organization	Middle
SK	Active learning	Middle
SK	Service orientation	Middle
KN	Telecommunications	Lower
KN	Transportation	Lower

Table 3.2

Dimensions with Higher Future Levels—Computer Systems Specialists

Domain	Dimension	Past Level (Quartile)
WC	Degree of automation	Upper
WC	Consequence of error	Upper
WC	Importance of being exact or accurate	Upper
KN	Computers and electronics	Upper
SK	Troubleshooting	Upper
AB	Originality	Upper
GW	Inspecting equipment, structures, or materials	Middle
GW	Performing for or working directly with the public	Middle
WC	Providing a service to others	Middle
WC	Using hands on objects, tools, controls	Middle
WC	Importance of being aware of new events	Middle
WC	Pace determined by speed of equipment	Middle
WC	Frustrating circumstances	Middle
WC	Dealing with unpleasant/angry people	Middle
SK	Technology design	Middle
SK	Systems evaluation	Middle
SK	Identification of downstream consequences	Middle
SK	Installation	Middle
SK	Service orientation	Middle
SK	Equipment selection	Middle
AB	Fluency of ideas	Middle

point to instances of selection or training or education for it. However, in the case of a dimension that required relatively low levels in the past but is projected to be higher in the future, the occupational manager might not have incorporated selection, training, education for the dimension in workforce planning efforts. It may not have shown up previously on the proverbial "radar screen."

CHANGES ACROSS DOMAINS WITHIN OCCUPATIONAL CLUSTERS

Having examined significant change at the level of individual dimensions, we also found it useful to examine whether change in any occupational cluster can be broadly identified with specific domains. We did this because, as will be discussed in Chapter Four, occupational managers might structure their human resource management responses differently depending on the domain requiring attention. Accordingly, we sought to determine which occupational clusters have significant predicted change by domain (generalized work activities, work context, knowledge, skills, and abilities). To be certain that an occupation could be labeled as changing significantly in one or more domains, we used an additional test of statistical significance.[3]

Table 3.3 lists the occupational clusters with significant change at the domain level along with the numbers of occupations they include and the number of personnel in each.

These occupational clusters represent a relatively large proportion of all personnel in the military services (32 percent in the Navy to 48 percent in the Army) and about 15 percent of all personnel in the civil service. They also represent a large, but somewhat lesser, proportion of all occupations in the military services (22 percent or more) and about 13 percent of all defense civil service occupations. Moreover, there are differences among the services in the number of people in each. In particular, combat arms and communications operators are large occupational clusters for the Army and Marine Corps; maintenance specialists is large for all; intelligence specialists is large for the Army and Air Force; and computer systems specialists is large for civil service, Navy, and Air Force. The others vary from very small to relatively small.

Note that none of the occupational clusters on the list have significant changes concentrated in the abilities domain. This point will be revisited below. Also note that no occupational cluster on the list is expected to change significantly in more than two domains.

_____

[3]Significant change within an occupational cluster was achieved if a sufficient number of dimensions for that cluster showed statistically significant change as determined by the binomial confidence interval for the number of dimensions at $p < .05$. In most cases, this meant that approximately 15 percent of the dimensions within a given domain had to have statistically significant change for the domain change to be considered statistically significant.

Table 3.3

Occupational Clusters with Significant Domain Changes and the Numbers of Included Occupations and Personnel

Occupational Cluster	Domains with Significant Change					Army		Navy		Air Force		Marine Corps		Civil Service	
	GW	WC	KN	SK	AB	No. of Occup.	No. of People	No. of Occup.	No. of People	No. of Occup.	No. of People	No. of Occup.	No. of People	No. of Occup.	No. of People
Combat Arms	x					32	121,589	53	1,245			34	34,697		
Aircraft, Automotive, and Electrical Maintenance Specialists		x		x	x	35	48,472	140	32,273	92	45,891	61	18,733	49	54,609
Communications Operators	x		x			7	17,552	28	4,739	56	9,302	16	9,264	4	1,875
Intelligence Specialists		x				28	16,623	80	5,375	24	30,461	16	2,986	2	3,030
Computer Systems Specialists	x		x			7	1,094	48	7,454	41	17,690	8	1,934	4	31,250
Physicians, Surgeons, and Optometrists			x			42	4,989	31	3,186	140	3,737			3	768
Dental and Pharmacy Technicians			x			12	3,300	18	3,021	28	4,152			5	2,329
Recruiting Specialists	x					4	4,996	9	3,572	3	695	1	397		
Air Traffic Controllers		x		x		1	1,143	12	1,545	30	5,020	5	718	2	1,216
Environmental Health and Safety Specialists	x					2	1,648	4	2,288	14	1,813			5	4,099
Sum of clusters						170	221,406	423	64,698	428	118,761	141	68,729	74	99,446
% of workforce						39	48	25	32	22	34	32	45	13	15

CHANGES ACROSS WORKFORCES

A look at the dimensions of work and workers when all occupational clusters are pooled across workforces yields some interesting potential trends. To highlight these trends, we have identified dimensions which, when ranked by mean *change score,* fall within the top 10 percent of all dimensions across all five domains. These are the dimensions that analysts judged likely to require the largest increases in level for the future. All the dimensions in the top 10 percent list carry change scores that are statistically significant at the $p < .05$ level.

These changes can be examined for the defense workforce as a whole as well as for segments within it (e.g., military service and civil service workforces). Occupational analysts did not provide ratings for each military service and the civil service workforces separately. However, to average the analysts' change scores across occupational clusters, we weighted change scores by the population within each occupational cluster. Since occupational distributions differ between the military and civil service workforces, we can derive segment-specific rankings by weighted average change score. Results are reported in this manner in Table 3.4.

For the entire workforce and the military subset, no changes in ability dimensions were high enough to be included in the top 10 percent list. Only one ability (speech clarity) was expected to change enough to reach the top 10 percent of changed dimensions for the civil service workforce. Among the military services, only the Army had significant changes in ability dimensions. In contrast, significant change was far more prevalent among generalized work activity, work context, knowledge, and skill dimensions.

Themes

Many of the dimensions with high change scores can be grouped to form four broad themes (see Table 3.5). One theme is the need for *an enhanced service orientation* such as providing services to identified constituents and stakeholders. A second theme indicates that *more advanced technical knowledge and skills* (understanding, using, and managing technology) will be needed. Third, *better problem-solving skills* (critical thinking, analyzing and evaluating information and situations) will be required across the board. Finally, a number

Table 3.4

Dimensions with Greatest Expected Change by Workforce Segment

	Workforce Segment					
	Army	Navy	Air Force	Marine Corps	Civil Service	Total
Generalized work activities (of 42 dimensions)						
Operating vehicles, mechanized devices, equipment	x	x	x	x	x	x
Interacting with computers	x	x	x	x	x	x
Updating and using job-relevant knowledge	x	x	x	x	x	x
Interpreting meaning of information for others					x	x
Analyzing data or information	x	x	x	x	x	x
Thinking creatively	x	x		x		x
Getting information needed to do the job	x			x		
Repairing and maintaining electronic equipment	x			x		
Work context (of 59 dimensions)						
Degree of automation	x	x	x	x	x	x
Importance of providing a service to others		x	x	x	x	x
Frequency of dealing with external customers		x	x	x	x	x
Degree to which pace determined by speed of equipment			x		x	x
Responsibility for outcomes and results			x			
Knowledge (of 33 dimensions)						
Computers and electronics	x	x	x	x	x	x
Foreign language	x	x	x	x	x	x
Telecommunications	x	x	x	x	x	x
Public safety and security	x	x	x	x	x	x
Engineering and technology	x	x	x	x		x
Mechanical		x	x			
Skills (of 46 dimensions)						
Service orientation	x	x	x	x	x	x
Active learning	x	x	x	x	x	x
Systems evaluation					x	x
Negotiation					x	x

Table 3.4 (continued)

	Army	Navy	Air Force	Marine Corps	Civil Service	Total
Technology design		x	x		x	x
Visioning					x	
Monitoring					x	x
Identification of downstream consequences	x	x	x		x	x
Synthesis/reorganization			x	x	x	
Critical thinking					x	
Reading comprehension	x	x	x	x		x
Information gathering	x	x	x	x		
Science	x	x		x		
Operations analysis		x				
Information organization		x				
Problem identification			x	x		
Abilities (of 52 dimensions)						
Speech clarity					x	
Speed of closure	x					
Inductive reasoning	x					
Originality	x					
Problem sensitivity	x					

NOTE: An "x" in this table indicates that the dimension is in the top 10 percent of changed dimensions within the workforce segment indicated when ranked by weighted average change score.

of dimensions can be associated with an increase in *the need to stay current*, including the ability and willingness to learn, adapt, be flexible, and work in ambiguous environments.

Corresponding Change in the Private Sector

The four broad themes seen in Table 3.5 reflect a need for workers to increase their skills to stay competitive in a rapidly changing world. The projected need for workers with high proficiency in work-related knowledge, skills, and abilities is not a new phenomenon but rather a continuation of a pattern that has been evident since shortly after the end of World War II. The past 50 years have seen a consistent increase in employers' demand for high-skill workers. Occupations

Table 3.5
Themes Among Dimensions Requiring Greatest Change

An Enhanced Service Orientation	More Advanced Technical Skills and Knowledge Skills	Better Problem-Solving Skills	The Need to Stay Current
Generalized Work Activities			
Interpreting the meaning of information for others	Operating vehicles, mechanized devices, or equipment	Analyzing data or information	Updating and using job-relevant information
	Interacting with computers	Thinking creatively	Getting information needed to do the job
Work Context			
Importance of providing a service to others	Degree of automation		
Frequency of dealing with external customers	Degree to which pace is determined by speed of equipment		
Knowledge			
	Computers and electronics		
	Telecommunications		
	Engineering and technology		
Skills			
Service orientation	Technology design	Identification of downstream consequences	Active learning
Negotiation		Systems evaluation	Reading comprehension
		Critical thinking	Information gathering
		Problem identification	Synthesis/reorganization

requiring a college degree are growing twice as fast as those that require lower educational attainment (U.S. DoL, 1999). The increasing globalization of commerce puts greater pressure on U.S. workers to acquire and maintain those skills necessary to compete in a rapidly changing global market (NCES, 1997). This international competition has created more high-tech jobs in the United States and decreased the demand for low-skill workers (U.S. DoL, 1999).

Many analysts think that declining demand for low-skill workers is the greatest challenge facing the U.S. labor market (Urban Institute, 1996). The rising level of educational attainment in the United States and increasing competition abroad have led manufacturers to replace labor-intensive production systems with technologically advanced, labor-saving systems. This cycle has increased the demand for high-skilled workers and compelled many workers to enter the service sector (NCES, 1997; NCES, 1998). This may explain why an enhanced service orientation is one of the themes we found in our data.

Enhanced Service Orientation. Most job growth in the last 20 years has been in the service-based sector (U.S. DoL, 1999). The shift from a manufacturing to service-based economy is expected to increase in the future. High-tech service professions are expected to grow more rapidly than in the past and to account for a larger proportion of overall job growth (Hecker, 1999). This expansion of service employment appears to require workers with an enhanced service orientation. The growth in the service sector has occurred during a period of rapid technological advance that is putting pressure on workers to strengthen their technical skills.

More Advanced Technical Knowledge and Skills. The new century is projected to include an increasing expansion in the use of computers and rapid technological change that will redefine work. By 2006, almost half of all workers will be in occupations that produce or use information technology (U.S. DoL, 1999). Although many of today's jobs will exist in the new century, they will require a much different and more advanced package of knowledge and skills (U.S. DoL, 1999). Workers must increase their technological knowledge or risk being left behind. There is evidence of this problem even today. Forty percent of top U.S. businesses claim that they cannot modernize equipment because their workers do not have the necessary technological skills (Century Foundation, 1999). The rising demand for workers with high levels of knowledge and technical skills can be seen in the rapid growth in wages found in computer-related occupations (NCES, 1997). These trends make it unsurprising that the need for more advanced technical skills would emerge from our data.

Better Problem-Solving Skills. Technological advances have led to increased complexity and a demand for workers with better problem-solving skills (NCES, 1997). The rapid pace of today's economy requires workers with the flexibility to respond quickly to changes in work (U.S. DoL, 1999). The increase in worker autonomy that has accompanied technological advances is expected to increase in the future. For example, many manufacturing firms are moving to systems that give great responsibility to frontline workers (Century Foundation, 1999). These independent workers will need the ability to solve problems on their own (U.S. DoL, 1999). As the margins of competitive advantage shrink, employers are trying to find workers with the problem-solving skills needed to increase work efficiency (U.S. DoL, 1999). In a recent survey, 77 percent of chief executive officers stated that they wanted workers with a liberal arts education because of the problem-solving skills that they bring to their work (*Fortune*, 1997).

Need to Stay Current. The Department of Labor projects a greater need for workers to stay current to maintain the skills needed in our increasingly information-based economy (U.S. DoL, 1999). Technology allows workers with the right skills to stay current through use of email, pagers, and the Internet (U.S. DoL, 1999).

Chapter Four

WORKFORCE SHAPING AND DEVELOPMENT

In view of our predicted changes in work and worker characteristics, DoD HR managers might contemplate the kinds of shifts in workforce shaping and development tools needed to accommodate the expected changes. In this chapter, we discuss those issues.

WORKFORCE SHAPING AND DEVELOPMENT TOOLS

Workforce shaping may be defined as a conscious effort to use human resource management tools to change the characteristics of the workforce in a purposeful way. Some tools might be used to change the mix of available workers, and others might be used to develop new human capital within the existing workforce. Tools useful for these purposes include:

- *Classification*: division of work into distinctly defined occupations and identification of required knowledge, skills, and abilities for each occupation;

- *Recruiting/selection*: bringing new members into the workforce; can occur at typical entry levels or at higher-grade (lateral entry) levels;

- *Promotion*: filling higher-grade requirements from within the organization;

- *Training*: providing additional skills to members of the workforce;

- *Education*: providing additional knowledge to members of the workforce;

- *Compensation*: using extrinsic rewards to motivate and retain members of the workforce;

- *Acculturation*: influencing the values, attitudes, and awareness of organizational needs among members of the workforce; can be accomplished in many ways, e.g., through leadership, mentoring, focusing of rewards, training and education programs, and developmental job rotation; and

- *Retention/separation*: using retention incentives, disincentives, or controls to keep or sever selected segments of the workforce.

These workforce shaping and development tools can help to bring about required changes in work and worker characteristics, as outlined below and as illustrated in Figure 4.1.

- Changes in work or worker characteristics will be formally cataloged in the job descriptions found in various military and civil service classification systems.

- If general work activities or work context change, HR managers may need to adjust programs to acculturate members of the workforce so that they readily accept and exploit the new conditions. Additionally, they can integrate other workforce shaping and development tools to help produce the desired changes in the workforce. They can adjust recruiting/selection and promotion processes to acquire and advance those who are better suited to new work contexts. Retention/separation programs can be used to extend the service of those with suitable adaptations and sever those who adapt less well. Promotion and compensation programs can attach incentives to appropriate adaptation.

- If required knowledge changes, HR managers can modify education programs to develop required human capital among both new and current members of the workforce. Additionally, an integrated HR strategy, similar to that described above for adaptation to the work activities and context, can be used to reshape the workforce along its educational dimensions.

- If required skills change, HR managers can employ the same integrated approach as for a change in required knowledge, except

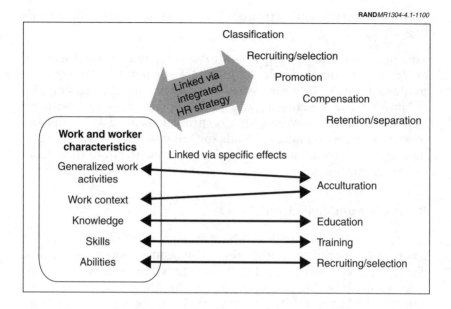

Figure 4.1—Relationship of Workforce Shaping and Development Tools to
Domains of Work and Worker Characteristics

that training programs, rather than education programs, are the
specific means for developing new skills.

- If required abilities change in ways that tend to exceed the abilities of current workers, recruiting/selection and reten-
  tion/separation programs must be adjusted, because abilities are
  personal traits that are somewhat stable over time—they generally cannot be developed to a higher level within the existing
  workforce.

POTENTIAL EFFECTS

Classification

Since predicted changes in work and worker characteristics are expected to be modest, they pose no impetus for radical restructuring
of classification systems. Incremental changes in knowledge and

skill requirements, and in related aptitude requirements, should suffice.

This does not rule out impetus for classification restructuring for other reasons—for example, to find more efficient or effective ways to organize work. However, since we predict generally higher levels of knowledge and technical skill, more emphasis on staying current in one's field, and more emphasis on problem solving, HR managers might take a second look at trends toward multi-skilling and multi-tasking, which could make some jobs too broad to afford the necessary technical focus.

Recruiting and Selection

Since we predict no significant shifts in required abilities, we find no absolute necessity to modify recruiting and selection processes. However, in view of expected shifts in required knowledge and skills, changes in recruiting and selection can be used as part of a broad strategy of adaptation. The military workforce generally acquires its occupation-specific skills through post-accession training; revised aptitude requirements reflected in classification systems should bring in members capable of responding to the generally higher levels of knowledge and skill that we predict will be needed. Members of the civilian workforce are generally acquired with a ready set of skills; changes in the classification system will similarly induce required changes in recruiting/selection criteria.

For military or civilian occupations with more pronounced changes in knowledge and skill requirements (see Tables 3.1, 3.2, 3.3, and Appendix E), aptitudes among members of the current workforce could be insufficient to meet new requirements. If so, increased lateral entries or cross-flow from other high-aptitude occupations might be appropriate.

Promotion

Promotions are generally based on a variety of considerations, including occupation-specific knowledge, skills, and abilities; broader managerial and leadership skills; experience; suitability to work activities and contexts; and potential for increased responsibility.

Through appropriate weighting and focusing of these factors, promotion programs can contribute to required reshaping of the workforce.

Training

Clearly, changes in skill requirements should be reflected in changes in training programs. Tables 3.1, 3.2, 3.3, and Appendix E identify the affected occupations.

Education

Military HR managers have traditionally linked professional and academic education to promotions, providing military members a strong incentive to continually expand and renew their knowledge sets. For military HR managers, the challenge is to ensure that existing incentives are properly focused on organizational needs. For civilian members of the workforce, incentives are generally much weaker. Thus, strengthening the linkages between education and promotion could provide needed incentives for civilians to meet new or changing knowledge requirements. Increased knowledge requirements might also be addressed through greater access to organizationally funded professional and academic development programs, especially for civilian members of the workforce, who generally receive much less assistance in this sphere than military members. Again, Tables 3.1, 3.2, 3.3, and Appendix E identify the affected occupations.

Note that aircraft, automotive, and electrical maintenance specialists—a very large occupational group (see Table 3.1)—is identified as having significant upward shifts in both knowledge and skill requirements, which leads to corresponding increases in both education and training requirements. These changes can be traced to the increasingly sophisticated technology embedded in the military equipment these specialists maintain. A trend toward greater use of contractors to maintain the most sophisticated equipment, extending even into battlefield theaters, suggests that in-house maintenance workforces (primarily enlisted and wage grade) may already lag in acquiring critical knowledge and skills or may lack the aptitude to acquire them.

Compensation

Compensation is tied in large part to promotions and thus serves as part of the motivation for behaviors, including knowledge and skill acquisition, that are associated with promotion. Compensation can also be used more directly to motivate individual development, through a mechanism that compensation experts refer to as *competency pay*. This mechanism is used very sparingly in military and civil service pay systems but could be expanded if needed.

Acculturation

Changes in general work activities and context, as highlighted in Tables 3.1, 3.2, 3.3, and Appendix E, might require adjustment of acculturation processes. This could be particularly important in the case of combat arms occupations and special operations forces (see Table 3.3 and Table E.1). Our findings suggest that individuals in these occupations must become more accustomed to acquiring, processing, and acting upon information, in contrast to an older model that emphasized centralized control and processing of information and decentralized execution of orders.

Retention/Separation

In cases where some members of the current workforce lack the aptitude for required changes, where retraining, reeducation, or reacculturation of the workforce is extremely expensive, or where it is difficult to motivate acquisition of new knowledge, skills, or attitudes, prudent HR managers will look for ways to increase severances and make room for a greater flow of new, more qualified entrants into the workforce.

Chapter Five

CONCLUSIONS AND OBSERVATIONS

We have found that expected changes in required work and worker characteristics during the first decade of the 21st century will be much more modest than is implied by prevailing descriptions of the changing environment. The revolutions in military and business affairs that are affecting DoD, including concepts such as precision weaponry, information warfare, leaner logistics, and openness to new business practices, may be changing DoD processes in dramatic ways but are actually changing work and workers in very measured ways. Reassuringly, we predict no significant changes in required abilities. This means that current and prospective workforces, given existing selection instruments and appropriate training and education, should generally be able to adapt to needed changes.

We have also highlighted some general themes that extend broadly through the whole range of DoD occupations. These themes are an enhanced service orientation, an increase in the need to stay current, more advanced technical knowledge and skills, and better problem-solving skills.

DoD HR managers have access to a variety of workforce shaping and development tools. Given sufficient resources for their programs, HR managers are generally well equipped to bring about the necessary changes in work and workers. The challenge may lie in articulating the needs and obtaining the resources.

This work required extensive use of crosswalks between multiple occupational classification systems and clustering of occupational categories. These steps suggest a potential need for refinement of federal civilian and military classification systems. Among the one

Table A.1 (continued)

Performing administrative activities
Performing for or working directly with the public
Performing general physical activities
Processing information
Providing consultation and advice to others
Repairing and maintaining mechanical electronic equipment
Repairing and maintaining mechanical equipment
Resolving conflicts and negotiating with others
Scheduling work and activities
Selling or influencing others
Staffing organizational units
Teaching others
Thinking creatively
Updating and using job-relevant knowledge

Table A.2

Dimensions Within the Work Context Domain

Bending or twisting the body
Climbing ladders, scaffolds, poles, etc.
Common protective or safety attire
Consequence of error
Contaminants
Coordinate or lead others
Cramped work space, awkward positions
Deal with external customers
Deal with physically aggressive people
Deal with unpleasant/angry people
Degree of automation
Diseases/infections degree of injury
Diseases/infections frequency
Diseases/infections injury
Extremely bright or inadequate
Frequency in conflict situations
Frustrating circumstances
Hazardous conditions degree of injury
Hazardous conditions frequency
Hazardous conditions injury
Hazardous equipment degree of injury
Hazardous equipment frequency
Hazardous equipment injury
Hazardous situations degree of injury

Table A.2 (continued)

Hazardous situations frequency
Hazardous situations injury
High places degree of injury
High places frequency of injury
High places injury
Importance of being aware of new events
Importance of being exact or accurate
Importance of being sure all is done
Importance of repeating same tasks
Job-required social interaction
Keeping or regaining balance
Kneeling, crouching, or crawling
Lighting
Making repetitive motions
Objective or subjective information
Pace determined by speed of equipment
Persuade someone to a course of action
Provide a service to others
Radiation degree of injury
Radiation frequency
Radiation injury
Responsibility for outcomes and results
Responsible for others' health and safety
Sitting
Sounds, noise levels are distracting, etc.
Special uniform
Specialized protective or safety attire
Standing
Supervise, coach, train others
Take a position opposed to others
Using hands on objects, tools, controls
Very hot
Walking or running
Whole body vibration

Table A.3

Dimensions Within the Knowledge Domain

Administration and management	History and archeology
Biology	Law, government, and jurisprudence
Building and construction	Mathematics
Chemistry	Mechanical
Clerical	Medicine and dentistry
Communications and media	Personnel and human resources
Computers and electronics	Philosophy and theology
Customer and personal service	Physics
Design	Production and processing
Economics and accounting	Psychology
Education and training	Public safety and security
Engineering and technology	Sales and marketing
English language	Sociology and anthropology
Fine arts	Telecommunications
Food production	Therapy and counseling
Foreign language	Transportation
Geography	

Table A.4

Dimensions Within the Skills Domain

Active learning	Operation and control
Active listening	Operation monitoring
Coordination	Operations analysis
Critical thinking	Persuasion
Equipment maintenance	Problem identification
Equipment selection	Product inspection
Idea evaluation	Programming
Idea generation	Reading comprehension
Identification of downstream consequences	Repairing
Identification of key causes	Science
Implementation planning	Service orientation
Information gathering	Social perceptiveness
Information organization	Solution appraisal
Installation	Speaking
Instructing	Synthesis/reorganization
Judgment and decisionmaking	Systems evaluation
Learning strategies	Systems perceptions
Management of financial resources	Technology design
Management of material resources	Testing
Management of personnel resources	Time management
Mathematics	Troubleshooting
Monitoring	Visioning
Negotiation	Writing

Table A.5

Dimensions Within the Abilities Domain

Auditory attention	Oral comprehension
Category flexibility	Oral expression
Control precision	Originality
Deductive reasoning	Perceptual speed
Depth perception	Peripheral vision
Dynamic flexibility	Problem sensitivity
Dynamic strength	Rate control
Explosive strength	Reaction time
Extent flexibility	Response orientation
Far vision	Selective attention
Finger dexterity	Sound localization
Flexibility of closure	Spatial orientation
Fluency of ideas	Speech clarity
Glare sensitivity	Speech recognition
Gross body coordination	Speed of closure
Gross body equilibrium	Speed of limb movement
Hearing sensitivity	Stamina
Inductive reasoning	Static strength
Information ordering	Time sharing
Manual dexterity	Trunk strength
Mathematical reasoning	Visual color discrimination
Memorization	Visualization
Multilimb coordination	Wrist-finger speed
Near vision	Written comprehension
Night vision	Written expression
Number facility	

DIFFERENCES BETWEEN GROUPS OF RATERS

Before considering the results of the rating task, we undertook an analysis of differences between the ratings provided by groups of raters. The results of that analysis are reported here.

The overall mean change scores for the 34 civilian analysts did not differ appreciably from the mean for the 18 military analysts (see Table B.1). In fact, the percentages of ratings for which they projected change were almost identical (28 percent for civilians, and 30 percent for military analysts). However, when they did project change, the magnitude of that change was rated somewhat higher by civilians than by military analysts. The mean nonzero change scores for civilian and military raters were .86 and .65, respectively. Because in our analysis we did not consider magnitude of change in an absolute sense, this latter difference did not alter our treatment of the results.

Across all raters, the median years of experience in occupational analysis was three years. Interestingly, the mean change scores

Table B.1

Number and Mean Change Score of Civilian and Military Analysts by Affiliation

	AFOMS	IJOA	NCSU	Mean Change
Civilian	17	6	11	.24
Military	18			.20
Mean change	.19	.22	.37	

NOTE: Mean change is on a scale from 0 to 7 for most dimensions.

for raters above and below the median were similar (.20 and .26, respectively). Raters above the median years of experience projected change in 24 percent of their ratings. The mean change score for that 24 percent of ratings was .83. Raters below the median years of experience projected change in 35 percent of their ratings, with a somewhat smaller mean nonzero change score of .75.

There were somewhat larger differences between the mean change scores for analysts with different institutional affiliations. In particular, NCSU raters predicted a greater amount of change overall than did raters from AFOMS and IJOA. Further investigation revealed that on average, NCSU raters predicted change more often than did other raters and the magnitudes of their predicted changes were somewhat higher (see Table B.2). Again, these differences were not considered to be large enough to warrant any changes in the treatment of the results.

Table B.2

Proportion of Ratings Predicting Change and Mean Nonzero
Change Score by Affiliation

	NCSU	AFOMS/ IJOA	Mean
Change proportion	.45	.26	.30
Mean nonzero change score	.86	.76	.79

NOTE: NCSU proportional change was driven predominantly by two raters.

CLUSTER ANALYSIS

This appendix presents the details of the hierarchical agglomerative cluster analysis of MOTD occupations using data and job analysis concepts from O*NET. One goal of this analysis was to explore the utility of the O*NET data as a basis for development of MOTD classification structures. The second goal was to develop occupational families that would serve as units of analysis in later stages of the research. Characterization of future defense work based on every MOTD occupation was not practical from a resource standpoint and the results would be cumbersome to interpret or summarize.

The analysis classified a combined set of MOTD occupations that included enlisted, officer, warrant officer, and defense civil service occupations. The use of a combined dataset resulted in a comprehensive occupational classification of defense- and military-related jobs that could be analyzed to reveal occupational similarities and differences across services and DoD.

Occupations were clustered according to occupational and worker characteristics as measured in the O*NET process.[1] Characteristics were organized according to O*NET domains.[2] Separate classifica-

---

[1] The O*NET measures of characteristics were assigned to military and defense civil service occupations by matching similar occupations using crosswalks developed by DoL for O*NET and by DMDC.

[2] Variables from the work context domain were not used in the cluster analysis because of a lack of uniformity in the rating scales. After the clustering was complete, work context ratings were coupled with their corresponding occupational clusters.

tion systems were developed according to each of these domains. Separate systems are useful because occupations cluster differently depending on what characteristics are used as the basis for classification. A classification system based on abilities could be used for selection and placement of individuals into occupations based on a battery of test scores. This system may be different from one developed from required knowledge or skills that would be used to group occupations according to training similarities. The separate classification structures can be compared to reveal the extent to which occupations are similar across multiple domains. These comparisons can be used to develop an overall classification structure. The resulting occupational families consist of occupations that are alike in generalized work activities, knowledge, skills, and abilities.

O*NET includes measures of 42 generalized work activities, 33 knowledge areas, 46 skills, and 52 abilities. These characteristics may be measured in terms of level, importance, and frequency. For the cluster analyis, we used only the level variables from O*NET, because there are typically high correlations between level, importance, and frequency ratings. Second, the labor requirements and cost of later steps in the project can be substantially reduced if unnecessary variables can be dropped from the analysis.

In any clustering analysis choices must be made relating to treatment of data and specific methods to be used. These choices involve possible transformation or standardization of data, different measures of similarity, and methods to determine the number of clusters and place jobs into clusters. Our choices were guided by previous clustering efforts in the job analysis field and by methods used in the O*NET technical analysis that tested the utility of their data for just such an exercise (Peterson et al., 1996, Chapter 12). Whereas we report results from one combination of methods, we explored some alternative methods and found that they produced classification solutions that were less useful for our purposes.

We standardized the descriptive scores within each occupation so that all scores would have a mean of 0 and a standard deviation of 1. The result of this data standardization is that the profiles across work and worker characteristics for each occupation are compared, and information about the level of scores is eliminated. This is consistent with the purpose of our clustering effort. We are interested in clusters based on similar profiles where within occupations, scores are relatively higher in some areas and lower in others. Such clusters contain occupations that share an emphasis on a particular set of skills or activities. Without standardization, our clusters would be more likely to separate by rank or seniority (overall level of a dimension) rather than by the relative emphases of the occupations on skills or work activities. As a result of the standardization, the results of the analysis do not include a consideration of future changes based on shifts in seniority, nor do they allow us to detect cases where more senior jobs in an occupation would change in a different way from more junior jobs.

For our measure of similarity in the cluster analysis, we used Euclidean distance. When comparing two occupations, the Euclidean distance is the square root of the sum of the squared differences between the scores for all descriptors for those two occupations.[3] Squared Euclidean distance is sometimes used in cluster analyses, but was not used here because it exaggerates larger differences between scores.

We used Ward's minimum-variance method as the specific procedure for our hierarchical agglomerative clustering analyses. Ward's method is commonly used for occupational clustering and has properties making it particularly useful for our purposes.[4] Although Ward's method is effective in properly placing occupations into clusters, it has been shown to be less useful for identifying the correct number of clusters present in a dataset.[5] For this reason, we used Q-type factor analysis to determine the number of clusters. For this

---

[3]See Colihan and Burger (1995) or *O*NET Final Technical Report* for more detailed discussion of distance measures.

[4]Ward's method is slightly biased to produce clusters of equal size. Some other methods, such as within-groups average linkage, tend to produce a few large clusters and other very small clusters. We found that the average linkage method produced sets of clusters where most clusters consisted of only one occupation, which is a less useful way of combining occupations for our study.

[5]See Colihan and Burger (1995) for a Monte Carlo study that examines the performance of different grouping strategies for occupational classification. Clustering methods alone were found to have problems identifying the correct number of clusters, in particular when measurement error and overlapping clusters were introduced. This study found that Ward's method was effective when combined with a Q-type factor analysis that identifies the number of clusters.

analysis, we constructed a correlation matrix of occupations based on descriptor scores. We performed a factor analysis of this matrix and determined the number of job families to be extracted based on the number of factors with eigenvalues greater than one. This value was then used as an input parameter for the Ward's cluster analysis.

Table C.1 lists occupational clusters that were obtained from the clustering procedures. They are based on subclustering using each of three dimensions: GW, a combination of KN and SK (KNSK), and AB. Solutions of 11, 10, and 9 subclusters were produced from the individual sets of measures, respectively. For example, the numbers in the GW column show to which of the 11 subclusters based on generalized work activities each MOTD occupation was assigned. Combining the three subcluster schemes produced 41 unique clusters that have unique requirements in terms of work activities, knowledge, skills, and abilities.[6] Descriptive labels were assigned to each occupational cluster.

One adjustment was made to these results. The occupational cluster consisting of firefighters and vehicle drivers was split into two separate clusters, firefighters and vehicle drivers, thereby increasing the number of clusters to 42. Some of the work activities of these two occupations are sufficiently different that rating them separately allowed raters to make more accurate judgments.

There are also 10 MOTD occupations with mostly military content that cannot be matched accurately with O*NET classifications because there are no equivalent civilian jobs. These occupations were placed into four occupational clusters based on general similarities and convenience for rating purposes (see Table C.2). When combined with the results above, we have a set of 46 occupational clusters that serve as the units of analysis in the other parts of this study.

------

[6]Analyses reported in the *O*NET Final Technical Report* support the use of this sort of multistage clustering as a desirable alternative to clustering in a single step. Multistage clustering produces higher effect size estimates, a higher percentage of correct reclassifications, and smaller error terms.

Table C.1

Clusters of MOTD Occupations

Cluster Assignment			MOTD	
GW	KNSK	AB	No.	Occupational Cluster and MOTD Occupations
				Air Traffic Controllers
1	1	1	3920012	Air Traffic Control Managers
1	1	1	3920021	Air Traffic Controllers
				Airplane Navigators
1	1	9	8250032	Airplane Navigators
				Communications Operators
1	3	6	3930011	Communications Equipment Operators
1	3	6	3930021	Radio Intelligence Operators
				Photographic and Audiovisual Specialists
1	4	1	3220991	Graphic Designers and Illustrators
1	4	1	3260011	Photographic Specialists
1	4	1	3290021	Audiovisual and Broadcast Technicians
				Surveyors and Mappers
1	6	4	1643992	Surveying and Mapping Managers
1	6	4	3733991	Surveying, Mapping, and Drafting Technicians
				Emergency Management and Laboratory Specialists
1	6	6	3831991	Chemical Laboratory Technicians
1	6	6	3990011	Emergency Management Specialists
				Environmental Health and Safety Specialists
1	10	6	1473011	Environmental Health and Safety Specialists
				Precision Equipment Repairers
2	3	2	3900011	Space Operations Specialists
2	3	2	6150011	Radar and Sonar Equipment Repairers
2	3	2	6150021	Communications Equipment Repairers
2	3	2	6150031	Weapons Maintenance Technicians
2	3	2	6150051	Computer Equipment Repairers
2	3	2	6150081	Electronic Instrument Repairers
2	3	2	6171011	Precision Instrument Repairers
				Radar and Sonar Operators
2	3	6	3900031	Radar and Sonar Operators
				Computer Systems Specialists
3	4	4	1260012	Computer Systems Officers
3	4	4	3971991	Computer Programmers
3	4	4	4793981	Computer Systems Specialists

Table C.1 (continued)

Cluster Assignment			MOTD	
GW	KNSK	AB	No.	Occupational Cluster and MOTD Occupations
				Intelligence Specialists
3	5	3	1919012	Intelligence Officers
3	5	3	1919021	Intelligence Specialists
				Scientists and Engineers
3	6	4	1622002	Aerospace Engineers
3	6	4	1627002	Nuclear Engineers
3	6	4	1628992	Civil Engineers
3	6	4	1633002	Electrical and Electronics Engineers
3	6	4	1634002	Industrial Engineers
3	6	4	1637002	Marine Engineers
3	6	4	1843002	Physicists
3	6	4	1845002	Chemists
3	6	4	1847002	Oceanographers
3	6	4	1849002	Environmental Health and Safety Officers
3	6	4	3900022	Space Operations Officers
3	6	4	9100032	Missile Systems Officers
				Life Scientists
3	10	4	1850002	Life Scientists
				Recruiting Specialists
4	2	3	1430011	Recruiting Specialists
4	2	3	1430022	Recruiting Managers
				Functional Specialty Managers
5	2	3	1131022	Law Enforcement and Security Directors
5	2	3	1230992	Personnel Managers
5	2	3	1240992	Purchasing and Contracting Managers
5	2	3	1342012	Transportation Managers
5	2	3	1342022	Transportation Maintenance Managers
5	2	3	1342032	Supply and Warehousing Managers
5	2	3	1351002	Food Service Managers
5	2	3	1420002	Management Analysts
5	2	3	4020992	Store Managers
5	2	3	5211991	Food Service Specialists
				Communications Managers
5	2	4	1341992	Communications Managers
				Postal Directors
5	2	5	1344002	Postal Directors
				Musicians and Media Directors
5	4	1	3230001	Musicians
5	4	1	3230022	Music Directors
5	4	1	3240002	Audiovisual and Broadcast Directors

Table C.1 (continued)

Cluster Assignment			MOTD	
GW	KNSK	AB	No.	Occupational Cluster and MOTD Occupations
				Public Information Managers and Journalists
5	5	3	1131012	Emergency Management Officers
5	5	3	1139992	International Relations Officers
5	5	3	3320002	Public Information Officers
5	5	3	3331001	Broadcast Journalists and News-Writers
				Non-Destructive Testers
6	6	2	3990981	Non-Destructive Testers
				Flight Engineers
6	7	6	8250041	Flight Engineers
				Aircraft, Automotive, and Electrical Maintenance Specialists
6	7	7	6116991	Aircraft Mechanics
6	7	7	6117001	Automotive and Heavy Equipment Mechanics
6	7	7	6130011	Marine Engine Mechanics
6	7	7	6130021	Powerhouse Mechanics
6	7	7	6150101	Aircraft Electricians
6	7	7	6150111	Power Plant Electricians
6	7	7	6150121	Ship Electricians
6	7	7	6150131	Electrical Products Repairers
6	7	7	6160001	Heating and Cooling Mechanics
6	7	7	6432001	Building Electricians
				Preventive Maintenance Analysts
6	8	2	4752011	Preventive Maintenance Analysts
6	8	2	6171021	Photographic Equipment Repairers
				Divers
7	7	8	6179021	Divers
				Machinists, Technicians, and Cargo Specialists
7	8	2	6813991	Machinists
7	8	2	6865001	Dental and Optical Laboratory Technicians
7	8	2	6910001	Water and Sewage Treatment Plant Operators
7	8	2	6930001	Power Plant Operators
7	8	2	7443991	Printing Specialists
7	8	2	7676991	Compressed Gas Technicians
7	8	2	7714001	Welders and Metal Workers
7	8	2	8313991	Cargo Specialists
7	8	2	8319991	Petroleum Supply Specialists
				Ship Engineers and Air Crew Members
7	8	6	8244002	Ship Engineers
7	8	6	9100131	Air Crew Members

Table C.1 (continued)

Cluster Assignment			MOTD	
GW	KNSK	AB	No.	Occupational Cluster and MOTD Occupations
				Construction and Engineering Operators
7	8	7	6422001	Construction Specialists
7	8	7	6450001	Plumbers and Pipe Fitters
7	8	7	7759991	Survival Equipment Specialists
7	8	7	8243021	Seamen
7	8	7	8312001	Construction Equipment Operators
7	8	7	9100321	Combat Engineers
				Finance and Accounting Managers
8	2	5	1220002	Finance and Accounting Managers
				Administrative, Personnel, Supply Specialists
8	9	5	2049001	Religious Program Specialists
8	9	5	3640991	Medical Record Technicians
8	9	5	4362001	Sales and Stock Specialists
8	9	5	4630991	Administrative Support Specialists
8	9	5	4692001	Personnel Specialists
8	9	5	4712991	Finance and Accounting Specialists
8	9	5	4742001	Postal Specialists
8	9	5	4752021	Flight Operations Specialists
8	9	5	4754001	Supply and Warehousing Specialists
				Transportation Specialists
8	9	6	4644991	Transportation Specialists
				Optometric Specialists
9	10	1	3690061	Optometric Technicians
				Dentists and Pharmacy Specialists
9	10	2	2620002	Dentists
9	10	2	3630991	Dental Specialists
9	10	2	3690011	Pharmacy Technicians
				Medical Service and Medical Care Technicians
9	10	6	3040002	Physician Assistants
9	10	6	3650001	Radiologic (X-Ray) Technicians
9	10	6	3660991	Medical Care Technicians
9	10	6	3690021	Medical Laboratory Technicians
9	10	6	3690041	Cardiopulmonary and EEG Technicians
9	10	6	3690071	Medical Service Technicians
				Law Enforcement Specialists
10	1	8	5132021	Military Police
10	1	8	5133001	Law Enforcement and Security Specialists

Table C.1 (continued)

Cluster Assignment			MOTD	
GW	KNSK	AB	No.	Occupational Cluster and MOTD Occupations
				Health, Education, and Welfare Workers
10	5	3	1283992	Training and Education Directors
10	5	3	1310982	Health Services Administrators
10	5	3	1915002	Psychologists
10	5	3	2032012	Social Workers
10	5	3	2032021	Caseworkers and Counselors
10	5	3	2042002	Chaplains
10	5	3	2110002	Lawyers
10	5	3	2200992	Teachers and Instructors
10	5	3	2390001	Training Specialists and Instructors
10	5	3	3010002	Pharmacists
10	5	3	3020002	Dietitians
10	5	3	3034002	Speech Therapists
10	5	3	3290011	Interpreters and Translators
				Legal Specialists and Court Reporters
10	5	5	3960001	Legal Specialists and Court Reporters
				Nurses and Physical Therapists
10	5	6	2900002	Registered Nurses
10	5	6	3033982	Physical and Occupational Therapists
10	5	6	5233011	Physical and Occupational Therapy Specialists
				Weather Personnel
10	6	4	1846992	Meteorologists
10	6	4	3890981	Meteorological Specialists
				Physicians, Surgeons, Optometrists
10	10	6	2610002	Physicians and Surgeons
10	10	6	2810002	Optometrists
				Firefighters
11	1	8	5123991	Firefighters
				Vehicle Drivers
11	1	8	8212991	Vehicle Drivers
				Pilots and Ship/Submarine Operators
11	1	9	8241002	Ship and Submarine Officers
11	1	9	8243011	Quartermasters and Boat Operators
11	1	9	8250012	Airplane Pilots
11	1	9	8250022	Helicopter Pilots

Table C.2

Clusters of Uniquely Military Occupations

MOTD	Occupational Cluster and MOTD Occupations
	Special Operations Forces
9100251	Special Operations Forces
9100262	Special Operations Officers
	Combat Arms
9100191	Infantry
9100042	Infantry Officers
9100012	Artillery Crew Members
9100161	Artillery Officers
9100281	Tank Crew Members
9100102	Tank Officers
	Aircraft Launch and Recovery Specialists
9100301	Aircraft Launch and Recovery Specialists
	Ordnance Specialists
6179011	Ordnance Specialists

DISTRIBUTION OF EXPECTED DIMENSION-LEVEL INCREASES BY OCCUPATIONAL CLUSTER

Table D.1 shows, by occupational cluster, the number of dimensions that are expected to have higher-level requirements in the future, broken out by military and civil service workforces. The codes in the table partially correspond to the sectors in Figure 3.2. The codes appearing in the table are as follows:

1 indicates a large occupational cluster with many changed dimensions. Corresponds to sector I in Figure 3.2.

2 indicates a small occupational cluster with many changed dimensions. Corresponds to sector II in Figure 3.2.

3 indicates a large occupational cluster with few changed dimensions. Corresponds to sector III in Figure 3.2.

4 indicates a small occupational cluster with few changed dimensions. Corresponds to sector IV in Figure 3.2.

5 indicates that there are no people in that occupational cluster for that service.

6 indicates no changed dimensions.

The distinction between *small* and *large* in this taxonomy is based on 3 percent of the total population in a service or in the aggregate. That is, large was characterized as 14,000 in the Army, 6,000 in the Navy, 10,000 in the Air Force, 4,500 in the Marine Corps, 20,000 in the civil service, and 50,000 in the aggregate.

Occupational clusters with over 20 significant changes in dimension levels were considered to have *many* changes. Those with 20 or less were considered to have *few*.

Table D.1

Distribution of Occupational Clusters by Service, Size, and Number of Changed Dimensions

	Sector Code					
Occupational Cluster	Army	Navy	USAF	USMC	Civil Service	All
Aircraft, Automotive, and Electrical Maintenance Specialists	1	1	1	1	1	1
Computer Systems Specialists	2	1	1	2	1	1
Communications Operators	1	2	2	1	2	2
Air Traffic Controllers	2	2	2	2	2	2
Environmental Health and Safety Specialists	2	2	2	5	2	2
Administrative, Personnel, and Supply Specialists	3	3	3	3	3	3
Functional Specialty Managers	3	3	3	3	3	3
Precision Equipment Repairers	3	3	3	3	3	3
Construction and Engineering Operators	3	4	4	3	3	3
Health, Education and Welfare Workers	4	3	3	4	3	3
Machinists, Technicians, and Cargo Specialists	4	3	4	4	3	3
Scientists and Engineers	4	4	4	4	3	3
Medical Service and Medical Care Technicians	3	3	3	5	4	3
Combat Arms	3	4	5	3	4	3
Law Enforcement Specialists	3	4	3	4	4	3
Intelligence Specialists	3	4	4	4	4	4
Pilots and Ship/Submarine Operators	4	3	3	3	4	4
Radar and Sonar Operators	4	3	4	4	4	4
Communications Managers	4	4	4	4	4	4
Dental and Pharmacy Specialists	4	4	4	5	4	4
Emergency Management and Laboratory Specialists	4	4	4	4	4	4
Ordnance Specialists	4	4	4	4	4	4
Photographic and Audiovisual Specialists	4	4	4	4	4	4
Physicians, Surgeons, Optometrists	4	4	4	5	4	4
Ship Engineers and Air Crew Members	4	4	4	4	4	4

Table D.1 (continued)

Occupational Cluster	Army	Navy	USAF	USMC	Civil Service	All
Surveyors and Mappers	4	4	4	4	4	4
Transportation Specialists	4	4	4	4	4	4
Weather Personnel	4	4	4	4	4	4
Non-Destructive Testers	5	4	4	5	4	4
Airplane Navigators	5	5	4	4	4	4
Vehicle Drivers	5	5	4	3	4	4
Special Operations Forces	4	4	4	5	5	4
Divers	4	4	5	5	5	4
Recruiting Specialists	4	4	4	4	5	4
Postal Directors	5	4	5	5	5	4
Flight Engineers	5	5	4	4	5	4
Optometric Technicians	5	5	6	5	5	6
Aircraft Launch and Recovery Specialists	5	6	5	5	5	6
Firefighters	5	6	6	6	6	6
Legal Specialists and Court Reporters	6	5	6	6	6	6
Finance and Accounting Managers	6	6	6	6	6	6
Life Scientists	6	6	6	5	6	6
Musicians and Media Directors	6	6	6	6	6	6
Nurses and Physical Therapists	6	6	6	5	6	6
Preventive Maintenance Analysts	6	6	6	6	6	6
Public Information Managers and Journalists	6	6	6	6	6	6

DIMENSIONS WITH EXPECTED HIGHER LEVELS
WITHIN OCCUPATIONAL CLUSTER

This appendix contains tables for each occupational cluster with dimensions that are projected to require significantly higher levels in the future than in the past. In addition to identifying these dimensions (and their associated domains), the tables also show the past relative level (upper, middle two, and lower quartiles) of the dimension compared to all other dimensions for the occupational cluster. For example, in the occupational cluster for Administrative, Personnel, and Supply Specialists, a dimension in the work context domain, Provide a Service to Others, was in the middle quartiles of all dimensions for this occupational cluster in the past but is projected to have a higher level in the future.

Military service and civil service occupational managers can link information in this appendix to the workforce data in Appendices F through J and the index in Appendix K to determine how each of their occupations might be changing.

Table E.1

Dimensions with Higher Future Levels—Special
Operations Forces

Domain	Dimension	Past Level (Quartile)
SK	Information organization	Middle

Table E.2

Dimensions with Higher Future Levels—Administrative, Personnel, and Supply Specialists

Domain	Dimension	Past Level (Quartile)
GW	Performing administrative activities	Upper
WC	Degree of automation	Upper
SK	Critical thinking	Upper
WC	Provide a service to others	Middle
KN	Computers and electronics	Middle
KN	Telecommunications	Middle

Table E.3

Dimensions with Higher Future Levels—Aircraft, Automotive, and Electrical Maintenance Specialists

Domain	Dimension	Past Level (Quartile)
GW	Updating and using job-relevant knowledge	Upper
WC	Consequence of error	Upper
WC	Degree of automation	Upper
KN	Mechanical	Upper
KN	Engineering and technology	Upper
SK	Repairing	Upper
SK	Equipment maintenance	Upper
SK	Troubleshooting	Upper
SK	Problem identification	Upper
SK	Equipment selection	Upper
SK	Testing	Upper
SK	Reading comprehension	Upper
SK	Critical thinking	Upper
SK	Mathematics	Upper
SK	Information gathering	Upper
SK	Identification of key causes	Upper
WC	Responsible for others' health and safety	Middle
WC	Responsibility for outcomes and results	Middle
WC	Provide a service to others	Middle
KN	Computers and electronics	Middle
KN	Public safety and security	Middle
SK	Active learning	Middle
SK	Information organization	Middle
SK	Service orientation	Middle
KN	Telecommunications	Lower
KN	Transportation	Lower

Table E.4

Dimensions with Higher Future Levels—Air Traffic Controllers

Domain	Dimension	Past Level (Quartile)
GW	Making decisions and solving problems	Upper
GW	Updating and using job-relevant knowledge	Upper
GW	Thinking creatively	Upper
WC	Responsible for others' health and safety	Upper
WC	Job-required social interaction	Upper
WC	Responsibility for outcomes and results	Upper
WC	Importance of being sure all is done	Upper
WC	Importance of being exact or accurate	Upper
WC	Importance of being aware of new events	Upper
WC	Degree of automation	Upper
KN	Transportation	Upper
SK	Speaking	Upper
SK	Monitoring	Upper
SK	Problem identification	Upper
AB	Time sharing	Upper
AB	Speech clarity	Upper
AB	Speed of closure	Upper
AB	Selective attention	Upper
GW	Providing consultation and advice to others	Middle
WC	Frustrating circumstances	Middle
KN	Computers and electronics	Middle
KN	Telecommunications	Middle
KN	Engineering and technology	Middle
KN	Communications and media	Middle
KN	Public safety and security	Middle
KN	Law, government, and jurisprudence	Middle
AB	Perceptual speed	Middle
AB	Information ordering	Middle
KN	Psychology	Lower
KN	Customer and personal service	Lower

Table E.5

Dimensions with Higher Future Levels—Airplane Navigators

Domain	Dimension	Past Level (Quartile)
WC	Responsible for others' health and safety	Upper
WC	Degree of automation	Upper
WC	Importance of being aware of new events	Upper
KN	Geography	Upper
SK	Active listening	Upper
SK	Coordination	Upper
AB	Speed of closure	Upper
AB	Oral comprehension	Upper
AB	Selective attention	Upper
GW	Updating and using job-relevant knowledge	Middle
GW	Interpreting the meaning of information for others	Middle
WC	Responsibility for outcomes and results	Middle
KN	Computers and electronics	Middle
KN	Telecommunications	Middle
AB	Response orientation	Middle

Table E.6

Dimensions with Higher Future Levels—Communications Managers

Domain	Dimension	Past Level (Quartile)
AB	Problem sensitivity	Upper
GW	Developing and building teams	Middle
WC	Degree of automation	Middle
WC	Provide a service to others	Middle
KN	Computers and electronics	Middle
KN	Law, government, and jurisprudence	Middle
KN	Customer and personal service	Middle
SK	Synthesis/reorganization	Middle
SK	Equipment selection	Middle
SK	Service orientation	Middle
SK	Critical thinking	Middle
AB	Speed of closure	Middle
AB	Speech clarity	Middle
KN	Public safety and security	Lower

Table E.7

Dimensions with Higher Future Levels—Communications Operators

Domain	Dimension	Past Level (Quartile)
WC	Consequence of error	Upper
WC	Importance of being exact or accurate	Upper
WC	Importance of being sure all is done	Upper
WC	Using hands on objects, tools, controls	Upper
WC	Degree of automation	Upper
KN	Telecommunications	Upper
SK	Active listening	Upper
SK	Problem identification	Upper
SK	Information gathering	Upper
SK	Critical thinking	Upper
SK	Troubleshooting	Upper
SK	Judgment and decisionmaking	Upper
AB	Information ordering	Upper
AB	Speed of closure	Upper
WC	Importance of being aware of new events	Middle
WC	Pace determined by speed of equipment	Middle
KN	Communications and media	Middle
KN	Engineering and technology	Middle
KN	Clerical	Middle
SK	Testing	Middle
SK	Technology design	Middle
AB	Perceptual speed	Middle

Table E.8

Dimensions with Higher Future Levels—Computer Systems Specialists

Domain	Dimension	Past Level (Quartile)
WC	Degree of automation	Upper
WC	Consequence of error	Upper
WC	Importance of being exact or accurate	Upper
KN	Computers and electronics	Upper
SK	Troubleshooting	Upper
AB	Originality	Upper
GW	Inspecting equipment, structures, or materials	Middle
GW	Performing for or working directly with the public	Middle
WC	Frustrating circumstances	Middle
WC	Provide a service to others	Middle
WC	Using hands on objects, tools, controls	Middle
WC	Importance of being aware of new events	Middle
WC	Pace determined by speed of equipment	Middle
WC	Deal with unpleasant/angry people	Middle
SK	Equipment selection	Middle
SK	Technology design	Middle
SK	Systems evaluation	Middle
SK	Identification of downstream consequences	Middle
SK	Installation	Middle
SK	Service orientation	Middle
AB	Fluency of ideas	Middle

Table E.9

Dimensions with Higher Future Levels—Construction and Engineering Operators

Domain	Dimension	Past Level (Quartile)
WC	Responsible for others' health and safety	Upper
KN	Building and construction	Upper
WC	Upper places frequency	Lower
WC	Upper places injury	Lower

Table E.10

Dimensions with Higher Future Levels—Combat Arms

Domain	Dimension	Past Level (Quartile)
GW	Getting information needed to do the job	Middle
GW	Updating and using job-relevant knowledge	Middle
GW	Analyzing data or information	Middle
GW	Thinking creatively	Middle
SK	Social perceptiveness	Middle
AB	Speed of closure	Middle
AB	Inductive reasoning	Middle
AB	Oral comprehension	Middle
GW	Repairing and maintaining electronic equipment	Lower
GW	Evaluating information for compliance to standards	Lower
KN	Personnel and human resources	Lower

Table E.11

Dimensions with Higher Future Levels—Dental and Pharmacy Specialists

Domain	Dimension	Past Level (Quartile)
GW	Updating and using job-relevant knowledge	Upper
WC	Provide a service to others	Upper
KN	Medicine and dentistry	Upper
KN	Chemistry	Upper
AB	Oral comprehension	Upper
AB	Written comprehension	Upper
GW	Interacting with computers	Middle
GW	Teaching others	Middle
GW	Resolving conflicts and negotiating with others	Middle
KN	Biology	Middle
KN	Customer and personal service	Middle
KN	Computers and electronics	Middle
KN	Engineering and technology	Lower

Table E.12

Dimensions with Higher Future Levels—Divers

Domain	Dimension	Past Level (Quartile)
GW	Updating and using job-relevant knowledge	Middle
GW	Analyzing data or information	Middle
KN	Engineering and technology	Middle
GW	Operating vehicles, mechanized devices, or equipment	Lower
GW	Interacting with computers	Lower

Table E.13

Dimensions with Higher Future Levels—Emergency Management and Laboratory Specialists

Domain	Dimension	Past Level (Quartile)
AB	Written comprehension	Upper
AB	Oral expression	Upper
AB	Written expression	Upper
KN	Administration and management	Middle
SK	Identification of key causes	Middle
SK	Solution appraisal	Middle
SK	Implementation planning	Middle
AB	Fluency of ideas	Middle
AB	Originality	Middle

Table E.14

Dimensions with Higher Future Levels—Environmental Health and Safety Specialists

Domain	Dimension	Past Level (Quartile)
GW	Getting information needed to do the job	Upper
GW	Identifying objects, actions, and events	Upper
GW	Updating and using job-relevant knowledge	Upper
GW	Monitoring processes, materials, or surroundings	Upper
GW	Processing information	Upper
GW	Analyzing data or information	Upper
GW	Evaluating information for compliance to standards	Upper
SK	Implementation planning	Upper
SK	Solution appraisal	Upper
SK	Identification of downstream consequences	Upper
AB	Written comprehension	Upper
AB	Written expression	Upper
AB	Problem sensitivity	Upper
AB	Inductive reasoning	Upper
AB	Deductive reasoning	Upper
GW	Teaching others	Middle
GW	Coaching and developing others	Middle
KN	Chemistry	Middle
KN	Public safety and security	Middle
KN	Biology	Middle
KN	Law, government, and jurisprudence	Middle

Table E.15

Dimensions with Higher Future Levels—Finance and Accounting Managers

Domain	Dimension	Past Level (Quartile)
	None significant	

Table E.16

Dimensions with Higher Future Levels—Firefighters

Domain	Dimension	Past Level (Quartile)
	None significant	

Table E.17

Dimensions with Higher Future Levels—Flight Engineers

Domain	Dimension	Past Level (Quartile)
KN	Computers and electronics	Upper
KN	Engineering and technology	Upper
AB	Perceptual speed	Upper

Table E.18

Dimensions with Higher Future Levels—Functional Specialty Managers

Domain	Dimension	Past Level (Quartile)
KN	Administration and management	Upper
KN	Personnel and human resources	Upper
SK	Management of personnel resources	Upper
SK	Time management	Upper
AB	Written expression	Upper
KN	Customer and personal service	Middle
KN	Computers and electronics	Middle

Table E.19

Dimensions with Higher Future Levels—Aircraft Launch and Recovery Specialists

Domain	Dimension	Past Level (Quartile)
	None significant	

Table E.20

Dimensions with Higher Future Levels—Health, Education, and Welfare Workers

Domain	Dimension	Past Level (Quartile)
GW	Getting information needed to do the job	Upper
GW	Making decisions and solving problems	Upper
GW	Processing information	Upper
SK	Writing	Upper
SK	Visioning	Upper

Table E.21

Dimensions with Higher Future Levels—Intelligence Specialists

Domain	Dimension	Past Level (Quartile)
GW	Getting information needed to do the job	Upper
GW	Identifying objects, actions, and events	Upper
GW	Updating and using job-relevant knowledge	Upper
SK	Information gathering	Upper
SK	Reading comprehension	Upper
SK	Information organization	Upper
SK	Active learning	Upper
SK	Active listening	Upper
SK	Problem identification	Upper
SK	Judgment and decisionmaking	Upper
SK	Synthesis/reorganization	Upper
SK	Idea evaluation	Upper
SK	Monitoring	Upper
KN	Telecommunications	Middle

Table E.22

Dimensions with Higher Future Levels—Law Enforcement Specialists

Domain	Dimension	Past Level (Quartile)
GW	Resolving conflicts and negotiating with others	Upper
WC	Importance of being exact or accurate	Upper
KN	Public safety and security	Upper
KN	Law, government, and jurisprudence	Upper
AB	Inductive reasoning	Upper
GW	Interpreting the meaning of information for others	Middle
KN	Sociology and anthropology	Middle
SK	Persuasion	Middle
SK	Negotiation	Middle

Table E.23

Dimensions with Higher Future Levels—Legal Specialists and Court Reporters

Domain	Dimension	Past Level (Quartile)
	None significant	

Table E.24

Dimensions with Higher Future Levels—Life Scientists

Domain	Dimension	Past Level (Quartile)
	None significant	

Table E.25

Dimensions with Higher Future Levels—Machinists, Technicians, and Cargo Specialists

Domain	Dimension	Past Level (Quartile)
GW	Monitoring processes, materials, or surroundings	Upper
GW	Controlling machines and processes	Upper
GW	Evaluating information for compliance to standards	Upper
SK	Coordination	Upper
SK	Equipment selection	Upper
SK	Troubleshooting	Upper
GW	Thinking creatively	Middle
KN	Engineering and technology	Middle
KN	Computers and electronics	Middle
SK	Operations analysis	Middle
GW	Operating vehicles, mechanized devices, or equipment	Lower

Table E.26

Dimensions with Higher Future Levels—Medical Service and Medical Care Technicians

Domain	Dimension	Past Level (Quartile)
GW	Communicating with supervisors, peers, or subordinates	Upper
GW	Making decisions and solving problems	Upper
SK	Reading comprehension	Upper
SK	Active listening	Upper
GW	Analyzing data or information	Middle
GW	Interpreting the meaning of information for others	Middle
GW	Thinking creatively	Middle
KN	Customer and personal service	Middle
SK	Information organization	Middle
SK	Equipment selection	Middle

Table E.27

Dimensions with Higher Future Levels—Musicians and Media Directors

Domain	Dimension	Past Level (Quartile)
	None significant	

Table E.28

Dimensions with Higher Future Levels—Non-Destructive Testers

Domain	Dimension	Past Level (Quartile)
KN	Mechanical	Upper
KN	Physics	Upper
WC	Radiation injury	Lower

Table E.29

Dimensions with Higher Future Levels—Ordnance Specialists

Domain	Dimension	Past Level (Quartile)
KN	Public safety and security	Upper
KN	Engineering and technology	Middle
KN	Computers and electronics	Middle

Table E.30

Dimensions with Higher Future Levels—Nurses and Physical Therapists

Domain	Dimension	Past Level (Quartile)
	None significant	

Table E.31

Dimensions with Higher Future Levels—Optometry Technicians

Domain	Dimension	Past Level (Quartile)
	None significant	

Table E.32

Dimensions with Higher Future Levels—Photographic and Audiovisual Specialists

Domain	Dimension	Past Level (Quartile)
GW	Updating and using job-relevant knowledge	Upper
KN	Computers and electronics	Middle
KN	Telecommunications	Middle

Table E.33

Dimensions with Higher Future Levels—Physicians, Surgeons, and Optometrists

Domain	Dimension	Past Level (Quartile)
WC	Responsible for others' health and safety	Upper
KN	Medicine and dentistry	Upper
KN	Biology	Upper
KN	Chemistry	Upper
KN	Therapy and counseling	Middle
KN	Administration and management	Middle
KN	Psychology	Middle
KN	Computers and electronics	Middle
KN	Foreign language	Lower

Table E.34

Dimensions with Higher Future Levels—Pilots and Ship/ Submarine Operators

Domain	Dimension	Past Level (Quartile)
SK	Instructing	Upper
AB	Response orientation	Upper
AB	Reaction time	Upper
AB	Problem sensitivity	Upper
KN	Mechanical	Middle
KN	Computers and electronics	Middle
KN	Engineering and technology	Middle
KN	Foreign language	Lower

Table E.35

Dimensions with Higher Future Levels—Postal Directors

Domain	Dimension	Past Level (Quartile)
WC	Degree of automation	Upper
KN	Computers and electronics	Middle

Table E.36

Dimensions with Higher Future Levels—Precision Equipment Repairers

Domain	Dimension	Past Level (Quartile)
GW	Repairing and maintaining electronic equipment	Upper
KN	Computers and electronics	Upper
KN	Mechanical	Upper

Table E.37

Dimensions with Higher Future Levels—Preventive Maintenance Analysts

Domain	Dimension	Past Level (Quartile)
	None significant	

Table E.38

Dimensions with Higher Future Levels—Public Information Managers and Journalists

Domain	Dimension	Past Level (Quartile)
	None significant	

Table E.39

Dimensions with Higher Future Levels—Radar and Sonar Operators

Domain	Dimension	Past Level (Quartile)
GW	Interacting with computers	Middle

Table E.40

Dimensions with Higher Future Levels—Recruiting Specialists

Domain	Dimension	Past Level (Quartile)
GW	Communicating with persons outside the organization	Upper
SK	Persuasion	Upper
GW	Selling or influencing others	Middle
GW	Developing objectives and strategies	Middle
GW	Thinking creatively	Middle
GW	Performing for or working directly with the public	Middle
GW	Operating vehicles, mechanized devices, or equipment	Middle
WC	Persuade someone to a course of action	Middle

Table E.41

Dimensions with Higher Future Levels—Scientists and Engineers

Domain	Dimension	Past Level (Quartile)
GW	Processing information	Upper
GW	Thinking creatively	Upper
SK	Mathematics	Upper
SK	Science	Upper
KN	Building and construction	Middle
SK	Systems evaluation	Middle
SK	Technology design	Middle

Table E.42

Dimensions with Higher Future Levels—Ship Engineers and Air Crew Members

Domain	Dimension	Past Level (Quartile)
SK	Operation monitoring	Upper
SK	Problem identification	Upper
GW	Repairing and maintaining electronic equipment	Middle
SK	Information gathering	Middle
SK	Information organization	Middle
SK	Science	Middle
GW	Interacting with computers	Lower

Table E.43

Dimensions with Higher Future Levels—Surveyors and Mappers

Domain	Dimension	Past Level (Quartile)
GW	Analyzing data or information	Upper
WC	Degree of automation	Middle

Table E.44

Dimensions with Higher Future Levels—Transportation Specialists

Domain	Dimension	Past Level (Quartile)
GW	Interacting with computers	Middle

Table E.45

Dimensions with Higher Future Levels—Vehicle Drivers

Domain	Dimension	Past Level (Quartile)
GW	Repairing and maintaining mechanical equipment	Upper
GW	Interacting with computers	Lower

Table E.46

Dimensions with Higher Future Levels—Weather Personnel

Domain	Dimension	Past Level (Quartile)
WC	Importance of being aware of new events	Upper
KN	Geography	Upper
KN	Computers and electronics	Middle

ARMY OCCUPATIONS BY OCCUPATIONAL CLUSTER

1 Special Operations Forces

MOC	MOC Title	Personnel
180A	Special Forces Warrant Officer	388
18A	Special Forces	1,169
18B	Special Forces Weapons Sergeant	782
18F	Special Forces Assistant Operations/Intelligence Sergeant	396
18Z	Special Forces Senior Sergeant	684
921A	Airdrop Systems Technician	56

2 Administrative, Personnel, and Supply Specialists

MOC	MOC Title	Personnel
55B	Ammunition Specialist	2,574
57E	Laundry and Shower Specialist	781
71G	Patient Administration Specialist	922
71L	Administrative Specialist	9,957
71M	Chaplain Assistant	1,267
73C	Finance Specialist	1,877
73D	Accounting Specialist	621
73Z	Finance Senior Sergeant	108
75B	Personnel Administration Specialist	3,278
76J	Medical Supply Specialist	1,454
92A	Automated Logistical Specialist	12,763
92M	Quartermaster	390
92Y	Unit Supply Specialist	12,325
92Z	Senior Noncommissioned Logistician	137
93P	Aviation Operations Specialist	1,738

3 Aircraft, Automotive, and Electrical Maintenance Specialists

MOC	MOC Title	Personnel
44B	Metal Worker	851
51R	Interior Electrician	181
52C	Utilities Equipment Repairer	1,346
52D	Power-Generation Equipment Repairer	3,239
52E	Prime Power Production Specialist	190
52X	Special Purpose Equipment Repairer	196
62B	Construction Equipment Repairer	1,983

63B	Light-Wheel Vehicle Mechanic	10,209
63D	Self-Propelled Field Artillery System Mechanic	653
63E	M1 ABRAMS Tank System Mechanic	1,930
63G	Fuel and Electrical Systems Repairer	503
63H	Track Vehicle Repairer	3,271
63N	M60A1/A3 Tank System Mechanic (Reserve Components)	1
63S	Heavy-Wheel Vehicle Mechanic	2,701
63T	BRADLEY Fighting Vehicle System Mechanic	3,135
63W	Wheel Vehicle Repairer	3,393
63Y	Track Vehicle Mechanic	732
63Z	Mechanical Maintenance Supervisor	847
67G	Utility Airplane Repairer (Reserve Components)	6
67N	UH-1 Helicopter Repairer	214
67R	AH-64 Attack Helicopter Repairer	1,658
67S	OH-58D Helicopter Repairer	1,015
67T	UH-60 Helicopter Repairer	3,540
67U	CH-47 Helicopter Repairer	1,706
67V	Observation/Scout Helicopter Repairer	126
67Y	AH-1 Attack Helicopter Repairer	111
67Z	Aircraft Maintenance Senior Sergeant	449
68B	Aircraft Powerplant Repairer	619
68D	Aircraft Powertrain Repairer	443
68F	Aircraft Electrician	523
68G	Aircraft Structural Repairer	591
68H	Aircraft Pneudraulics Repairer	391
68K	Aircraft Components Repair Supervisor	259
68X	AH-64 Armament/Electrical Systems Repairer	1,044
88L	Watercraft Engineer	416

4 Air Traffic Controllers

MOC	MOC Title	Personnel
93C	Air Traffic Control (ATC) Operator	1,143

6 Communications Managers

MOC	MOC Title	Personnel
25C	Communications-Electronics (C-E) Operations	1,626

7 Communications Operators

MOC	MOC Title	Personnel
18E	Special Forces Communications Sergeant	804
31F	Network Switching Systems Operator-Maintainer	4,232
31U	Signal Support Systems Specialist	7,360
31W	Telecommunications Operations Chief	1,591
74C	Record Telecommunications Operator-Maintainer	2,449
98H	Morse Interceptor	607
98K	Non-Morse Interceptor/Analyst	509

8 Computer Systems Specialists

MOC	MOC Title	Personnel
251A	Data Processing Technician	82
25B	Communications-Electronics (C-E) Automation	106
53A	Systems Automation Management	43

53B	Systems Automation Officer, Hardware Engineering	8
53C	Systems Automation Acquisition	5
74Z	Record Information Systems Chief	154
75F	Personnel Information System Management Specialist	696

9 Construction and Engineering Operators

MOC	MOC Title	Personnel
12B	Combat Engineer	8,974
12C	Bridge Crewmember	724
12Z	Combat Engineering Senior Sergeant	310
18C	Special Forces Engineer Sergeant	748
43M	Fabric Repair Specialist	205
51H	Construction Engineering Supervisor	480
51K	Plumber	155
51Z	General Engineering Supervisor	160
62E	Heavy Construction Equipment Operator	1,526
62F	Crane Operator	353
62G	Quarrying Specialist	48
62H	Concrete and Asphalt Equipment Operator	101
62J	General Construction Equipment Operator	772
62N	Construction Equipment Supervisor	473

10 Combat Arms

MOC	MOC Title	Personnel
11A	Infantry	6,726
11B	Infantryman	28,391
11C	Indirect Fire Infantryman	5,568
11H	Heavy Antiarmor Weapons Infantryman	2,589
11M	Fighting Vehicle Infantryman	13,780
11X	Infantry MOS to Be Determined	2,449
11Z	Infantry Senior Sergeant	244
12A	Armor, General	4,003
12B	Armor	6
12C	Cavalry	2
13A	Field Artillery, General	5,213
13B	Cannon Crewmember	11,361
13C	Automated Fire Support Systems Specialist	817
13E	Cannon Fire Direction Specialist	1,919
13F	Fire Support Specialist	4,278
13M	Multiple Launch Rocket System Crewmember	3,464
13P	Multiple Launch Rocket System Operations/Fire Direction Specialist	1,008
13Z	Field Artillery Senior Sergeant	621
14A	Air Defense Artillery, General	1,643
14B	Short-Range Air Defense Artillery (SHORAD)	212
14D	HAWK Missile System Crewmember	1
14D	HAWK Missile Air Defense Artillery	4
14E	PATRIOT Missile Air Defense Artillery	263
14E	PATRIOT Fire Control Enhanced Operator/Maintainer	1,227
14J	Air Defense C4I Tactical Operations Center Enhanced Operator/Maintainer	1,219
14M	Man Portable Air Defense System Crewmember	14
14R	BRADLEY Linebacker Crewmember	1,504

14S	AVENGER Crewmember	3,079
19D	Cavalry Scout	6,620
19K	M1 Armor Crewman	12,670
19Z	Armor Senior Sergeant	625
913A	Armament Repair Technician	69

11 Dental and Pharmacy Specialists

MOC	MOC Title	Personnel
63A	General Dentist	341
63B	Comprehensive Dentist	297
63D	Periodontist	53
63E	Endodontist	41
63F	Prosthodontist	102
63H	Public Health Dentist	7
63K	Pediatric Dentist	38
63M	Orthodonist	34
63N	Oral and Maxillofacial Surgeon	89
63P	Oral Pathologist	17
91E	Dental Specialist	1,648
91Q	Pharmacy Specialist	633

12 Divers

MOC	MOC Title	Personnel
00B	Diver	88

13 Emergency Management and Laboratory Specialists

MOC	MOC Title	Personnel
54B	Chemical Operations Specialist	6,386
77L	Petroleum Laboratory Specialist	149

14 Environmental Health and Safety Specialists

MOC	MOC Title	Personnel
91R	Veterinary Food Inspection Specialist	967
91S	Preventive Medicine Specialist	681

15 Finance and Accounting Managers

MOC	MOC Title	Personnel
44A	Finance, General	590
45A	Comptroller	19

18 Functional Specialty Managers

MOC	MOC Title	Personnel
151A	Aviation Maintenance Technician (Nonrated)	220
15D	Aviation Logistics	174
311A	CID Special Agent	326
31A	Military Police General	1,617
420A	Military Personnel Technician	215
42A	Adjutant General, General	455
42B	Personnel Systems Management	1,121
49B	Operations Research, Personnel	19
640A	Veterinary Services Technician	60
74C	Chemical Munitions and Materiel Management	636

88A	Transportation, General	1,909
88B	Traffic Management	1
88C	Marine and Terminal Operations	2
88D	Motor/Rail Transportation	2
90A	Logistics	23
910A	Ammunition Technician	106
914A	Allied Trades Technician	54
915A	Unit Maintenance Technician (Light)	486
915D	Unit Maintenance Technician (Heavy)	126
915E	Support Maintenance Technician	340
91A	Ordnance, General	330
91B	Maintenance Management	2,139
91D	Munitions Materiel Management	456
91M	Hospital Food Service Specialist	558
920A	Property Accounting Technician	444
920B	Supply Systems Technician	304
922A	Food Service Technician	174
92A	Quartermaster, General	836
92B	Supply and Materiel Management	1,737
92D	Aerial Delivery and Materiel	206
92F	Petroleum and Water	203
92G	Quartermaster	10,589

20 Health, Education and Welfare Workers

MOC	MOC Title	Personnel
47A	USMA Professor	28
55A	Judge Advocate, General	1,391
55B	Military Judge	1
56A	Command and Unit Chaplain	1,238
56D	Clinical Pastoral Educator	2
61E	Clinical Pharmacologist	8
65C	Dietitian	141
67A	Health Services	2,591
67D	Behavioral Sciences	252
67E	Pharmacy	144
70A	Health Care Administration	1
70B	Health Services Administration	2
73B	Clinical Psychology	4
96Z	Intelligence Senior Sergeant	32
97E	Interrogator	826
98G	Voice Interceptor	2,968
98X	Linguist MOS to Be Determined	443
98Z	Signals Intelligence/Electronic Warfare Chief	148

21 Intelligence Specialists

MOC	MOC Title	Personnel
131A	Field Artillery Targeting Technician	172
25A	Signal, General	2,000
350B	All Source Intelligence Technician	137
350D	Imagery Intelligence Technician	78
351B	Counterintelligence Technician	293
351E	Human Intelligence Collection Technician	108
352C	Traffic Analysis Technician	145

352D	Emitter Location/Identification Technician	12
352G	Voice Intercept Technician	44
352H	Morse Intercept Technician	19
352J	Emanations Analysis Technician	44
352K	Non-Morse Intercept Technician	16
353A	IEW Equipment Technician	48
35B	Strategic Intelligence	311
35D	All Source Intelligence	3,414
35E	Counterintelligence	143
35F	Human Intelligence	6
35G	Signals Intelligence/Electronic Warfare	162
37F	Psychological Operations Specialist	440
96B	Intelligence Analyst	3,120
96D	Imagery Analyst	764
96H	Imagery Ground Station (IGS) Operator	329
96R	Ground Surveillance Systems Operator	764
96U	Unmanned Aerial Vehicle Operator	154
97B	Counterintelligence Agent	1,076
97Z	Counterintelligence/Human Intelligence Senior Sergeant	10
98C	Signals Intelligence Analyst	2,116
98J	Noncommunications Interceptor/Analyst	698

22 Law Enforcement Specialists

MOC	MOC Title	Personnel
95B	Military Police	14,072
95C	Corrections Specialist	948
95D	CID Special Agent	463

23 Legal Specialists and Court Reporters

MOC	MOC Title	Personnel
550A	Legal Administrator	61
71D	Legal Specialist	1,570

24 Life Scientists

MOC	MOC Title	Personnel
64A	Veterinarian	417
67B	Laboratory Sciences	270
75A	Field Veterinary Service	7

25 Machinists, Technicians, and Cargo Specialists

MOC	MOC Title	Personnel
42E	Optical Laboratory Specialist	182
44E	Machinist	410
77F	Petroleum Supply Specialist	8,586
77W	Water Treatment Specialist	862
81L	Lithographer	301
88H	Cargo Specialist	1,657
92R	Quartermaster	1,598

26 Medical Service and Medical Care Technicians

MOC	MOC Title	Personnel
18D	Special Forces Medical Sergeant	730
65D	Physician Assistant	478

91B	Medical Specialist	16,975
91C	Practical Nurse	3,073
91D	Operating Room Specialist	1,068
91K	Medical Laboratory Specialist	1,977
91P	Radiology Specialist	959
91T	Animal Care Specialist	458
91V	Respiratory Specialist	298

27 Musicians and Media Directors

MOC	MOC Title	Personnel
02B	Band Member Coronet or Trumpet Player	258
02C	Band Member Baritone or Euphonium Player	74
02D	Band Member French Horn Player	105
02E	Band Member Trombone Player	149
02F	Band Member Tuba Player	102
02G	Band Member Flute or Piccolo Player	75
02H	Band Member Oboe Player	35
02J	Band Member Clarinet Player	177
02K	Band Member Bassoon Player	43
02L	Band Member Saxophone Player	149
02M	Band Member Percussion Player	107
02N	Band Member Piano Player	71
02S	Special Band Member	551
02T	Band Member Guitar Player	43
02U	Electric Bass Guitar Player	55
02Z	Bands Senior Sergeant	61
420C	Bandmaster	46
42C	Army Bands	22
46B	Broadcast	13

29 Ordnance Specialists

MOC	MOC Title	Personnel
55D	Explosive Ordnance Disposal (EOD) Specialist	1,065

30 Nurses and Physical Therapists

MOC	MOC Title	Personnel
65A	Occupational Therapy	72
65B	Physical Therapy	177
66A	Nurse Administrator	2
66C	Psychiatric/Mental Health Nurse	91
66E	Operating Room Nurse	285
66F	Nurse Anesthetist	221
66H	Medical Surgical Nurse	2,739
66J	Clinical Nurse	1

32 Photographic and Audiovisual Specialists

MOC	MOC Title	Personnel
25M	Multimedia Illustrator	332
25V	Combat Documentation/Production Specialist	472
25Z	Visual Information Operations Chief	107

33 Physicians, Surgeons, Optometrists

MOC	MOC Title	Personnel
60B	Nuclear Medicine Officer	23
60C	Preventive Medicine Officer	78
60D	Occupational Medicine Officer	22
60F	Pulmonary Disease Officer	58
60G	Medical Corps Officer, Gastroenterologist	47
60H	Cardiologist	64
60J	Obstetrician and Gynecologist	269
60K	Urologist	72
60L	Dermatologist	71
60M	Allergist, Clinical Immunologist	21
60N	Anesthesiologist	171
60P	Pediatrician	287
60Q	Pediatric Cardiologist	7
60R	Child Neurologist	14
60S	Ophthalmologist	103
60T	Otolaryngologist	77
60U	Child Psychiatrist	40
60V	Neurologist	60
60W	Psychiatrist	165
61A	Nephrologist	14
61B	Medical Oncologist/Hematologist	36
61C	Endocrinologist	22
61D	Rheumatologist	15
61F	Internist	445
61G	Infectious Disease Officer	35
61H	Family Physician	563
61J	General Surgeon	302
61K	Thoracic Surgeon	19
61L	Plastic Surgeon	20
61M	Orthopedic Surgeon	223
61N	Flight Surgeon	147
61P	Physiatrist	36
61Q	Therapeutic Radiologist	16
61R	Diagnostic Radiologist	216
61U	Pathologist	143
61W	Peripheral Vascular Surgeon	15
61Z	Neurosurgeon	26
62A	Emergency Physician	177
62B	Field Surgeon	354
67C	Preventive Medicine Sciences	372
67F	Optometry	122
67G	Podiatry	22

34 Pilots and Ship/Submarine Operators

MOC	MOC Title	Personnel
152B	OH-58A/C Scout Pilot	79
152C	OH-6 Pilot	52
152D	OH-58D Pilot	702
152F	AH-64 Attack Pilot	862
152G	AH-1 Attack Pilot	50
153B	UH-1 Pilot	158

153D	UH-60 Pilot	1,943
154C	CH-47D Pilot	516
155A	Fixed Wing Aviator	4
155D	U-21 Pilot	37
155E	C-12 Pilot	302
15A	Aviation, General	4,337
15B	Aviation Combined Arms Operations	159
15C	Aviation All-Source Intelligence	26
67J	Aeromedical Evacuation	286
880A	Marine Deck Officer	88
88K	Watercraft Operator	591

36 Precision Equipment Repairers

MOC	MOC Title	Personnel
140E	PATRIOT Systems Technician	161
14T	PATRIOT Launching Station Enhanced Operator/Maintainer	2,372
14Z	Air Defense Artillery Senior Sergeant	253
25R	Visual Information Equipment Operator-Maintainer	221
27E	Land Combat Electronic Missile System Repairer	600
27M	Multiple Launch Rocket System (MLRS) Repairer	451
27T	AVENGER System Repairer	276
27X	PATRIOT System Repairer	160
27Z	Missile Systems Maintenance Chief	36
31C	Radio Operator-Maintainer	1,421
31L	Cable Systems Installer-Maintainer	2,123
31P	Microwave Systems Operator-Maintainer	1,515
31R	Multichannel Transmission Systems Operator-Maintainer	7,196
31S	Satellite Communication Systems Operator-Maintainer	2,047
31T	Satellite/Microwave Systems Chief	69
31Z	Senior Signal Sergeant	127
35B	Land Combat Support System (LCSS) Test Specialist	56
35C	Surveillance Radar Repairer	41
35E	Radio and Communications Security (COMSEC) Repairer	1,766
35F	Special Electronic Devices Repairer	354
35H	Test, Measurement, and Diagnostic Equipment (TMDE) Maintenance Support Specialist	262
35J	Telecommunication Terminal Device Repairer	424
35M	Radar Repairer	194
35N	Wire Systems Equipment Repairer	390
35Q	Avionic Flight Systems Repairer	119
35W	Electronic Maintenance Chief	455
35Y	Integrated Family of Test Equipment (IFTE) Operator and Maintainer	294
35Z	Senior Electronics Maintenance Chief	27
39B	Automatic Test Equipment Operator/Maintainer	108
45B	Small Arms/Artillery Repairer	503
45D	Self-Propelled Field Artillery Turret Mechanic	181
45E	M1 ABRAMS Tank Turret Mechanic	700
45G	Fire Control Repairer	355
45K	Armament Repairer	922
45N	M60A1/A3 Tank Turret Mechanic	3

45T	BRADLEY Fighting Vehicle System Turret Mechanic	558
52G	Transmission and Distribution Specialist	2
63J	Quartermaster and Chemical Equipment Repairer	1,272
670A	Health Services Maintenance Technician	77
68J	Aircraft Armament/Missile Systems Repairer	616
68N	Avionic Mechanic	624
74G	ADP Systems Analyst	390
91A	Medical Equipment Repairer	650

37 Preventive Maintenance Analysts

MOC	MOC Title	Personnel
74B	Card and Tape Writer	2,673

38 Public Information Managers and Journalists

MOC	MOC Title	Personnel
350L	Attaché Technician	54
38A	Civil Affairs Specialist (Reserve Components)	7
39A	PSYOP or CA, General	32
39B	Psychological Operations	7
39C	Civil Affairs	3
46A	Public Affairs, General	18
46Q	Journalist	378
46R	Broadcast Journalist	247
46Z	Public Affairs Chief	53
48A	Foreign Area Officer, General	50
48B	Latin America	7
48C	West Europe	1
48D	Foreign Area Officer, South Asia	3
48E	Russia/East Europe	3
48F	Foreign Area Officer, China	1
70H	Health Services Plans, Operations, Intelligence, Security, and Training	2
91E	Explosive Ordnance Disposal	28

39 Radar and Sonar Operators

MOC	MOC Title	Personnel
13R	Field Artillery (FA) Firefinder Radar Operator	487

40 Recruiting Specialists

MOC	MOC Title	Personnel
00Z	Command Sergeant Major	1,119
79R	Recruiter	3,158
79S	Career Counselor	719

41 Scientists and Engineers

MOC	MOC Title	Personnel
140A	Command and Control Systems Technician	22
210A	Utilities Operation and Maintenance Technician	41
21A	Engineer General	1,004
21B	Combat Engineer	2,593
21D	Facilities/Contract Construction Management Engineer (FCCME) Officer	6

25D	Communications-Electronics (C-E) Engineering	58
25E	Information Systems and Networking	21
49A	Operations Research/Systems Analysis Officer, Operations Research, General	63
49C	Operations Research, Combat Operations/Weapon Systems	9
49D	Operations Research, Planning, Programming, and Resource Management	8
49E	Operations Research, Test, and Evaluation	1
51A	Research and Development	1
52A	Nuclear Weapons Officer, General	6
52B	Nuclear Weapons Research	5
72D	Environmental Science	1
72E	Sanitary Engineer	2
74A	Chemical, General	508
74B	Chemical Operations and Training	84
912A	Land Combat Missile Systems Technician	59
916A	High-to-Medium Air Defense (HIMAD) Direct Support/General Support Maintenance Technician	20
917A	Maneuver Forces Air Defense Systems (MFADS) Technician	74
918A	TMDE Maintenance Support Technician	20
918B	Electronic Systems Maintenance Technician	185
919A	Engineer Equipment Repair Technician	136

42 Ship Engineers and Air Crew Members

MOC	MOC Title	Personnel
881A	Marine Engineering Officer	95

43 Surveyors and Mappers

MOC	MOC Title	Personnel
215D	Terrain Analysis Technician	34
21C	Topographic Engineer	12
35C	Imagery Intelligence	195
51T	Technical Engineering Specialist	290
81T	Topographic Analyst	379
81Z	Topographic Engineering Supervisor	26
82C	Field Artillery Surveyor	895
82D	Topographic Surveyor	121

44 Transportation Specialists

MOC	MOC Title	Personnel
88M	Motor Transport Operator	10,756
88N	Transportation Management Coordinator	1,444
88Z	Transportation Senior Sergeant	274

46 Weather Personnel

MOC	MOC Title	Personnel
93F	Field Artillery Meteorological Crewmember	226

NAVY OCCUPATIONS BY OCCUPATIONAL CLUSTER

1 Special Operations Forces

MOC	MOC Title	Personnel
5323	SDV Pilot/Navigator/DDS Operator	82
5326	Combatant Swimmer (SEAL)	669
5332	EOD Technician	64
5333	EOD Technician/Parachutist	8
5350	Special Warfare Combatant Crewman (SWCC) Basic	10
5351	Special Warfare Combatant Crewman (SWCC) Intermediate	169
5352	Special Warfare Combatant Crewman (SWCC) Advanced	57
8673	Squadron Special Missions Officer	54
9062	Amphibious Operations Officer	36
9231	Explosive Ordnance Disposal Mobile Unit Officer	1
9291	Executive Officer, Special Warfare Team	2
9291	Executive Officer, Special Warfare Team	22
9293	Sea-Air-Land Officer	11
9293	Sea-Air-Land Officer	181
9294	Seal Delivery Vehicle Officer	36
9480	Search and Rescue Officer	11
9554	Master Naval Parachutist	1

2 Administrative, Personnel, and Supply Specialists

MOC	MOC Title	Personnel
2514	Flag Officer Writer	180
2612	Classification Interviewer	409
2813	Independent Duty Ashore Storekeeper	25
2814	SNAP II Supply and Financial Management (SFM) Storekeeper	840
2815	Independent Duty Afloat Storekeeper	237
2820	SNAP II Supply and Financial Management (SFM) Functional Area Supervisor	632
2824	Supply and Accounting (SUADPS R/T) Technical Specialist	822

2825	Supply and Accounting (SUADPS-R/T) Advanced Technical Specialist	458
2905	Disbursing Afloat Automated Systems Specialist	684
3111	Automated Afloat Sales and Service Manager	875
3115	Resale Management Specialist	36
3122	Barber	801
3154	Dry Cleaning Specialist	138
8012	Aviation Supply Systems Specialist	430
8424	Medical Department Administration Technician	277
8496	Mortician	17
9190	Special Security Assistant	877
9580	Command Master Chief	190
9590	Support Equipment Asset Manager	138

3 Aircraft, Automotive, and Electrical Maintenance Specialists

MOC	MOC Title	Personnel
0982	Guided Missile Launching System (GMLS) MK-26 Obsolescence Recovery Program (ORP) Technician	19
0983	MK-41 Vertical Launching System (VLS) Advanced Technician	16
1103	AEGIS Combat System Maintenance Supervisor	21
1104	AEGIS Combat System (BL4) Maintenance Supervisor	71
1105	AEGIS Weapon System MK-7 Technician	155
1157	Improved Self Defense Surface Missile System Technician	111
1158	TARTAR Missile Fire Control System (MK-74 MOD 14) Technician	22
1159	TERRIER Missile Fire Control System (MK-76 MOD 10) Technician	9
1194	AN/BSY-2(V) Advanced Maintainer	1
1323	AGFCS MK-86 MOD 8/10 Systems Technician	154
1324	AGFCS MK-86 MOD 9 Systems Technician	4
1332	Over the Horizon-Targeting (OTH-T) Supervisor	16
1333	Advanced TOMAHAWK Weapon Control System (ATWCS) AN/SWG-4 Operator and Maintenance Technician	37
3354	Submarine Nuclear Propulsion Plant Operator—Electrical	950
3355	Submarine Nuclear Propulsion Plant Operator—Mechanical	1,004
3384	Surface Ship Nuclear Propulsion Plant Operator—Electrical	580
3385	Surface Ship Nuclear Propulsion Plant Operator—Mechanical	903
3386	Surface Ship Nuclear Propulsion Plant Operator—Engineering Laboratory Technician	213
4123	DD-963/DDG-993/CG-47 Gas Turbine Electrical Maintenance Technician	413
4124	DD-963/DDG-993/CG-47 and DDG-51 Gas Turbine Mechanical Maintenance Technician	757
4125	DDG-51/AOE-6 Gas Turbine Electrical Maintenance Technician	101
4126	AOE-6 Gas Turbine Mechanical Maintenance Technician	33

4128	FFG-7 Gas Turbine Mechanical Maintenance Technician	130
4129	FFG-7 Gas Turbine Electrical Maintenance Technician	145
4131	LCAC Craft Engineer/Assistant Operator	65
4133	LCAC Mechanical Systems Maintenance Technician	172
4135	LCAC Electrical Systems Maintenance Technician	77
4136	Marine Gas Turbine Inspector	72
4204	Steam Propulsion Maintenance Supervisor	507
4206	Shipboard Engineering Plant Program Manager	610
4230	SSN/SSBN Auxiliary Equipment Operator	1,012
4231	SSN/SSBN Auxiliary Equipment Technician	1,115
4232	SSN/SSBN Weapons Equipment Operator	388
4233	SSN/SSBN Weapons Equipment Technician	598
4245	SSN/SSBN Basic Auxiliary Equipment Technician	53
4246	SSN/SSBN Diesel Engine (Fairbanks-Morse) Maintenance Technician	76
4291	Refrigeration and Air Conditioning Systems Technician	1,768
4295	UNREP Equipment Mechanic	237
4296	Shipboard Elevator Hydraulic/Mechanical System Mechanic	578
4302	PAXMAN Valenta Diesel Engine Operator	23
4303	Cummins/Volvo Penta Diesel Engines Technician	226
4308	Causeway Section Powered/Side Loadable Warping Tug (CSP/SLWT) Engineer	46
4310	ALCO (251C) and General Motors EMD (645) Diesel Engine Technician	291
4313	Outboard Engine Mechanic	584
4314	Diesel Engine Inspector	54
4316	MCM 1 & 2 Propulsion Technician	43
4324	MCM Propulsion Technician	209
4333	Fairbanks Morse (38D 8-1/8) and Colt Pielstick (PC2.5V) Diesel Engine Technician	207
4355	LAMPS MK III RAST Mechanical Maintenanceman	252
4361	ARS-50 Class Propulsion Technician	11
4366	LSD-41 Class Propulsion System Technician	101
4615	Electrical Motor Rewinder	557
4621	IMA Electrical Shop Journeyman	235
4626	DD-963/LHD-1 Electrical Component Maintenance Technician	211
4632	FFG-7 Class Auxiliaries Electrical System Technician	146
4666	Minesweeping Electrician	73
4668	UNREP Electrical-Electronics Control Maintenance	217
4671	Shipboard Elevator Electronic/Electrical System Maintenance Technician	485
4672	Steam Catapult Electrician	71
4673	LAMPS MK III RAST/HRS Electrical Maintenanceman	235
4709	Mission Briefing System AN/SXQ-8 Maintenance Technician	59
4731	Auxiliary Electrician	10

4743	Integrated Launch and Recovery Television Surveillance (ILARTS) System Maintenance Technician	95
4752	Electrolytic Oxygen Generator (MODEL 6L16) Maintenance Technician	7
4755	LSD-41 Console Maintenance	33
4756	AO-177 Console Maintenance	71
4757	ARS-50 Console Maintenance	32
4758	Stabilized Glide Slope Indicator System Maintenance	436
4775	MK-9 MOD 4 DRAI/MK-6 MOD 4B DRT Technician	58
4776	MK-9 MOD 4/MK-10 MOD 0 DRAI and MK-6 MOD 4B DRT Technician	59
4777	MK-6 MOD 4D Digital Dead Reckoning Trace (DDRT) Technician	59
5601	Uninterruptible Power Supply (UPS) Maintenance	42
5633	Mobile Utilities Support Equipment (MUSE) Technician	37
5635	Advanced Construction Electrician	245
5805	Advanced Construction Mechanic	379
5908	Tool and Equipment Technician	48
6104	Shore Based Refrigeration and Air Conditioning Technician	74
6410	F-110 Turbofan Jet Engine First Degree Repair/IMA Technician	73
6415	TF-30 Turbofan Jet Engine First Degree Repair/IMA Mechanic	117
6416	J-52 Turbojet Engine First Degree/IMA Mechanic	165
6417	T-400 Turboshaft Jet Engine First Degree Repair/IMA Mechanic	14
6418	T-56 Turboprop Engine and 54H60 Series Propeller First Degree/IMA Mechanic	270
6419	T-58 Turboshaft Jet Engine First Degree/IMA Mechanic	139
6420	F-404 Turbofan Jet Engine First Degree/IMA Mechanic	190
6421	TF-34 Turbofan Jet Engine First Degree/IMA Mechanic	96
6422	Test Cell Operator/Maintainer	140
6423	T-56-425/427 Turboprop Engine and Propeller IMA Mechanic	58
6424	T-64 Turboshaft Jet Engine First Degree/IMA Mechanic	29
6426	T-700 Turboshaft Jet Engine First Degree/IMA Mechanic	69
6428	Helicopter Rotors/Related Components IMA Mechanic	6
7105	Attitude Heading Reference System IMA Technician	140
7131	Power Generating Systems IMA Technician	39
7133	A6/EA6 Electrical Component IMA Technician	19
7136	P-3C Automatic Flight Control Systems (AFCS) IMA Technician	91
7137	Aircraft Instrument IMA Technician	178
7144	Helicopter ASE/AFCS IMA Technician	90
7173	ASM-175 Electronic Module Test Console IMA Technician	81
7174	AFCS/ADC/INS/DRS and Flight Systems Mini-SACE GT-4 Test Console Intermediate Technician	64
7175	P-3/C-130/E-2/C-2 Electrical Component IMA Technician	65

7182	P-3A/B Integrated Electrical System OMA Specialist	59
7184	F/A-18 Electrical Systems IMA Technician	89
7197	ASM-608 Inertial Measurement Unit Test Set Maintenance Technician	191
7212	Stationary Hydraulics Test Stand Operator/Maintenanceman	177
7213	Hydraulic, Pneumatic, Servocylinder Test (STS) Operator/Maintainer	32
7232	Structural Repair IMA Technician	498
7603	Support Equipment Air Conditioning and Mobile Maintenance Facility (MMF) Technician	73
7606	Support Equipment Gas Turbine Mechanic	167
7607	Shore Support Equipment Tow Tractor Technician	288
7610	Weapons Handling/Loading Equipment Mechanic	59
7612	Afloat SE Hydraulic Equipment IMA Technician	134
7613	Shore Based SE Hydraulic Equipment IMA Technician	127
7614	Shore Based Mobile Electric Power Plant IMA Technician	255
7615	Afloat Mobile Electric Power Plant Technician	148
7616	Maintenance Crane IMA Technician (Shore)	31
7617	Crash and Material Handling Technician (Sea)	64
7618	Afloat Support Equipment Technician	138
8361	Unmanned Air Vehicle (UAV) Systems Organizational Maintenance Technician	42
8362	Unmanned Air Vehicle (UAV) Systems Operator	23
8375	H-2 (LAMPS) Systems Organizational Maintenance Technician	69
8376	SH-60 (LAMPS MK III) Systems Organizational Maintenance Technician	604
8377	SH-3 Systems Organizational Maintenance Technician	316
8378	SH-60F/HH-60H Systems Organizational Maintenance Technician	1,347
8379	H-46 Systems Organizational Maintenance Technician	756
8380	UH-1N Systems Organizational Maintenance Technician	32
8391	Airborne Mine Countermeasure Systems Maintenance (AMCM) Technician (Level I and O)	79
8803	CH/MH-53 Systems Organizational Apprentice Maintenance Technician	154
8805	C-2/E-2 Systems Organizational Apprentice Maintenance Technician	228
8806	E-2C Group II Systems Organizational Apprentice Maintenance Technician	131
8819	P-3 Systems Organizational Apprentice Maintenance Technician	666
8832	EA-6B Systems Organizational Apprentice Maintenance Technician	485
8835	F-14D Systems Organizational Apprentice Maintenance Technician	179

8842	F/A-18 Systems Organizational Apprentice Maintenance Technician	1,489
8843	E-6A Systems Organizational Apprentice Maintenance Technician	29
8845	F-14 Systems Organizational Apprentice Maintenance Technician	853
8847	S-3 Systems Organizational Apprentice Maintenance Technician	502
8877	H-3 Systems Organizational Apprentice Maintenance Technician	46
8878	SH-60F/HH-60H Systems Organizational Apprentice Maintenance Technician	200
8891	Airborne Mine Countermeasure (AMCM) Systems Organization Apprentice Maintenance Technician	43
9583	Locksmith	95
9594	Intermediate Maintenance Activity (IMA) Nuclear Worker	28

4 Air Traffic Controllers

MOC	MOC Title	Personnel
6901	Facility Rated Approach Controller	396
6902	Carrier Air Traffic Control Center Controller	637
6903	Amphibious Air Traffic Control Center Controller	244
8621	Strike Operations Officer	63
8644	Radar Air Traffic Control Center Officer	49
8647	Air Traffic Control Officer	18
8658	Controlled Approach Officer	1
8662	Landing Signal Officer	112
8960	Navy Airspace Officer	8
8972	Staff Air Tactical Officer	14
8976	Target Aircraft Controller	1
8976	Target Aircraft Controller	2

6 Communications Managers

MOC	MOC Title	Personnel
9510	Communication Officer, Ashore	19
9510	Communication Officer, Ashore	61
9512	Automated Message Processing Exchange Officer	2
9515	Communications Plans and Operations Officer	8
9515	Communications Plans and Operations Officer	97
9517	Communication Security Officer	2
9517	Communication Security Officer	12
9525	Communication Watch Officer	13
9525	Communication Watch Officer	34
9535	Custodian of Communications Material	28
9543	Director of Communications	5
9560	Satellite Communications Officer	3
9560	Satellite Communications Officer	14

9565	Radio Officer	6
9565	Radio Officer	26
9567	Radio Station Officer	2
9567	Radio Station Officer	8
9575	Circuit Control Officer	7
9575	Circuit Control Officer	9
9582	Communication Officer, Afloat	8
9582	Communication Officer, Afloat	373
9585	Signal Officer	12
9590	Staff Communications Officer	9
9590	Staff Communications Officer	141
9595	Communications Traffic Officer	4
9595	Communications Traffic Officer	18

7 Communications Operators

MOC	MOC Title	Personnel
0342	Navy Tactical Command System Afloat (NTCS-A) Operator	1,401
0344	Navy Command and Control System (NCCS) Ashore System/Operator	53
1447	Communications Security Devices (T/SEC/KW-46 T/R) Technician	75
14RO	SSN Radio Frequency (RF) Equipment Operator	135
14TM	TRIDENT I/II Radio Frequency (RF) Equipment Maintenance Technician	27
14TO	TRIDENT I/II Radio Frequency (RF) Equipment Operator	196
1573	AIMS (TSEC/CRYPTO) Technician	1
1733	Electronic Warfare Systems Technician (AN/SLQ-32(V)2)	313
1734	Electronic Warfare Systems Technician (AN/SLQ-32(V)3)	435
1737	Electronics Warfare Systems Technician (AN/SLQ-32A(V)5/AN/SLQ-32(V)5)	68
1743	Electronic Warfare Systems Technician (AN/WLR-1H)	44
1781	Electronic Warfare Technician (Advanced Application)	283
2301	Enlisted Frequency Manager	20
2321	Surface Communication Systems Operator	365
2350	NAVMACS(V)5 Ship System Operator	117
2354	FLTSATCOM (SSIXS-OPCONCEN) Operator	45
2358	SHF SATCOM Systems Operator	33
2375	Tactical Support Communications (TSCOMM) Replacement Program System Operator	95
2376	LHD Class Radio Communications Systems Controller	22
2378	VERDIN/ISABPS Shore Communications System Operator	17
6634	Aircraft Communications Security Devices Equipment IMA Technician	142
9133	HFDF Network Manager	49
9177	CLASSIC OWL Operator	79
9178	NEWSDEALER Communications Operator	123
9185	TACINTEL Communications Operator	534

9188	Navy Integrated Cryptologic Communications Systems Specialist	12
9401	EP-3E In-Flight Technician	31
9403	EP-3E Electronic Warfare Operator	24

8 Computer Systems Specialists

MOC	MOC Title	Personnel
0336	Tactical Support Center (TSC) Operations Control Operator	95
2306	Computer Based Training Technician	4,553
2708	OSIS Baseline Upgrade (OBU) System Manager	25
2709	Joint Force Air Component Commander (JFACC) System Administrator	5
2720	NTCS-A System Administrator	72
2730	SNAP III System Administrator	263
2735	Information Systems Administrator	305
2739	Information Center Supervisor	2
2743	Computer Programmer (FORTRAN)	4
2750	Small Computer System Specialist	66
2755	AN/UYK-65 System Supervisor (SNAP I)	67
2756	AN/UYK-65(V) System Operator (SNAP I)	117
2757	CV-ASWM Data Processing System Operator	21
2776	Navy Command and Control System (NCCS) Ashore System Manager	45
2777	Tactical Support Center (TSC) Data Processing System Operator	26
2778	Mission Distribution System Operator	49
6314	Naval Aviation Logistics Command Management Information System (NALCOMIS) Database Administrator/Analyst (DBA/A)	136
6315	Naval Aviation Logistics Command Management Information System (NALCOMIS) System Administrator/Analyst (SA/A)	200
8013	Naval Aviation Logistics Command Management Information System (NALCOMIS) Supply Database Administrator (DBA)	36
9170	CLASSIC WIZARD Basic Operator	216
9174	CLASSIC WIZARD Configuration Maintenance Analyst	28
9176	CLASSIC WIZARD System Support Operator	5
9301	Entry Level Programmer/Analyst	102
9302	Cryptologic Network and Systems Configuration Manager	82
9303	Integrated Data Network Exchange Operations and Maintenance	97
9304	Database Administrator	23
9512	3-M System Coordinator	83
9517	Ship's 3-M System Coordinator	252
9705	ADP System Director	5
9705	ADP System Director	80
9710	ADP Programs Officer	1

9710	ADP Programs Officer	42
9715	ADP Production Officer	4
9715	ADP Production Officer	15
9720	ADP Plans Officer	3
9720	ADP Plans Officer	69
9730	Database Management Officer	27
9735	Computer Systems Analyst	4
9735	Computer Systems Analyst	101
9740	Digital Computer System Programmer	2
9740	Digital Computer System Programmer	11
9745	ADP Systems Maintenance Officer	14
9745	ADP Systems Maintenance Officer	44
9750	ADP Customer Liaison Officer	5
9755	Shipboard Nontactical Automatic Data Processing System Coordinator	4
9755	Shipboard Nontactical Automatic Data Processing System Coordinator	13
9781	ADP Systems Security Officer	6
9781	ADP Systems Security Officer	29

9 Construction and Engineering Operators

MOC	MOC Title	Personnel
0107	Minesweeping Boatswain's Mate	175
0110	IMA Rigging and Weight Testing Shop Journeyman	106
0164	Assault Boat Coxswain	765
5501	Construction Inspector	348
5707	Water Well Drilling Technician	60
5708	Blaster	59
5710	Advanced Equipment Operator	296
5712	Elevated Causeway System (Modular) Specialist	1
5907	Advanced Builder	270
5915	Construction Planner and Estimator Specialist	219
6010	Advanced Steelworker	89
6021	Safety Inspector	456
7353	Special Operations Parachute Rigger	164
7356	Aircrew Survival Equipment (IMA) Technician	190

10 Combat Arms

MOC	MOC Title	Personnel
0332	TOMAHAWK Weapon System (Surface) Operator	214
6090	Surface Munitions Project Officer	1
6380	Weapons Equipment Project Officer	9
6457	Fire Control Inspection and Repair Officer	4
6470	Weapons Control Systems Project Officer (General)	10
6472	Weapons Control Systems Project Officer (Surface)	16
6503	Degaussing Officer	1
6516	Mine Assembly and Repair Officer	1

6516	Mine Assembly and Repair Officer	7
6537	Torpedo Weapons Officer	4
6537	Torpedo Weapons Officer	15
6582	Undersea Weapons Project Officer	5
6704	Weapons Maintenance Officer	1
6704	Weapons Maintenance Officer	4
6715	Weapons Material Officer (General)	5
6715	Weapons Material Officer (General)	11
6717	Program Manager, Weapons Systems	20
6920	Weapons Design Officer	4
6936	Weapons Systems Inspection and Survey Officer	3
6940	Weapons Installation and Repair Superintendent	4
6942	Weapons Logistics Officer	3
6942	Weapons Logistics Officer	23
6948	Weapons Military Characteristics Officer	4
6960	Weapons Officer, Naval Activity	6
6960	Weapons Officer, Naval Activity	21
6978	Weapons Repair Officer	3
6978	Weapons Repair Officer	14
6982	Weapons Technical Officer	2
6990	Weapons Safety Officer	8
6999	Staff Weapons Material Officer	1
9046	Staff Electronic Warfare Officer	40
9053	Staff Weapons Officer	50
9064	Staff Mine Warfare Officer	31
9066	Anti-Air Warfare Operations Officer	10
9080	Staff Nuclear Weapons Officer	1
9080	Staff Nuclear Weapons Officer	28
9202	Gunnery/Ordnance Officer	10
9202	Gunnery/Ordnance Officer	23
9230	Explosive Ordnance Disposal Officer	22
9230	Explosive Ordnance Disposal Officer	89
9238	Fire Control Officer (Surface-to-Air Missiles)	18
9238	Fire Control Officer (Surface-to-Air Missiles)	131
9247	Strike Warfare/Missile Systems Officer (Surface-to-Air Missiles)	85
9250	Division Officer, Weapons Department (General)	19
9250	Division Officer, Weapons Department (General)	132
9272	Naval Gunfire Liaison Officer	29
9289	Special Weapons Unit Officer	3
9292	Special Weapons Technical Repair Officer	1
9292	Special Weapons Technical Repair Officer	3
9296	Special Weapons Assembly Officer (General)	2
9296	Special Weapons Assembly Officer (General)	12
9540	Stinger Anti-Terrorist Weapon (ATW) Operator and Maintenanceman	76

11 Dental and Pharmacy Specialists

MOC	MOC Title	Personnel
0335	Dental Officer General Practitioner	530
0340	Operative Dentist	15
0510	Endodontist	60
0525	Comprehensive Dentist	167
0530	Maxillofacial Prosthetist	4
0535	Orthodontist	14
0545	Oral Diagnostician	13
0550	Oral Maxillofacial Surgeon	81
0560	Periodontist	47
0569	Prosthodontist	68
0575	Public Health/Preventive Dentistry Officer	6
0579	Pedodontist	11
0580	Oral Pathologist	8
8482	Pharmacy Technician	884
8703	Dental Department Administrative Technician	267
8707	Field Service Dental Technician	736
8708	Dental Hygienist	8
8783	Dental Surgical Technologist	102

12 Divers

MOC	MOC Title	Personnel
5311	Saturation Diver	100
5320	Basic Combatant Swimmer	116
5330	Explosive Ordnance Disposal (EOD) Apprentice Diver	41
5334	Senior EOD Technician	96
5335	Senior EOD Technician/Parachutist	87
5336	Master EOD Technician	53
5337	Master EOD Technician/Parachutist	136
5341	Master Diver	60
5342	Diver First Class	372
5343	Diver Second Class	177
5344	Submarine SCUBA Diver	15
5345	Scuba Diver	59
5346	Master Saturation Diver	8
5375	Salvage/Construction Demolition Diver	1
5931	Advanced Underwater Construction Technician	67
5932	Basic Underwater Construction Technician	60
9562	Deep Submergence Vehicle Operator	3
9563	Deep Submergence Vehicle Crewmember	7

13 Emergency Management and Laboratory Specialists

MOC	MOC Title	Personnel
0303	ACDS Block 1 Operator	17
0310	AEGIS Operations Specialist (CG 65-DDG 79)	188
6403	Oil Analysis Operator/Evaluator	138

| 9597 | Radiac Technician | 25 |
| 9598 | Disaster Preparedness Operations and Training Specialists | 33 |

14 Environmental Health and Safety Specialists

MOC	MOC Title	Personnel
4805	Shipboard Chemical, Biological and Radiological-Defense (CBR-D) Operations and Training Specialist	485
4811	Senior Enlisted Damage Control Program Management and Training Specialist	543
8432	Preventive Medicine Technician	617
9595	Hazardous Material Control Management Technician	643

15 Finance and Accounting Managers

MOC	MOC Title	Personnel
1005	Accounting Officer	46
1015	Internal Review Officer	11
1025	Budget Officer	67
1045	Disbursing Officer	3
1045	Disbursing Officer	285
1050	Comptroller	199
2164	Designated Project Business Administrator	38
9052	Military Assistance Programs Officer	17

16 Firefighters

MOC	MOC Title	Personnel
7011	Aircraft Firefighting and Salvage Specialists	502

18 Functional Specialty Managers

MOC	MOC Title	Personnel
0814	Food Service Officer, Medical Facility	17
1105	Mess Treasurer/Caterer	1
1105	Mess Treasurer/Caterer	16
1112	Bachelor Quarters Manager	3
1112	Bachelor Quarters Manager	13
1130	Food Service Officer	38
1130	Food Service Officer	105
1205	Air Traffic Officer	1
1205	Air Traffic Officer	17
1215	Cargo Handling Officer	13
1242	Passenger Transportation Officer	3
1245	Household Goods Officer	1
1272	Transportation Logistics Officer	1
1272	Transportation Logistics Officer	29
1295	Transportation Director	19
1302	Issue Control Officer	1
1302	Issue Control Officer	43
1306	Material Division Officer	66

1345	Naval Supply Control Officer	7
1370	Warehouse and Storage Officer	1
1370	Warehouse and Storage Officer	7
1476	Procurement Management Officer	44
1480	Procurement Contracting Officer	93
1485	Administrative Contracting Officer	51
1515	Inventory Control Methods Officer	40
1530	Stock Control Officer, Requirements	5
1530	Stock Control Officer, Requirements	84
1913	Stores Officer	55
1918	General Supply Officer	5
1918	General Supply Officer	821
1920	Equipment Program Support Officer	33
1933	Navy Exchange Officer	9
1935	Ships Store Officer	2
1935	Ships Store Officer	45
1940	Fuel Logistics Planning Officer	19
1946	Fuel Depot Officer	2
1946	Fuel Depot Officer	14
1955	Staff Supply Officer	3
1955	Staff Supply Officer	107
1976	Supply Field Services Officer	10
1978	Supply Logistics Officer	2
1978	Supply Logistics Officer	98
1984	Supply Plans Officer	1
1984	Supply Plans Officer	62
1990	Technical Supply Officer (General)	1
1990	Technical Supply Officer (General)	26
1991	Technical Supply Officer (Aviation)	2
1991	Technical Supply Officer (Aviation)	70
2163	Manager, Designated Project Functional Element	108
2605	Administrative Assistant	11
2605	Administrative Assistant	98
2610	Management Analysis and Control Officer	36
2612	Management Information Systems Officer	1
2612	Management Information Systems Officer	23
2614	Management Information Center Officer	4
2615	Administrative Officer	53
2615	Administrative Officer	373
2642	Maintenance and Material Management Data Analyst	22
2670	Records Management Officer	2
2748	Security Manager, Information Security Program	2
2748	Security Manager, Information Security Program	17
2750	Law Enforcement and Security Officer, Staff	6
2750	Law Enforcement and Security Officer, Staff	32
2771	Law Enforcement and Security Officer, Afloat	1
2775	Law Enforcement and Security Officer, Shore Activity	3
2775	Law Enforcement and Security Officer, Shore Activity	53

3120	Personnel Classification Officer	1
3125	Personnel Distribution Officer (General)	1
3125	Personnel Distribution Officer (General)	6
3126	Personnel Distribution Officer (Officer)	165
3127	Personnel Distribution Officer (Enlisted)	4
3127	Personnel Distribution Officer (Enlisted)	49
3320	Human Resource Management Officer	33
3330	Equal Opportunity Program Officer	6
3412	Brig Officer	5
3415	Discipline Administration and Review Officer	9
3420	Personnel Performance Officer (General)	9
3421	Personnel Performance Officer (Officer)	16
3422	Personnel Performance Officer (Enlisted)	4
3525	Private Mess Specialist	630
3527	Culinary Specialist	1,142
3529	Wardroom/Galley Supervisor	1,112
3535	Special Services Officer	3
3538	Bachelor Quarter Specialist	754
3910	Transient Personnel Unit Officer	1
3910	Transient Personnel Unit Officer	1
3925	Military Manpower Requirements Control Officer	6
3943	Manpower Planning Officer	2
3943	Manpower Planning Officer	85
3950	Personnel Research Officer	14
3965	Personnel/Manpower Management Officer	14
3965	Personnel/Manpower Management Officer	135
3970	Personnel Planning Officer	105
3980	Personnel Plans and Policy Chief	15
3981	Personnel Plans and Policy Director	1
3981	Personnel Plans and Policy Director	92
3985	Staff Personnel Officer	25
4265	Public Works Transportation Officer	3
4265	Public Works Transportation Officer	4
5761	Training Device Program Coordinator	21
6083	Ammunition Material Officer	7
6083	Ammunition Material Officer	19
6702	Weapons Distribution Officer	4
6708	Weapons Procurement Officer	3
6914	Naval Plant Representative	12
6962	Weapons Planning and Progress Officer	20
6966	Weapons Plans and Policies Director	7
6974	Weapons Technical Information Officer	1
6980	Weapons Research Planning Officer	5
8074	Ground Support Equipment and Ship Facilities Arrangement Officer	9
8112	Aviation Maintenance Field Representative	1
8115	Aviation Maintenance Management Engineer	9
8116	Aviation Maintenance Planning Officer	2

8116	Aviation Maintenance Planning Officer	42
8118	Aviation Maintenance Engineering Officer	13
8125	Aviation Overhaul Schedules Officer	1
8141	Depot Maintenance Engineering and Quality Officer	3
8152	Depot Maintenance Production Officer	11
8175	Aircraft Intermediate Maintenance/Material Control Officer	16
8175	Aircraft Intermediate Maintenance/Material Control Officer	33
8176	Aircraft Organizational Maintenance/Material Control Officer	56
8176	Aircraft Organizational Maintenance/Material Control Officer	185
8177	Aircraft Maintenance Quality Control Officer	6
8177	Aircraft Maintenance Quality Control Officer	79
8180	Air Wing Maintenance Officer	28
8189	Aircraft Intermediate Maintenance Officer, General	5
8189	Aircraft Intermediate Maintenance Officer, General	83
8190	Aircraft Organizational Maintenance Officer, General	6
8190	Aircraft Organizational Maintenance Officer, General	254
8618	Air Officer	90
8620	Air Operations Officer, Afloat	45
8625	Aircraft Handling Officer	38
8638	Aircraft Fueling Officer	19
8638	Aircraft Fueling Officer	33
8653	Officer in Charge, Aviation Unit or Detachment	9
8653	Officer in Charge, Aviation Unit or Detachment	298
8654	Flight Deck Officer	43
8660	Hangar Deck Officer	30
8668	Operations Officer, Aviation Shore Activity	41
8670	Squadron Commanding Officer	236
8672	Squadron Executive Officer	175
8675	Squadron Department Head	429
8680	Squadron Operations Officer	5
8680	Squadron Operations Officer	125
8685	Staff Air Operations and Planning Officer	120
8687	Staff Air Defense Officer	8
8925	Aircraft Material Control and Allocation Officer	62
8925	Aircraft Material Control and Allocation Officer	80
9034	Staff Administration Officer	8
9034	Staff Administration Officer	84
9050	Shipping Control Officer	13
9051	Logistics Officer	3
9051	Logistics Officer	117
9405	Beachmaster	5
9405	Beachmaster	5
9420	Officer in Charge, Naval Shore Activity	15
9420	Officer in Charge, Naval Shore Activity	404
9421	Commander/Commanding Officer, Shore Activity	489
9422	Commanding Officer, Naval Shore Activity (Selected)	86

9424	Naval Control of Shipping Officer	5
9430	Drydocking Officer (General)	9
9431	Drydocking Officer (Floating Drydocks)	5
9436	Executive Officer, Shore Activity	449
9456	Coastal/Harbor Defense Officer	4
9466	Operations Officer, Ashore	7
9466	Operations Officer, Ashore	37
9467	Shipping Operations Officer	6
9470	Commanding Officer, Military Sealift Command Office	13
9471	Executive Officer, Military Sealift Command Office	10
9476	Port Services Officer	4
9476	Port Services Officer	22
9486	Operations Control Center Briefing Officer	3
9497	Yard Boatswain	4
9580	Communications Security Material Issuing Officer	1
9580	Communications Security Material Issuing Officer	3
9930	Executive Assistant	178
9935	Aide	97
9950	Military Sealift Command Commander	4
9960	Inspector General	1
9960	Inspector General	53
9965	Inspector, Technical	4
9965	Inspector, Technical	65
9970	Plans and Policies Chief	22
9980	Plans and Policies Director	87
9981	Naval Plans and Policies Director, Naval Command Systems	30
9990	Joint Strategic Plans and Policy Officer	77
9992	Deputy/Vice Commander	28

19 Aircraft Launch and Recovery Specialists

MOC	MOC Title	Personnel
7004	C-13 Catapult Operator	279
7005	MK-7 Arresting Gear Operator	239
7006	Aircraft Launch and Recovery Equipment Maintenance Technician	151
7609	Support Equipment Maintenance Manager	293

20 Health, Education and Welfare Workers

MOC	MOC Title	Personnel
0002	Medical Department Staff Officer	215
0005	Director, Health Service or Program	63
0020	Health Services Department Head	252
0026	Health Services Branch Clinic Director	72
0028	Health Services Division Officer	304
0030	Health Science Research Officer	62
0031	Plans, Operations and Medical Intelligence	86
0049	Health Services Quality Assurance Coordinator	40

0055	Commanding Officer, Fleet Marine Force Company	22
0109	Emergency Medical Specialist	71
0800	Health Care Administrator	224
0801	Administrative Officer, Dental Service	10
0808	Patient Administrator	63
0812	Small Arms Marksmanship Instructor	755
0820	Operations Management Officer, Medical Facility	38
0822	Medical Facilities Liaison Officer	16
0851	Clinical Psychologist	85
0852	Aerospace Experimental Psychologist	23
0854	Research Psychologist	11
0868	Social Worker	28
0871	Audiologist	21
0876	Dietitian	23
0887	Pharmacist	123
2505	General Attorney	283
2510	Administrative Law Attorney	19
2515	Admiralty Attorney	5
2517	Appellate Military Judge	2
2518	Appellate Counsel	25
2520	Claims Attorney	23
2525	Acquisition/Procurement Attorney	2
2529	International Law Attorney	39
2530	Legislative Counsel	15
2535	Legal Assistance Attorney	24
2554	Military Judge, General Courts-Martial	14
2556	Military Judge, Special Courts-Martial	1
2557	Trial Counsel	76
2558	Defense Counsel	78
2591	Legal Officer	67
2592	Military Justice Management Officer	11
3215	Education/Training Planning and Program Officer (General)	3
3215	Education/Training Planning and Program Officer (General)	187
3217	Training Planning and Program Officer (Aviation, Flight)	105
3219	Training Planning and Program Officer (Aviation, Ground)	4
3219	Training Planning and Program Officer (Aviation, Ground)	25
3220	Leadership/Management Training Program Officer	45
3230	Educational Services Officer	18
3236	Ground School Instructor	1
3236	Ground School Instructor	31
3240	Officer Candidate Company Officer	47
3242	Indoctrination Training Officer	5
3242	Indoctrination Training Officer	33
3245	Instructor, General	3
3245	Instructor, General	57
3250	Instructor, Technical	18
3250	Instructor, Technical	411
3251	Instructor, Academic	4

3251	Instructor, Academic	134
3254	Instructor, Academic (Social Science)	36
3255	Instructor, Academic (Physical Science)	41
3260	Instructor, Engineering	2
3260	Instructor, Engineering	93
3262	Instructor Training Officer	3
3265	Advanced Command and Staff School Instructor	95
3270	Instructor, Naval Science	7
3270	Instructor, Naval Science	263
3274	Physical Training Officer	16
3277	Professor of Naval Science	34
3283	School Administrator	17
3283	School Administrator	236
3290	Training Officer	39
3290	Training Officer	211
3298	Training Publications and Curriculum Officer	1
3298	Training Publications and Curriculum Officer	11
3350	Counseling and Assistance Center Director	8
3525	Family Services Center Director	7
3701	Chaplain	640
3740	Supervisory Chaplain	192
3745	Force Chaplain	11
3750	Claimant Chaplain	16
5348	Marine Mammal Systems Operator	4
7352	Senior Naval Parachutist	114
8591	Naval Flight Officer Instructor, Training Planes	67
8592	Flight Instructor, Training Planes	474
8593	Flight Instructor—Pilot, Fleet Operational Aircraft	227
8594	Flight Instructor—NFO, Fleet Operational Aircraft	131
8696	Naval Air Training and Operating Procedures Standardization Officer	128
9192	Basic Thai Linguist	8
9193	Basic Indonesian Linguist	3
9194	Basic Cambodian Linguist	3
9195	Basic Burmese Linguist	1
9197	Basic Serbo-Croatian Linguist	36
9201	Basic Russian Linguist	243
9202	Basic Tagalog Linguist	15
9203	Basic Spanish Linguist	197
9204	Basic French Linguist	19
9207	Basic German Linguist	1
9209	Basic Persian (Farsi) Linguist	49
9211	Basic Chinese (Mandarin) Linguist	98
9212	Basic Korean Linguist	32
9213	Basic North Vietnamese Linguist	13
9215	Basic Hebrew Linguist	25
9216	Basic Arabic Linguist	117
9311	Basic Georgian Linguist	3

9312	Basic Kurdish Linguist	2
9313	Basic Portuguese Linguist	10
9314	Basic Romanian Linguist	4
9315	Basic Ukrainian Linguist	5
9502	Instructor	2,281
9504	Aviation Water Survival Instructor	21
9505	Survival, Evasion, Resistance and Escape (SERE) Instructor	83
9508	Recruit/Assistant Recruit Company Commander/Recruit Instructor	453
9515	Equal Opportunity Program Specialist	49
9516	Correctional Counselor	101
9518	Naval Leadership Development Program (NAVLEAD) Instructor	104
9519	Navy Drug and Alcohol Counselor	69
9520	Consecutive Foreign Language Translator	1
9522	Navy Drug and Alcohol Counselor Intern	65

21 Intelligence Specialists

MOC	MOC Title	Personnel
0416	Acoustic Intelligence Specialist	54
0417	ASW Specialist	182
0450	Journeyman Level Acoustic Analyst	58
2240	Language Officer	4
3901	Satellite Sensor Interpreter	79
3905	Independent Surface Warfare Operational Intelligence (OPINTEL) Analyst	244
3907	OSIS Baseline Upgrade (OBU) User/Analyst	62
3910	Naval Imagery Interpreter	276
3912	Naval Special Warfare (NSW) Intelligence Specialist	2
3923	NTCS-A Strike Warfare Intelligence Applications Analyst	103
3924	Navy Tactical Command System-Afloat (NTCS-A) Operational Intelligence (OPINTEL) Analyst	181
3925	Digital Imagery Workstation Suite Afloat (DIWSA) Operator/Analyst	35
8506	Carrier Airborne Combat Information Center Officer	12
8606	Antisubmarine Classification and Analysis Officer, Aviation	14
8606	Antisubmarine Classification and Analysis Officer, Aviation	109
9102	Battle Force ELINT Analyst (BFEA)	102
9103	Fleet Cryptologic Systems Maintenance Technician	142
9104	Telemetry Collection and Analysis Technician	1
9105	C2 Tactical Analysis Technician	11
9116	Cryptologic Supervisor	48
9124	Direct Support (DIRSUP)/Ships Signals Exploitation Equipment Operator	187
9125	OUTBOARD System Operator	130
9126	SEAMARK Advanced Operator	26
9131	Combat Direction Finding System (AN/SRS-1) Operator	78
9132	Afloat Cryptologic Manager	42

9134	Subsurface Augmentee Operator	26
9135	Subsurface Augmentee ELINT Operator	52
9137	Apprentice Analysis and Reporting Specialist	283
9138	Journeyman Analysis and Reporting Specialist	84
9141	Intermediate Technical ELINT (TECHELINT) Analysis Technician	176
9147	Intermediate Signals Analyst	167
9149	Advanced Signals Analyst	14
9158	CLASSIC WIZARD Analyst	69
9160	CLASSIC WIZARD EDP Tuner	2
9166	Direction Finding Outstation Operator	81
9169	Morse Code Intercept Operator	470
9530	Cryptoboard Officer	3
9600	Intelligence Officer, Basic	39
9616	Intelligence Support Officer	22
9617	Intelligence Investigations Officer	2
9620	Geographic Area Intelligence Officer	3
9620	Geographic Area Intelligence Officer	38
9640	Operational Intelligence Officer (General)	4
9640	Operational Intelligence Officer (General)	425
9650	Electronic Intelligence Officer	1
9650	Electronic Intelligence Officer	22
9651	Automatic Data Processing Intelligence Officer	11
9660	Scientific and Technical Intelligence Officer	3
9660	Scientific and Technical Intelligence Officer	23
9670	Operational Intelligence Officer (Management)	149
9680	Operational Intelligence Officer (Analyst)	5
9680	Operational Intelligence Officer (Analyst)	287
9682	Tactical Intelligence Officer	92
9683	Photographic Intelligence Officer	5
9683	Photographic Intelligence Officer	54
9684	Multisensor Intelligence Officer	50
9686	Antisubmarine Warfare Intelligence Officer	37
9810	Head of Naval Security Group Department	11
9815	Operations Officer, Naval Security Group	3
9815	Operations Officer, Naval Security Group	89
9817	Operations Watch Officer, Naval Security Group	19
9825	Information Processing and Reporting Officer, Naval Security Group	2
9825	Information Processing and Reporting Officer, Naval Security Group	16
9835	High Frequency Direction Finding Analysis Officer	5
9835	High Frequency Direction Finding Analysis Officer	16
9840	Electronics Intelligence Technical Guidance Unit Officer	3
9840	Electronics Intelligence Technical Guidance Unit Officer	3
9845	CLASSIC WIZARD Operations Officer	4
9845	CLASSIC WIZARD Operations Officer	14
9850	Direct Support Coordinator, Naval Security Group	1

9850	Direct Support Coordinator, Naval Security Group	46
9851	Direct Support Officer, Naval Security Group (Surface)	34
9851	Direct Support Officer, Naval Security Group (Surface)	124
9852	Direct Support Officer, Naval Security Group (Air)	3
9852	Direct Support Officer, Naval Security Group (Air)	12
9853	Direct Support Officer, Naval Security Group (Subsurface)	1
9853	Direct Support Officer, Naval Security Group (Subsurface)	35
9860	Naval Security Group Special Operations Officer	5
9860	Naval Security Group Special Operations Officer	28
9865	Naval Security Group CLASSIC OWL Special Operations Officer	20

22 Law Enforcement Specialists

MOC	MOC Title	Personnel
2002	Military Investigator	177
2005	Dog Handler	242
2008	Afloat Corrections Specialist	369
9545	Navy Law Enforcement Specialist	2,810
9571	Safety Technician	164
9573	SNAP II Ship System Coordinator	48
9575	Correctional Custody Specialist Ashore	672

24 Life Scientists

MOC	MOC Title	Personnel
0840	Biochemist	24
0841	Microbiologist	40
0848	Physiologist	11
0849	Aerospace Physiologist	48

25 Machinists, Technicians, and Cargo Specialists

MOC	MOC Title	Personnel
3351	Submarine Nuclear Propulsion Plant Emergency Welder	7
3353	Submarine Nuclear Propulsion Plant Operator—Reactor Control	667
3356	Submarine Nuclear Propulsion Plant Operator—Engineering Laboratory Technician	340
3359	Submarine Nuclear Propulsion Plant Operator—Special Category	530
3363	Submarine Nuclear Propulsion Plant Supervisor—Reactor Control	679
3364	Submarine Nuclear Propulsion Plant Supervisor—Electrical	892
3365	Submarine Nuclear Propulsion Plant Supervisor—Mechanical	1,079
3366	Submarine Nuclear Propulsion Plant Supervisor—Engineering Laboratory Technician	488
3373	Nuclear Propulsion Plant Maintenance Supervisor—Electronics	3

3377	Nuclear Planner	2
3383	Surface Ship Nuclear Propulsion Plant Operator—Reactor Control	463
3389	Surface Ship Nuclear Propulsion Plant Operator—Special Category	418
3393	Surface Ship Nuclear Propulsion Plant Supervisor—Reactor Control	367
3394	Surface Ship Nuclear Propulsion Plant Supervisor— Electrical	364
3395	Surface Ship Nuclear Propulsion Plant Supervisor— Mechanical	714
3396	Surface Ship Nuclear Propulsion Plant Supervisor— Engineering Laboratory Technician	201
3601	Lithographic Equipment Repairman	42
4252	Electrolytic Oxygen Generator (Model 6L16) Operator	21
4283	High and Low Pressure Cryogenic Technician	402
4382	FFG-7 Class Auxiliaries Mechanical System Technician	238
4398	DD-963 Auxiliary Systems Technician	257
4402	Advanced Machinery Repairman	149
4403	Heat Treatment of Metals Machinist	153
4404	Computer Numerically Controlled Machinist	113
4502	Boiler Repair Technician	145
4503	Main Propulsion Steam Generating Plant Inspector	60
4505	Steam Propulsion Maintenance Supervisor	356
4954	General Maintenance	1,395
4955	Nonnuclear Welder	868
4956	Nuclear Power Plant Components Welder	358
6105	Advanced Utilitiesman	130
7022	Aviation Gasoline Handler	578
7222	Aeronautical Welder	131
7601	Support Equipment Cryogenic Mechanic	77
8463	Optician	270
8752	Dental Laboratory Technician, Basic	174
8753	Dental Laboratory Technician, Advanced	111
8765	Dental Laboratory Technician, Maxillofacial	6
9559	Engineering Bulk Fuel Systems (Shore) Technician	29
9570	Stevedore	62
9581	Rubber and Plastics Worker	12

26 Medical Service and Medical Care Technicians

MOC	MOC Title	Personnel
0113	Physician's Assistant	205
2006	Kennel Master	53
8401	Search and Rescue Medical Technician	92
8402	Submarine Force Independent Duty Corpsman	273
8403	Fleet Marine Force Reconnaissance Independent Duty Corpsman	26
8404	Field Medical Service Technician	7,744

8406	Aerospace Medical Technician	399
8407	Radiation Health Technician	108
8408	Cardiovascular Technician	113
8409	Aerospace Physiology Technician	135
8416	Nuclear Medicine Technician	79
8425	Surface Force Independent Duty Corpsman	954
8427	Fleet Marine Force Reconnaissance Corpsman	63
8434	Hemodialysis/Apheresis Technician	31
8445	Ocular Technician	100
8446	Otolaryngology Technician	106
8451	Basic X-Ray Technician	288
8452	Advanced X-Ray Technician	730
8454	Electroneurodiagnostic Technician	30
8483	Surgical Technologist	871
8485	Psychiatry Technician	286
8486	Urology Technician	69
8489	Orthopedic Cast Room Technician	106
8491	Special Operations Independent Duty Corpsman	103
8492	Special Operations Technician	244
8493	Medical Deep Sea Diving Technician	107
8494	Deep Sea Diving Independent Duty Corpsman	67
8495	Dermatology Technician	62
8503	Histopathology Technician	30
8505	Cytotechnologist	50
8506	Medical Laboratory Technician, Advanced	1,388
8541	Respiratory Therapy Technician	131

27 Musicians and Media Directors

MOC	MOC Title	Personnel
2445	Radio-Television Program Officer	4
3520	Music Director	18
3801	Flute/Piccolo Instrumentalist	26
3802	Oboe Instrumentalist	6
3803	Clarinet Instrumentalist	61
3804	Bassoon Instrumentalist	8
3805	Saxophone Instrumentalist	54
3806	Trumpet/Cornet Instrumentalist	96
3807	French Horn Instrumentalist	25
3808	Baritone/Euphonium Instrumentalist	14
3809	Trombone Instrumentalist	75
3811	Tuba Instrumentalist	25
3812	Guitar/Auxiliary Percussionist	24
3813	Percussion Instrumentalist	56
3814	Piano/Auxiliary Percussionist	27
3815	Electric Bass/String Bass Instrumentalist	24
3825	Vocalist/Auxiliary Percussionist	29
3851	Assistant Director	49
8804	Motion Picture and Television Project Officer	1

8815	Image Forming Systems Maintenance Officer	2
8815	Image Forming Systems Maintenance Officer	12
8853	Photographic Officer	4
8853	Photographic Officer	22

28 Non-Destructive Testers

MOC	MOC Title	Personnel
4935	NDT Radiographic Inspector (Nuclear)	10
4942	VT MT and PT NDT Inspector	98
4943	VT MT PT and RT NDT Inspector	106
4944	VT MT PT and UT Inspector	190
4946	Nonnuclear NDT Examiner	19
4947	Nuclear NDT Examiner	32
7225	Aircraft Maintenance Nondestructive Inspector (NDI)	257

29 Ordnance Specialists

MOC	MOC Title	Personnel
0749	MK-48 Heavyweight Torpedo Test Equipment Maintenance Technician	40
0750	MK-48 Heavyweight Torpedo Technician	281
0751	MK-48 Heavyweight Torpedo (ADCAP) Test Equipment Maintenance Technician	50
0801	IMA Ordnance Journeyman	5
1026	Warhead Maintenance Specialist	17
1202	CAPTOR MK-60 MOD 0 Weapons System Technician	30
6803	P-3 Armament/Ordnance IMA Technician	88

30 Nurses and Physical Therapists

MOC	MOC Title	Personnel
0873	Physical Therapist	71
0874	Occupational Therapist	16
0904	Critical Care Nurse	302
0925	Clinical Specialist, Nursing	22
0932	Perioperative Nurse	223
0935	Ambulatory Care Nurse	499
0944	Staff Nurse	11
0944	Staff Nurse	1,065
0952	Nurse Anesthetist	127
0963	Primary Care Nurse Practitioner	107
8466	Physical Therapy Technician	233
8467	Occupational Therapy Assistant	20

32 Photographic and Audiovisual Specialists

MOC	MOC Title	Personnel
8126	Photographic Quality Controlman	37
8143	Motion Media Cameraman	38
8144	Motion Media Director/Editor	28
8147	Photojournalism Specialist	51
8148	Photojournalist	26
8472	Biomedical Photography Technician	40

33 Physicians, Surgeons, Optometrists

MOC	MOC Title	Personnel
0101	Internist	242
0102	General Practice Medical Officer	426
0104	Intern	101
0105	Pediatrician	159
0106	Health Services Resident	381
0107	Undersea Medical Officer	108
0108	Family Practitioner	287
0110	Flight Surgeon	327
0111	Dermatologist	40
0115	Psychiatrist	84
0118	Anesthesiologist	126
0121	Neurologist	28
0131	Radiologist (Diagnostic)	82
0135	Radiologist (Therapeutic)	9
0140	Nuclear Medicine Specialist	7
0150	Pathologist	66
0160	Preventive Medicine Officer	11
0163	Preventive Medicine Officer (Aerospace)	36
0166	Preventive Medicine Officer (Occupational)	26
0214	General Surgeon	141
0224	Neurosurgeon	12
0229	Obstetrician-Gynecologist	107
0234	Ophthalmologist	59
0244	Orthopedic Surgeon	94
0249	Otolaryngologist	44
0254	Plastic Surgeon	7
0259	Colorectal Surgeon	8
0264	Thoracic and Cardiovascular Surgeon	4
0269	Urologist	33
0880	Optometrist	109
0892	Podiatrist	22

34 Pilots and Ship/Submarine Operators

MOC	MOC Title	Personnel
0160	Causeway Barge Ferry Pilot	107
0161	Tugmaster	203

0167	LCAC Operator	109
0169	Causeway Barge Ferry Coxswain	59
0215	Harbor/Docking Pilot	18
0343	AN/SYQ-13 NAV.C2 Operator	17
7285	Staff Machinery Material Officer	7
7998	Combat Systems Superintendent	1
7998	Combat Systems Superintendent	23
8501	Aviator	2,656
8543	Instrument Flight Instructor-Pilot	2
8588	Test Pilot	67
8614	Catapult and Arresting Gear Officer	6
8614	Catapult and Arresting Gear Officer	80
9005	Commander, Operating Forces Command	76
9006	Commander, Operating Forces (Selected)	47
9009	Area Commander	9
9015	Chief of Staff	98
9016	Chief Staff Officer	127
9018	Convoy Commodore	3
9019	Convoy Commodore Staff Officer	2
9021	Flag Lieutenant	82
9025	Advisor to Command in Combat	5
9038	Staff Special Projects Operations Officer	7
9040	Staff Antisubmarine Officer	19
9042	Staff Combat Information Center Officer	25
9044	Staff Naval Control of Shipping Officer	1
9045	Staff Operations Command Center Watch Officer	1
9045	Staff Operations Command Center Watch Officer	103
9063	Staff Material Officer	7
9063	Staff Material Officer	212
9084	Staff Submarine Warfare Officer	40
9206	Antisubmarine Weapons Officer	225
9209	Offshore Control and Surveillance System Officer	6
9212	Boat Group Officer	3
9212	Boat Group Officer	53
9214	Air Intercept Controller Supervisor	2
9216	Combat Information Center Officer	1
9216	Combat Information Center Officer	114
9217	Naval Tactical Data System—Combat Information Center Officer	12
9217	Naval Tactical Data System—Combat Information Center Officer	341
9222	Commanding Officer, Afloat	14
9225	Naval Tactical Data System—Combat Information Center Watch Officer, Carrier Controlled Approach Controller	1
9225	Naval Tactical Data System—Combat Information Center Watch Officer, Carrier Controlled Approach Controller	26
9227	Naval Tactical Data System—Combat Information Center Watch Officer, General	25

MOC	MOC Title	Personnel
9228	Executive Officer, Afloat	519
9233	Commanding Officer, Afloat (Lieutenant)	21
9234	Commanding Officer, Afloat (Lieutenant Commander)	52
9235	Commanding Officer, Afloat (Commander)	273
9236	Commanding Officer, Afloat (Captain)	143
9237	Fire Control Officer (General)	68
9242	First Lieutenant, Afloat	4
9242	First Lieutenant, Afloat	541
9246	Strike Warfare/Missile Systems Officer (General)	109
9252	Division Officer, Weapons Department (Gunnery)	3
9252	Division Officer, Weapons Department (Gunnery)	177
9253	Division Officer, Weapons Department (Antisubmarine Weapons)	10
9254	Division Officer, Weapons Department (Guided Missiles)	1
9254	Division Officer, Weapons Department (Guided Missiles)	1
9255	Surface Ship Watch/Division Officer (Basic)	15
9258	Weapons Officer (General)	2
9258	Weapons Officer (General)	117
9259	Weapons Officer (Fleet Ballistic Missiles)	76
9261	Combat Systems Officer	5
9261	Combat Systems Officer	312
9266	Military Department Officer	33
9268	Minesweeping Officer	3
9273	Officer in Charge, Afloat	16
9274	Operations Officer, Afloat (General)	354
9275	Operations Officer, Afloat (Naval Tactical Data Systems)	164
9278	Ship's Boatswain	24
9278	Ship's Boatswain	68
9279	Officer in Charge, Combat Craft	10
9282	Ship's Electronic Warfare Officer	50
9283	Ship's Electronic Material Officer	80
9283	Ship's Electronic Material Officer	199
9284	Ship's Navigator (General)	323
9286	Ship's Secretary	4
9286	Ship's Secretary	13
9290	Commanding Officer, Special Warfare Team	17
9313	Diving Officer (Deep Sea, HEO2)	8
9313	Diving Officer (Deep Sea, HEO2)	9
9533	Special Warfare Combatant Crewmember (SWCC)	56
9534	SEAL Delivery Vehicle (SDV) Team Technician	18
9579	Chief of the Boat (All Submarines)	7

35 Postal Directors

MOC	MOC Title	Personnel
2617	Postal Officer	4
9082	Flag Secretary	78

36 Precision Equipment Repairers

MOC	MOC Title	Personnel
0402	FFG-7 Class Sonar Subsystem Level II Technician	55
0404	AN/SQQ-28(V) Sonar Subsystem Level II Technician	15
0405	Sonar Auxiliary Maintenance and Operations Repairman	38
0406	AN/SQQ-89(V)2 Sonar Subsystem Level I Technician Operator	373
0407	AN/SQR-19(V)/SQQ-28(V) Sonar Subsystem Level II Technician	158
0410	AN/SLQ-48(V) Mine Neutralization Systems (MNS) Operator/Maintenance Technician	54
0411	AN/SQQ-89(V)4 Sonar Subsystem Level I Technician/Operator	314
0412	BQQ-5/5 (V) Submarine Sonar Basic Maintenance Technician	224
0413	AN/SQQ-89(V)1/3 Sonar Subsystem Level I Technician/Operator	238
0414	AN/SQS-53B Sonar Subsystem Level II Operator/Maintenance Technician	177
0415	AN/SQQ-89(V) Integrated Towed Array and Sonobuoy Sensors Level II Technician	262
0418	AN/BSY-1 (XN-1) (V) Basic Organizational Maintenance Technician	21
0419	AN/BSY-1 (XN-1) (V) Advanced Organizational Maintenance Technician	110
0421	Submarine Special Purpose Acoustic Equipment Maintenance Technician	197
0422	BQQ-5/5 Submarine Sonar Advanced Maintenance Technician	331
0424	AN/BQQ-6 TRIDENT LEVEL II Journeyman Operation and Maintenance Technician	29
0425	AN/BQQ-6 TRIDENT LEVEL III Master Operation and Maintenance Technician	220
0429	AN/SQQ-89(V) MK-116 Anti-Submarine Warfare Control System Maintenance	33
0430	Underwater Fire Control System MK-116 MOD 7 Anti-Submarine Warfare Control System Operator	222
0436	MK-116 MOD 4 Underwater Fire Control System Level II Technician	35
0438	MK-116 MOD 1 Underwater Fire Control System Level II Technician	4
0439	Underwater Fire Control System MK-116 MOD 6/8 Anti-Submarine Warfare Control System Operator	39
0443	AN/SQR-17/17A(V) Series Sonar Signal Processor Subsystem (SSPS) Level II Technician	19
0455	AN/SQS-53C Sonar Subsystem Level II Technician	129
0457	AN/SQS-53A Sonar Subsystem Level II Technician	46
0466	AN/SQQ-89(V) Sonar Watch Supervisor	2

1145	Rolling Airframe Missile (RAM) MK-31 Guided Missile Weapons Systems Technician	21
1147	NATO Sea Sparrow Surface Missile System MK-57 MOD 2, 3 Technician	418
1149	Improved Point Defense Target Acquisition System MK-23 (IPD/TAS)	75
1160	TARTAR Fire Control Radar Technician (MFCS MK-74 MOD)	28
1167	TARTAR Fire Control Radar (MFCS MK-74 MOD 14 W/RDP) Technician	12
1169	HARPOON (AN/SWG-1A) Maintenance Technician	104
1170	IMA Fire Control Shop Journeyman	2
1174	Combat Control System MK-1 Vertical Launch Subsystem Organizational/Intermediate Level Maintenance Technician	30
1175	Combat Control System MK-1 MOD 1 Organizational/Intermediate Level Maintenance Technician	302
1179	AN/BSY-1(XN-1)(V) Organizational/Intermediate Level Maintenance Technician	199
1196	Underwater Fire Control System MK-113 MOD 9 Technician	67
1204	Submarine Launched Mobile Mine Technician	51
1205	Underwater Mine Test Set Maintenance Technician	67
1312	CCS MK-2 MOD 0 Maintenance Technician	61
1313	CCS MK-2 MOD 1 Maintenance Technician	2
1315	CCS MK-2 MOD 3 Maintenance Technician	48
1320	TRIDENT MK-118 Combat Control System Maintenance Technician	122
1321	Combat Systems Senior Enlisted	229
1322	AEGIS Display Technician	38
1327	Fire Control Technician Basic Maintainer	67
1401	IMA Antenna/Mast Shop Journeyman	5
1412	Special Fixed Communications Maintenance Technician	81
1413	Meteorologist Equipment Maintenance Technician	131
1415	Combined Shore Communications Maintenance Technician	102
1416	SNAP II (AN/UYK-62(V)) Maintenance Technician	96
1419	Electromagnetic Compatibility Technician	120
1420	Surface HF Communications System Maintenance Technician	504
1421	Submarine Electromagnetic Compatibility Technician	19
1424	Communications Equipment (SRQ-4) Technician	125
1425	Communications Equipment (WSC-3/UHF DAMA) Technician	323
1427	Communications Equipment (Tactical Data Systems) Technician	48
1428	Small Combatant Communications Electronic Subsystem Technician	201

1429	Flight Deck Communications Systems (FDCS) Maintenance Technician	42
1430	AN/USC-38(V)2, 3 Maintenance Technician	204
1450	NAVMACS(V)5 Shipboard Maintenance Technician	40
1452	NAVMACS(V)3 Shipboard Maintenance Technician	132
1454	DD-963 Communications Systems Technician	51
1456	FLTSATCOM (CUDIXS/DAMA NAVCOMMSTA) Maintenance Technician	48
1458	VERDIN/ISABPS Communications Systems Technician	53
1460	Communications Security (COMSEC) Maintenance Technician	717
1461	Special Maintenance (FCS-78/79 SHF Satellite Terminal) Technician	48
1464	WSC-28(V) Satellite Communications Set Technician	22
1465	AN/GSC-52(V) State-of-the-Art Medium Terminal (SAMT) Technician	75
1468	Special Maintenance (SHF SATCOM System) Technician	54
1471	URN-25 Tactical Air Navigation Technician	96
1473	Tactical Air Navigation (URN-20) Technician	15
1479	Ships Navigation and Aircraft Inertial Alignment System (CVNS/SNAIS) Technician	66
1480	AN/FAC-6(V) Intersite System Maintenance Technician	18
1486	Single Audio System (SAS)	112
1491	FFG-7 Class Navigation Electronics Subsystem Technician	45
1493	Tactical Support Communications (TSCOMM) Replacement Program Maintenance Technician	14
1494	LHD Class Radio Communications System Maintenance Technician	9
1495	AN/SYQ-13 NAV/C2 Maintainer	3
14CM	SSN Radio Frequency (RF) Equipment Technician	3
14EB	SSN 688 Class ESM Technician	5
14EP	SSN 719-767 ESM Technician	1
14ET	ESM Technician (All Classes)	361
14FA	TRIDENT Submarine Electronics Technician Command and Control System (CCS)	22
14HB	SSN 637 Class ESM Technician	2
14IC	Former IC (SS)	617
14NM	Navigation Equipment Maintenance Technician	8
14QM	Former QM(SS)	608
14RD	SSN 637 Class Navigation Technician	21
14RM	Former RM (SS)	853
14SF	SSN 594/688 Class Navigation Technician	26
14TG	SSN 637/688 Class Navigation Technician	154
14ZA	AN/BRD-7 Submarine Radio Direction Finding (RDF) Set Maintenance Technician	38
1502	CATC Radar Technician	46
1503	Radar (SPS-49) Technician	66
1504	Radar (SPS-55) Technician	126

1507	Radar (SPS-67(V)) Technician	103
1510	Radar (AN/SPS-49(V)5 & 7) Technician	130
1511	Radar (AN/SPS-40E) Technician	78
1516	Radar (SPS-40B/C/D) Technician	64
1522	Radar (SPN-42) Technician	30
1523	Amphibious Air Traffic Control (AATC) Radar	10
1568	AN/TPX-42A(V)13 Shipboard DAIR Maintenance Technician	24
1570	Air Traffic Control Communications Technician	26
1571	AN/UPX-29(V) Ship System Maintainer	119
1572	AIMS System Technician	327
1574	DAIR/GCA (TPX-42) Maintenance Technician	31
1576	CATC DAIR Maintenance Technician	15
1578	RATCF DAIR Maintenance Technician	29
1579	Precision Approach Radar Technician	46
1580	ASR-8 Maintenance Technician	49
1589	Fleet Electronics Calibration (FECL) Technician	359
1590	AN/SPN-46(V) Radar Technician	24
1613	Command Center Maintenance Technician	98
1615	Shipboard Tactical Data Systems Technician	134
1622	CDS Upgrade Computer/Peripheral Maintenance Technician (CG-16/27 CGN-36 and DDG-993 Class)	30
1623	Data Communications Link Maintenance Technician	26
1624	AN/UYQ-21 Computer Display System Maintenance Technician	100
1633	ASWOC Fast Time Analyzer Subsystem (FTAS) Maintenance Technician	14
1646	FLTSATCOM (SSIXS-OPCONCEN) Maintenance Technician	14
1647	NCCS Ashore Maintenance Technician	31
1654	Intelligence Center Maintenance Technician	58
1656	CV/CVN Combat Direction System (CDS)/(ASWM) Computer/Peripheral Subsystem Maintenance Technician	107
1657	CV-ASWM Fast Time Analyzer Subsystem Upgrade (FTAS-U) Systems Technician	38
1658	LHD 1 Class ITAWDS Computer/Peripheral Subsystem Maintenance Technician	34
1664	SNAP I Computer System Maintenance Technician	65
1671	CG-26/CGN-9/CGN-38/DDG20/FFG-7/LHA-1 Class Computer/Peripheral Technician	62
1672	DD-963 Class Computer/Peripheral Technician	81
1673	LHA Class Computer and Associated Subsystem Technician	6
1674	LHA Integrated Tactical Amphibious Warfare Data System (ITAWDS) Maintenance Technician	5
1676	TOMAHAWK Command and Control System Maintenance Technician	26
1677	Tactical Advanced Computer (TAC-n) Maintenance Technician	588

4513	Automatic Combustion Control (General Regulator) Maintenanceman	198
4533	Automatic Combustion Control Console Operator (General Regulator)	225
4703	FFG-7 Class Interior Communications Subsystem Technician	59
4711	Interior Voice Communications System Maintenance Technician	15
4712	Integrated Voice Communications Technician	48
4716	Ship's Service Telephone System (Dimension 2000) PBX Repairman	175
4718	IC Journeyman	54
4720	Gyrocompass Maintenance	50
4721	MK-19 Gyrocompass Systems Maintenance Technician	111
4723	MK-23 Gyrocompass Systems Maintenance Technician	170
4727	WSN-2 Stabilized Gyrocompass Technician	74
4728	WSN-5 Inertial Navigation Set Technician	183
4737	TRIDENT Submarine Ship Control and Atmosphere Support Master Operation and Maintenance Technician (Level III)	3
4738	AN/USQ-82(V) Data Multiplex System Technician	40
4745	Optical Landing System Technician	84
4746	Closed Circuit TV Technician	187
4747	Broadcast Engineering Technician	82
4749	Physical Security Equipment Maintenance Technician	68
5642	Central Office Exchange Technician	22
5644	Cable Splicing Technician	39
6522	AKT-22 Data Link IMA Technician	12
6526	Aviation ASW (MAD) IMA Technician	36
6527	Aviation ASW (Airborne Sonar) IMA Technician	47
6529	ASW Sonobuoy Receivers and Recorder Group IMA Technician	47
6534	AQA-7 DIFAR System IMA Technician	35
6556	S-3B Computer System Specialist	14
6582	P-3A/B Weapons System OMA Technician	44
6605	Aircraft Radar Altimeter Equipment IMA Technician	84
6606	Aircraft Doppler Radar Navigation IMA Technician	27
6607	Digital Data Link Communications IMA Technician	82
6608	Aircraft Navigation Computers IMA Technician	36
6609	Aircraft Electronic Identification (IFF) IMA Technician	89
6611	Aircraft UHF Communications, Automatic Direction Finder (ADF) and Intercommunications Systems (ICS) Equipment IMA Technician	234
6612	Aircraft TACAN/Radio Navigation Equipment IMA Technician	107
6613	Aircraft HF Communications Equipment IMA Technician	28
6614	APS-116 IMA Technician	42
6615	P-3 FLIR IMA Technician	37
6618	USM-458 IMA Technician	90

6619	HATS (USM-403) IMA Operator	34
6621	APS-125 Radar IMA Technician	40
6622	Electronic Countermeasures (ECM) Technician/Weapons Replaceable Assembly (WRA) IMA Technician	29
6628	HATS (USM-403) IMA Maintenance Technician	25
6631	AN/USM-629 Electro-Optic Test Set (EOTS) Operator/Maintainer, IMA	64
6633	USM-467 RADCOM IMA Technician	171
6635	EP-3E/ES-3A ESM IMA Technician	76
6639	Countermeasures Receiving and Dispensing Equipment IMA Technician	29
6640	EP-3E/ES-3A ESM OMA Technician	125
6641	ALQ-126 ECM IMA Technician	13
6647	ALQ-99 Transmitter Test Station IMA Technician	52
6648	ALQ-99 Exciter IMA Technician	40
6649	ECM/Simulator IMA Technician	17
6650	AN/USM-470(V)1 Automatic Test System (ATS) Advanced IMA Technician	24
6653	VAST (USM-247(V)) On-Line Maintenance IMA Technician	52
6658	AN/USM-470(V)1 Automatic Test System (ATS) On-Line Maintenance Technician	90
6659	AN/USM-247 Versatile Avionic Shop Test (VAST) Advanced IMA Operator	89
6660	Dynamic Alignment Test Set IMA Technician	6
6663	VAST (USM-247(V)) Off-Line Maintenance/Calibration	29
6664	APS-115 Search Radar IMA Technician	64
6668	EA-6B ECM OMA System Analyst	150
6669	EA-6A ECM/ESM Organizational Maintenance Technician	2
6673	Field Calibration Activity Technician (Electrical/Electronic)	298
6680	ICAP Computer Group/ICAP II Digital Interface Unit IMA Technician	23
6684	AAM-60(V)6 Electro-Optical System Test Set IMA Technician	17
6686	USM-429 CAT IIID Maintenance Technician	175
6688	USM-484 Hybrid Test Set (HTS) IMA Technician	145
6689	USM-484 HTS Advanced IMA Technician	38
6694	USM-470(V)2 Automatic Test System On-Line Maintenance Technician	33
6695	USM-470(V)2 ATS Advanced IMA Technician	12
6701	Advanced Avionics Integrated Weapons System Maintenance Technician	332
6702	E-6A Mission Avionics System IMA Technician	6
6704	Consolidated Automated Support System (CASS) Test Station IMA Operator/Maintainer	348
6705	Consolidated Automated Support System (CASS) Test Station IMA Calibration/Advanced Maintenance Technician	78
6710	P-3 Navigation System Equipment Technician	24

6713	Video Test Set (VTS) AN/SSM-9 Test Set Operator	27
6714	Enhanced Comprehensive Asset Management System (ECAMS) Maintainer	15
6715	FLIR Systems IMA Technician	8
6716	P-3 Model Aircraft - AN/USM-449(V) Test Set Operator	23
6717	P-3 Peculiar Communications Equipment IMA Technician	46
6718	Electronics Standards Specialist	120
6719	Update III ASUW Improvement Program (AIP) OMA Weapons Systems Technician	17
6721	AN/USM-449(V), Series, ATE IMA Technician	57
6801	Air Launched Weapons Technician	519
6802	Strike Intermediate Armament Maintenanceman	661
6810	Armament Weapons Support Equipment (AWSE) Maintenance Manager	89
7835	Tactical Support Center (TSC) Systems Operator	47
7836	CV/CVN ASWMOD/TSC Watch Supervisor	46
7953	APQ-148/156 and APS-130 Radar, AAS-33 FLIR and APM-375 MSRTC IMA Technician	17
7955	Radar Systems Module Repair Intermediate Maintenance Technician	19
7958	A-6E TRAM Weapon System Organizational Maintenance Technician	90
7959	FLIR Systems Intermediate Maintenance Technician	22
7964	AVA-1 Analog Display Indicator and Test Console IMA Technician	19
7970	F-14D OMA Integrated Weapons Technician	3
7971	F-14A/B OMA Integrated Weapons Technician	10
7978	Radar Set Test Station IMA Technician	133
7984	AWG-9/AWM-23 Radio Frequency Test Console IMA Technician	51
7988	AWG-9/AWM-23 Low Frequency Test Station IMA Technician	36
7989	AWG-9/AWM-23 Computer Test Station IMA Technician	32
7991	AWG-9/AWM-23 Controls and Displays Test Station IMA Technician	41
7992	AWG-9/AWM-23 Module Test Station IMA Technician	33
8478	Advanced Biomedical Equipment Technician	235
8479	Basic Biomedical Equipment Systems Technician	87
8732	Dental Equipment Repair Technician	100
9226	CLASSIC OWL Maintenance Technician	31
9228	COMSAT Systems Maintenance Technician	51
9238	Submarine Carry-on Equipment Maintenance Technician	102
9244	WOLFERS/ROCKETEER System Maintenance Technician	14
9245	NEWSDEALER System Maintenance Technician	37
9249	OUTBOARD II System Maintenance Technician	90
9251	Wideband Acquisitions and Analysis (WBAA) Hardware Maintenance Technician	43

9252	High Frequency Direction Finding (HFDF) Hardware Maintenance Technician	59
9256	Radio Frequency Distribution (RFD) Maintenance Technician	26
9257	WOLFERS/ROCKETEER and Chainwork PTTI Maintenance Technician	1
9258	Outstation Communication (FLAGHOIST) System Maintenance Technician	38
9259	VAX Fundamentals Maintenance Technician	45
9267	MUSIC System Maintenance Technician	10
9283	Mobile Electronics Maintenance Technician (WLQ-4)	18
9285	HPW Fundamentals Technician	53
9286	Chainwork PTTI System Maintenance Technician	12
9289	Combat Direction Finding System (SRS-1) Maintenance Technician	34
9295	Network Systems Maintenance Technician	21
9296	Communications Electronics Equipment Installer	41
9297	CLASSIC WIZARD System Maintenance Technician	92
9402	P-3C Update III ASUW Improvement Program (AIP) In-Flight Technician	13
9503	Miniature/Microminiature Electronic Repair Inspector	3
9509	2M Instructor/Master Inspector	9
9526	Microminiature Electronic Repair Technician	42
9527	Miniature Electronic Repair Technician	139
9602	Amphibious Air Traffic Control (AATC) Radar Technician (AN/SPN-43C)	12
9604	JTIDS Shipboard Terminal Maintenance Technician	103
9605	Naval Modular Automated Communications Systems II (NAVMACS II) Maintenance Technician	71
9606	Carrier Air Traffic Control (CATC) Radar Technician (AN/SPN-43C)	33
9607	High Frequency Radio Group (HFRG) Maintenance Technician	36
9608	Radar Technician (AN/SPS-67(V)3)	39
9610	Radar (AN/SPS-49A(V)) Technician	25
9611	AN/SSN-2(V)4 Maintainer	19

37 Preventive Maintenance Analysts

MOC	MOC Title	Personnel
6301	Enhanced Comprehensive Asset Management Systems (ECAMS) Operator	183
6313	3-M System Data Analyst	336
6677	TARPS Camera Repair IMA Technician	29
8133	EH-38 Photographic Quality Control Technician	99

38 Public Information Managers and Journalists

MOC	MOC Title	Personnel
2410	Intragovernmental Inquiries Officer	33
2412	Public Affairs Officer	1
2412	Public Affairs Officer	193
2415	Historical Officer	7
2430	Press Officer	5
2690	Printing and Publications Officer	4
2715	Disaster Preparedness Officer	1
3221	Broadcast Operations Specialist	242
3251	Broadcast Operations Director	43
8608	Air Boatswain	7
8608	Air Boatswain	15
8656	Aviation Safety Officer	43
9059	Staff Liaison Officer	1
9059	Staff Liaison Officer	36
9060	Staff Command and Control Officer	87
9065	Staff Operations and Plans Officer	20
9065	Staff Operations and Plans Officer	702
9067	Staff Readiness Officer (General)	3
9067	Staff Readiness Officer (General)	174
9068	Staff Readiness Officer (Aviation)	75
9069	Staff Readiness Officer (Weapons)	3
9069	Staff Readiness Officer (Weapons)	33
9070	Staff Readiness Officer (Engineering)	34
9071	Staff Readiness Officer (Seamanship)	5
9071	Staff Readiness Officer (Seamanship)	6
9072	Staff Readiness Officer (Damage Control)	2
9072	Staff Readiness Officer (Damage Control)	9
9073	Staff Readiness Officer (Tactics)	36
9074	Staff Readiness Officer (Communications)	1
9074	Staff Readiness Officer (Communications)	8
9075	Staff Readiness Officer (Combat Information Center)	11
9076	Staff Readiness Officer (Antisubmarine Warfare)	23
9077	Staff Readiness Officer (Submarine Warfare)	58
9078	Staff Readiness Officer (Amphibious Warfare)	10
9079	Staff Readiness Officer (Electronic Warfare)	20
9462	Civil Affairs Officer	6
9635	Naval Attaché (Assistant)	56
9940	Head of Naval Mission	8
9942	International Affairs Officer	87

39 Radar and Sonar Operators

MOC	MOC Title	Personnel
0302	AN/SYS-2 Integrated Automatic Detection and Tracking (IADT) Systems Operator	247
0304	LCAC Radar Operator/Navigator	119

0311	AEGIS Operations Specialist (CG 47-64)	352
0318	Air Intercept Controller	458
0319	Supervisory Air Intercept Controller	316
0321	Antisubmarine Air Controller	105
0322	LAMPS MK-III Air Tactical Control Operator	69
0324	ASW/ASUW Tactical Air Controller (ASTAC)	652
0325	AN/SSN-2(V)4 Operator	28
0334	HARPOON (AN/SWG-1A) Engagement Planning Operator	318
0401	AN/SQQ-30 Mine Classifying-Detecting Set Maintenance Technician	5
0445	Intermediate Acoustic Analyst	443
0488	AN/SQQ-32 Minehunting Sonar Set Operator	41
0501	Submarine Sonar Master Analyst	39
0505	IUSS Analyst	225
0507	IUSS Master Analyst	97
0612	TDP Displays Analyst	4
0614	SURTASS Analyst	3
0619	IUSS Acoustic Analyst	41
14NO	Navigation Equipment Operator	494
7821	P-3B/C Acoustic Sensor Operator	96
7825	ASW Operations Center (ASWOC) Equipment Operator	66
7827	ASW Operations Center Electronic Warfare Analyst	59
7834	S-3B Multi-Sensor Operator	175
7841	P-3C Update III Acoustic Sensor Operator	444
7846	CV/CVN ASWMOD System Operator	165
7851	P-3/EP-3J Non-Acoustic Operator	3
7861	P-3C Non-Acoustic Operator	233
7872	SH-3H Multi-Sensor Operator	17
7873	SH-60B Multi-Sensor Operator	363
7874	SH-2G Multi-Sensor Operator	22
7876	SH-60F/HH-60H Multi-Sensor Operator	339
7877	P-3C Update III ASUW Improvement Program (AIP) Non-Acoustic Operator	18

40 Recruiting Specialists

MOC	MOC Title	Personnel
2186	Career Recruiter	816
3015	Mobilization and Selection Officer	1
3015	Mobilization and Selection Officer	3
3020	Procurement and Recruiting Officer	6
3020	Procurement and Recruiting Officer	247
3035	Induction and Enlistment Officer	17
9585	Navy Recruiter Canvasser	1,945
9586	Navy Recruiting District (NRD) Recruiter/Classifier	20
9588	Career Information Program Advisor	517

41 Scientists and Engineers

MOC	MOC Title	Personnel
0845	Radiation Health Officer	52
0847	Radiation Specialist	30
0860	Entomologist	26
0861	Environmental Health Officer	91
0862	Industrial Hygiene Officer	118
0866	Medical Technologist	81
2050	Mathematics Research Officer	6
2060	Physical Sciences Research Officer	1
2070	Physicist, General	3
2071	Physicist, Nuclear	2
2085	Statistical Data Analyst	5
2098	Space Projects Technologist	19
2105	Air Warfare Research Officer	7
2145	Armament Research Officer	1
2155	Naval Sciences Research Coordinator/Administrator	29
2160	Designated Project Manager	22
2161	Major Project Manager (Selected)	64
2162	Deputy Designated Project Manager	29
2165	Designated Project Systems Integration Coordinator	34
2166	Designated Project Engineering Coordinator	7
2167	Designated Project Test and Evaluation Coordinator	14
2168	Designated Project Integrated Logistics System Coordinator	12
2170	Designated Project Support Officer	6
2170	Designated Project Support Officer	191
2175	Undersea Warfare Research Officer (General)	9
2176	Undersea Warfare Research Officer (Antisubmarine)	6
2180	Preoperational Test and Evaluation Officer	8
2181	Operational Test and Evaluation Officer	133
2190	Liaison Officer, Naval Research and Development	17
2192	Space Acquisition Officer	16
2306	Oceanography Services Officer	161
2310	Hydrography Program Officer	14
2323	Oceanography Watch Officer	50
2365	Staff Oceanography Officer	55
2740	Safety Engineer	2
2740	Safety Engineer	22
4205	Facilities Engineering Officer	76
4210	Staff Civil Engineer	3
4210	Staff Civil Engineer	156
4215	Facilities Planning and Programming Officer	64
4220	Facilities Design Officer	10
4225	Facilities Research Officer	1
4230	Facilities Construction/Facilities Services Officer	1
4230	Facilities Construction/Facilities Services Officer	343
4240	Petroleum Production Engineering Officer	2
4250	Public Works Officer	158

4255	Public Works Operations Officer	38
4260	Public Works Maintenance Officer	25
4270	Public Works Utilities Officer	5
4275	Public Works Planning Officer	1
4275	Public Works Planning Officer	26
4305	Commanding Officer, Naval Construction Forces	13
4310	Executive Officer, Naval Construction Forces	16
4315	Operations Officer, Naval Construction Forces	1
4315	Operations Officer, Naval Construction Forces	72
4330	Company Officer, Naval Construction Forces	11
4330	Company Officer, Naval Construction Forces	119
4340	Officer in Charge, Naval Construction Battalion Unit	6
4340	Officer in Charge, Naval Construction Battalion Unit	16
5904	Electronics Engineering Officer	1
5904	Electronics Engineering Officer	14
5913	Electronic Engineering Plans and Policies Director	13
5917	Electronic Equipment Research Officer	58
5925	Electronics Installation and Maintenance Planning Officer (General)	4
5925	Electronics Installation and Maintenance Planning Officer (General)	11
5927	Electronics Installation and Maintenance Planning Officer (Aviation)	1
5930	Space Requirements Analyst	23
5960	Electronic Inspection and Survey Officer	3
5961	Aircraft Electronics Director	7
5965	Electronics Logistics Officer	2
5970	Electronic Equipment Military Characteristics Officer	3
5977	Electronic Equipment Installation, Maintenance, and Repair Officer	21
5977	Electronic Equipment Installation, Maintenance, and Repair Officer	79
5980	Electronics Research Administrator	1
5996	Staff Electronic Material Officer	3
5996	Staff Electronic Material Officer	29
6275	Guided Missile Test Officer	12
6280	Guided Missile Type Project Officer (General)	14
6281	Guided Missile Type Project Officer (Air-Launched)	4
6282	Guided Missile Type Project Officer (Ship-Launched)	4
6716	Weapons Material Officer (Nuclear)	4
6930	Naval Weapons Technical Liaison Officer	3
6968	Weapons and Ammunition Production Officer	2
6968	Weapons and Ammunition Production Officer	7
7120	Naval Engineering Hull Development Officer	1
7140	Hull Inspection Officer	3
7165	Hull Superintendent	3
7165	Hull Superintendent	7
7187	Staff Hull Material Officer	1

7241	Machinery Installation and Repair Superintendent	5
7241	Machinery Installation and Repair Superintendent	12
7245	Naval Engineering Machinery Development Officer	1
7249	Nuclear Systems and Components Repair Officer, Ship	1
7249	Nuclear Systems and Components Repair Officer, Ship	18
7251	Radiological Control Officer	4
7251	Radiological Control Officer	151
7273	Nuclear Power Research Project Officer	14
7273	Nuclear Power Research Project Officer	183
7420	Ship Type Planning and Estimating Superintendent	4
7420	Ship Type Planning and Estimating Superintendent	28
7435	Quality Assurance Superintendent	5
7435	Quality Assurance Superintendent	21
7445	Production Engineering Officer	2
7450	Shop Production Officer	1
7450	Shop Production Officer	5
7905	Ship Project Officer	1
7905	Ship Project Officer	48
7910	Engineering Liaison Officer	20
7927	Naval Engineering Inspection Officer	17
7930	Ship Electrical Repair Officer	3
7930	Ship Electrical Repair Officer	6
7931	Naval Engineering Logistics Officer	9
7936	Ship Construction and Repair Superintendent (General)	11
7937	Ship Construction and Repair Superintendent (Surface Ships)	3
7937	Ship Construction and Repair Superintendent (Surface Ships)	18
7938	Ship Construction and Repair Superintendent (Submarines)	20
7939	Ship Construction and Repair Superintendent (Nuclear)	2
7939	Ship Construction and Repair Superintendent (Nuclear)	17
7959	Naval Engineering Research Project Officer	4
7966	Naval Engineering Trials and Survey Officer	4
7968	Nuclear Power Superintendent	5
7970	Yard Planning Officer	14
7974	Naval Engineering Officer, Ship Design	19
7976	Ship Repair Officer	29
7976	Ship Repair Officer	103
7984	Ship Type Engineering Officer	1
7984	Ship Type Engineering Officer	12
7996	Supervisor of Shipbuilding, Conversion, and Repair	19
7997	Yard Production Officer	7
7999	Technical Assistant for Weapons	8
8002	Aerodynamics Engineering Officer	4
8004	Aeronautical Engineering Officer, A/C Mech, Electronic, Electrical and Safety Equip	1
8015	Aircraft Armament Development Officer	4
8018	Aircraft Production Officer	2

8026	Aircraft Test Engineer	2
8026	Aircraft Test Engineer	14
8035	Aircraft/Guided Missile Engine Project Officer	1
8050	Launching, Recovery, and Landing Aids Engineering Officer	1
8050	Launching, Recovery, and Landing Aids Engineering Officer	10
8076	Type Aircraft Design and Development Officer	25
8583	Special Project Pilot	34
8585	Special Project Airborne Electronics Evaluator	17
8694	Aviation Model Manager	11
8950	Aviation Tactical Readiness Officer	47
8995	Staff Aviation Safety Officer	43
9085	Operations Analyst	158
9086	Strategic Plans Officer	138
9087	Staff Plans Officer	217
9299	Special Weapons Assembly Officer (Nuclear)	3
9312	Diving Officer (General)	9
9312	Diving Officer (General)	17
9314	Diving Officer (Ship Salvage)	6
9314	Diving Officer (Ship Salvage)	9
9315	Diving Officer (Saturation)	2
9315	Diving Officer (Saturation)	4
9404	Tactical Deception Plans Officer	5
9442	Facilities Manager	4
9442	Facilities Manager	47
9450	Inshore Undersea Warfare Officer	4
9905	Atomic Energy Plans and Policies Officer	20
9920	Examiner, Reactor Safeguards	18
9967	Surface Safety Officer	3

42 Ship Engineers and Air Crew Members

MOC	MOC Title	Personnel
0170	Surface Rescue Swimmer	929
7815	Tactical Helicopter Search and Rescue Air Crew Swimmer	102
9302	Auxiliary Machinery Officer	27
9302	Auxiliary Machinery Officer	336
9305	Boiler Officer (General)	6
9305	Boiler Officer (General)	43
9306	Boiler Officer (1200 PSI Steam System)	1
9308	Damage Control Assistant	31
9308	Damage Control Assistant	341
9322	Deep Submergence Vehicle Operator	7
9336	Main Propulsion Assistant (Diesel)	29
9337	Main Propulsion Assistant (Gas Turbine)	191
9341	Main Propulsion Assistant (Steam)	13
9341	Main Propulsion Assistant (Steam)	70
9342	Main Propulsion Assistant (1200 PSI Steam System)	3
9343	Underway Replenishment Equipment Maintenance Officer	4
9343	Underway Replenishment Equipment Maintenance Officer	6

9345	Examiner, Surface Ship Propulsion Plant	3
9345	Examiner, Surface Ship Propulsion Plant	57
9348	Repair Division Officer	39
9348	Repair Division Officer	93
9353	Ship's Electrical Officer	17
9353	Ship's Electrical Officer	153
9362	Ship's Engineer Officer (General)	2
9362	Ship's Engineer Officer (General)	11
9363	Ship's Engineer Officer (Diesel)	9
9363	Ship's Engineer Officer (Diesel)	57
9364	Ship's Engineer Officer (Gas Turbine)	1
9364	Ship's Engineer Officer (Gas Turbine)	180
9369	Ship's Engineer Officer (Steam)	56
9370	Ship's Engineer Officer (1200 PSI Steam System)	5
9371	Ship's Engineer Officer, Nuclear (General)	1
9371	Ship's Engineer Officer, Nuclear (General)	211
9372	Ship's Engineer Officer, Nuclear (Main Propulsion)	1
9372	Ship's Engineer Officer, Nuclear (Main Propulsion)	145
9373	Ship's Engineer Officer, Nuclear (Damage Control)	114
9374	Ship's Engineer Officer, Nuclear (Electrical)	7
9374	Ship's Engineer Officer, Nuclear (Electrical)	164
9375	Ship Salvage Operations Officer	17
9378	Main Engine Officer (General)	2
9378	Main Engine Officer (General)	2
9384	Main Engine Officer (Steam)	2
9384	Main Engine Officer (Steam)	68
9390	Staff Engineer Officer	1
9390	Staff Engineer Officer	8
9392	Ship's Reactor Officer	23
9393	Ship's Reactor Mechanical Assistant	1
9393	Ship's Reactor Mechanical Assistant	76
9394	Ship's Reactor Control Assistant	2
9394	Ship's Reactor Control Assistant	156
9395	Engineering Maintenance Officer, 1200 PSI Steam	2
9464	Ocean Systems Operations Officer	2
9464	Ocean Systems Operations Officer	18
9465	Ocean Systems Watch Officer	7
9465	Ocean Systems Watch Officer	16

43 Surveyors and Mappers

MOC	MOC Title	Personnel
2153	Naval Observatory Officer	1
5503	Advanced Engineering Aide	81
9425	Survey and Inspection Officer (Non-Engineering)	1

44 Transportation Specialists

MOC	MOC Title	Personnel
2819	Personal Property Specialist	16
2821	Air Transportation Specialist	123
9566	Naval Control of Shipping Staff Assistant	1

46 Weather Personnel

MOC	MOC Title	Personnel
2332	Meteorological and Oceanographic Equipment Program Officer	3
7412	Analyst-Forecaster	490

AIR FORCE OCCUPATIONS BY OCCUPATIONAL CLUSTER

1 Special Operations Forces

MOC	MOC Title	Personnel
11S1A	Special Operations Pilot	6
11S1B	Special Operations Pilot	2
11S1G	Special Operations Pilot	3
11S2A	Special Operations Pilot	21
11S2B	Special Operations Pilot	4
11S2G	Special Operations Pilot	7
11S3A	Special Operations Pilot	131
11S3B	Special Operations Pilot	33
11S3G	Special Operations Pilot	70
11S3V	Special Operations Pilot	22
11S4A	Special Operations Pilot	3
11S4B	Special Operations Pilot	2
11S4G	Special Operations Pilot	1
11S4V	Special Operations Pilot	13

2 Administrative, Personnel, and Supply Specialists

MOC	MOC Title	Personnel
1C000	Air Operations Manager	18
1C011	Airfield Management	31
1C012	Operations Resource Management	73
1C031	Airfield Management	133
1C032	Operations Resource Management	289
1C051	Airfield Management	293
1C052	Operations Resource Management	696
1C071	Airfield Management	304
1C072	Operations Resource Management	665
1C091	Airfield Management	15
1C092	Operations Resource Management	34
2G000	Logistics Plans Manager	10

2G011	Logistics Plans	3
2G031	Logistics Plans	13
2G051	Logistics Plans	104
2G071	Logistics Plans	342
2G091	Logistics Plans	39
2S000	Supply Manager	111
2S011	Supply Management	390
2S031	Supply Management	2,433
2S051	Supply Management	4,546
2S071	Supply Management	5,370
2S090	Supply Management	374
2T000	Traffic Manager	16
2T011	Traffic Management	99
2T031	Traffic Management	418
2T051	Traffic Management	799
2T071	Traffic Management	693
2T091	Traffic Management	37
2T200	Air Transportation Manager	22
2T211	Air Transportation	184
2T231	Air Transportation	865
2T251	Air Transportation	1,682
2T271	Air Transportation	1,644
2T291	Air Transportation	79
3A011	Information Management	364
3A031	Information Management	2,095
3A051	Information Management	3,730
3A071	Information Management	5,727
3A091	Information Management	340
3S000	Personnel Manager	91
3S011	Personnel	275
3S031	Personnel	1,322
3S032	Personnel System Management (PSM)	2
3S051	Personnel	2,250
3S052	Personnel System Management (PSM)	87
3S071	Personnel	3,131
3S072	Personnel System Management (PSM)	273
3S090	Personnel	199
3S131	Equal Opportunity and Treatment	6
3S171	Equal Opportunity and Treatment	152
3S191	Equal Opportunity and Treatment	17
3U000	Manpower and Quality Management Manager	19
3U031	Manpower and Quality Management	24
3U071	Manpower and Quality Management	405
3U091	Manpower and Quality Management	54
4A000	Health Services Management Manager	23
4A011	Health Services Management	111
4A031	Health Services Management	926
4A051	Health Services Management	1,329

4A071	Health Services Management	1,270
4A091	Health Services Management	52
4A100	Medical Materiel Manager	9
4A111	Medical Materiel	31
4A131	Medical Materiel	243
4A151	Medical Materiel	437
4A171	Medical Materiel	517
4A191	Medical Materiel	21
5R000	Chaplain Service Support Manager	7
5R011	Chaplain Service Support	15
5R031	Chaplain Service Support	103
5R051	Chaplain Service Support	157
5R071	Chaplain Service Support	164
5R091	Chaplain Service Support	9
6C000	Contracting Manager	11
6C011	Contracting	11
6C031	Contracting	95
6C051	Contracting	352
6C071	Contracting	513
6C091	Contracting	40
6F000	Financial Manager	25
6F011	Financial Management	212
6F031	Financial Management	655
6F051	Financial Management	1,209
6F111	Financial Analysis	3
6F131	Financial Analysis	11
6F151	Financial Analysis	101
6F171	Financial Analysis	328
6F191	Financial Analysis	26
8F000	First Sergeant	704
8M000	Postal	512
8P000	Courier	37
9E000	Senior Enlisted Adviser	80

3 Aircraft, Automotive, and Electrical Maintanence Specialists

MOC	MOC Title	Personnel
2A111	Avionic Sensors Maintenance	89
2A112	Avionics Guidance and Control Systems	33
2A131	Avionic Sensors Maintenance	166
2A132	Avionics Guidance and Control Systems	58
2A151	Avionic Sensors Maintenance	322
2A152	Avionics Guidance and Control Systems	149
2A171	Avionic Sensors Maintenance	408
2A172	Avionics Guidance and Control Systems	188
2A313B	Tactical Aircraft Maintenance	406
2A313E	Tactical Aircraft Maintenance	87
2A313H	Tactical Aircraft Maintenance	23
2A333B	Tactical Aircraft Maintenance	607

2A333C	Tactical Aircraft Maintenance	9
2A333H	Tactical Aircraft Maintenance	125
2A353B	Tactical Aircraft Maintenance	1,415
2A353J	Tactical Aircraft Maintenance	590
2A373B	Tactical Aircraft Maintenance	1,832
2A373J	Tactical Aircraft Maintenance	1,218
2A512A	Helicopter Maintenance	22
2A512B	Helicopter Maintenance	18
2A532A	Helicopter Maintenance	97
2A532B	Helicopter Maintenance	92
2A532C	Helicopter Maintenance	22
2A552	Helicopter Maintenance	267
2A571	Aerospace Maintenance	5,715
2A572	Helicopter Maintenance	351
2A600	Systems Manager	146
2A611B	Aerospace Propulsion	82
2A611C	Aerospace Propulsion	143
2A611D	Aerospace Propulsion	103
2A611E	Aerospace Propulsion	92
2A612	Aerospace Ground Equipment	420
2A613	Aircrew Egress Systems	24
2A614	Aircraft Fuel Systems	87
2A615	Aircraft Hydraulic Systems	75
2A616	Aircraft Electrical and Environmental Systems	266
2A631B	Aerospace Propulsion	252
2A631C	Aerospace Propulsion	357
2A631D	Aerospace Propulsion	197
2A631E	Aerospace Propulsion	199
2A632	Aerospace Ground Equipment	754
2A633	Aircrew Egress Systems	109
2A634	Aircraft Fuel Systems	408
2A635	Aircraft Hydraulic Systems	366
2A636	Aircraft Electrical and Environmental Systems	584
2A651A	Aerospace Propulsion	1,429
2A651B	Aerospace Propulsion	426
2A652	Aerospace Ground Equipment	1,769
2A653	Aircrew Egress Systems	261
2A654	Aircraft Fuel Systems	695
2A655	Aircraft Hydraulic Systems	995
2A656	Aircraft Electrical and Environmental Systems	1,403
2A671A	Aerospace Propulsion	2,339
2A671B	Aerospace Propulsion	482
2A672	Aerospace Ground Equipment	2,150
2A673	Aircrew Egress Systems	280
2A674	Aircraft Fuel Systems	761
2A675	Aircraft Hydraulic Systems	765
2A676	Aircraft Electrical and Environmental Systems	1,687
2A690	Aircraft Systems	240

2A691	Aerospace Propulsion	181
2A692	Aerospace Ground Equipment	135
2A713	Aircraft Structural Maintenance	191
2A733	Aircraft Structural Maintenance	460
2A753	Aircraft Structural Maintenance	971
2A773	Aircraft Structural Maintenance	1,322
2T300	Vehicle Maintenance Manager	24
2T311	Special Purpose Vehicle and Equipment Maintenance	88
2T312A	Special Vehicle Maintenance	14
2T312B	Special Vehicle Maintenance	18
2T331	Special Purpose Vehicle and Equipment Maintenance	225
2T332A	Special Vehicle Maintenance	55
2T332B	Special Vehicle Maintenance	51
2T351	Special Purpose Vehicle and Equipment Maintenance	473
2T352A	Special Vehicle Maintenance	91
2T352B	Special Vehicle Maintenance	94
2T370	Special Purpose Vehicle and Equipment Maintenance	1,151
2T390	Vehicle Maintenance	54
3E011	Electrical Systems	217
3E012	Electrical Power Production	31
3E031	Electrical Systems	549
3E032	Electrical Power Production	367
3E051	Electrical Systems	497
3E052	Electrical Power Production	423
3E071	Electrical Systems	613
3E072	Electrical Power Production	520
3E090	Electrical	65
3E111	Heating, Ventilation, Air Conditioning, and Refrigeration	201
3E131	Heating, Ventilation, Air Conditioning, and Refrigeration	576
3E151	Heating, Ventilation, Air Conditioning, and Refrigeration	630
3E171	Heating, Ventilation, Air Conditioning, and Refrigeration	902
3E191	Heating, Ventilation, Air Conditioning, and Refrigeration	47

4 Air Traffic Controllers

MOC	MOC Title	Personnel
13B1B	Air Battle Management	50
13B1C	Air Battle Management	16
13B1J	Air Battle Management	1
13B1K	Air Battle Management	138
13B3B	Air Battle Management	471
13B3C	Air Battle Management	109
13B3J	Air Battle Management	6
13B3K	Air Battle Management	19
13B3L	Air Battle Management	9
13B4B	Air Battle Management	55
13B4C	Air Battle Management	26
13B4K	Air Battle Management	1
13D1	Combat Control	3

13D3	Combat Control	26
13D4	Combat Control	9
13M1	Air Traffic Control	58
13M3	Air Traffic Control	192
13M4	Air Traffic Control	44
1C100	Air Traffic Control Manager	26
1C111	Air Traffic Control	591
1C131	Air Traffic Control	487
1C151	Air Traffic Control	566
1C171	Air Traffic Control	1,607
1C191	Air Traffic Control	96
1C200	Combat Control Manager	1
1C211	Combat Control	73
1C231	Combat Control	41
1C251	Combat Control	108
1C271	Combat Control	177
1C291	Combat Control	14

5 Airplane Navigators

MOC	MOC Title	Personnel
12A1A	Airlift Navigator	5
12A1C	Airlift Navigator	85
12A1D	Airlift Navigator	2
12A1E	Airlift Navigator	21
12A1T	Airlift Navigator	3
12A1U	Airlift Navigator	1
12A1W	Airlift Navigator	2
12A1Y	Airlift Navigator	7
12A3A	Airlift Navigator	26
12A3B	Airlift Navigator	3
12A3C	Airlift Navigator	404
12A3D	Airlift Navigator	32
12A3E	Airlift Navigator	108
12A3T	Airlift Navigator	14
12A3U	Airlift Navigator	4
12A3V	Airlift Navigator	6
12A3Y	Airlift Navigator	27
12A3Z	Airlift Navigator	7
12A4A	Airlift Navigator	1
12A4C	Airlift Navigator	38
12A4D	Airlift Navigator	3
12A4E	Airlift Navigator	4
12A4U	Airlift Navigator	1
12A4V	Airlift Navigator	2
12A4W	Airlift Navigator	12
12A4Y	Airlift Navigator	92
12B1A	Bomber Navigator	23
12B1B	Bomber Navigator	3

12B1C	Bomber Navigator	2
12B1D	Bomber Navigator	18
12B1E	Bomber Navigator	27
12B1S	Bomber Navigator	2
12B1W	Bomber Navigator	2
12B1Y	Bomber Navigator	16
12B1Z	Bomber Navigator	2
12B2A	Bomber Navigator	2
12B2C	Bomber Navigator	1
12B2D	Bomber Navigator	2
12B2E	Bomber Navigator	36
12B3A	Bomber Navigator	28
12B3B	Bomber Navigator	53
12B3C	Bomber Navigator	167
12B3D	Bomber Navigator	124
12B3E	Bomber Navigator	203
12B3S	Bomber Navigator	16
12B3T	Bomber Navigator	13
12B3U	Bomber Navigator	3
12B3W	Bomber Navigator	8
12B3Y	Bomber Navigator	82
12B3Z	Bomber Navigator	1
12B4A	Bomber Navigator	7
12B4B	Bomber Navigator	10
12B4C	Bomber Navigator	2
12B4D	Bomber Navigator	17
12B4E	Bomber Navigator	33
12B4U	Bomber Navigator	5
12B4W	Bomber Navigator	14
12B4Y	Bomber Navigator	157
12E1A	Experimental Test Navigator	2
12E1B	Experimental Test Navigator	4
12E1Z	Experimental Test Navigator	2
12E3A	Experimental Test Navigator	6
12E3B	Experimental Test Navigator	8
12E3Z	Experimental Test Navigator	2
12E4A	Experimental Test Navigator	2
12E4Z	Experimental Test Navigator	1
12F1A	Fighter Navigator	7
12F1C	Fighter Navigator	12
12F1D	Fighter Navigator	3
12F1F	Fighter Navigator	35
12F1H	Fighter Navigator	7
12F1K	Fighter Navigator	2
12F1T	Fighter Navigator	3
12F1U	Fighter Navigator	5
12F1W	Fighter Navigator	7
12F1Y	Fighter Navigator	6

12F1Z	Fighter Navigator	2
12F3A	Fighter Navigator	20
12F3B	Fighter Navigator	1
12F3C	Fighter Navigator	17
12F3D	Fighter Navigator	8
12F3F	Fighter Navigator	327
12F3G	Fighter Navigator	2
12F3H	Fighter Navigator	48
12F3K	Fighter Navigator	34
12F3S	Fighter Navigator	4
12F3T	Fighter Navigator	11
12F3U	Fighter Navigator	10
12F3W	Fighter Navigator	22
12F3Y	Fighter Navigator	25
12F3Z	Fighter Navigator	8
12F4A	Fighter Navigator	12
12F4C	Fighter Navigator	8
12F4D	Fighter Navigator	2
12F4F	Fighter Navigator	22
12F4H	Fighter Navigator	19
12F4K	Fighter Navigator	2
12F4U	Fighter Navigator	23
12F4W	Fighter Navigator	53
12F4Y	Fighter Navigator	146
12F4Z	Fighter Navigator	1
12G3	Generalist Navigator	15
12G4	Generalist Navigator	60
12K1A	Trainer Navigator	1
12K1B	Trainer Navigator	1
12K3A	Trainer Navigator	2
12K3B	Trainer Navigator	1
12K3Z	Trainer Navigator	1
12K4Y	Trainer Navigator	5
12R1A	Reconnaissance/Surveillance/Electronic Warfare Navigator	14
12R1C	Reconnaissance/Surveillance/Electronic Warfare Navigator	7
12R1D	Reconnaissance/Surveillance/Electronic Warfare Navigator	6
12R1E	Reconnaissance/Surveillance/Electronic Warfare Navigator	1
12R1G	Reconnaissance/Surveillance/Electronic Warfare Navigator	1
12R1H	Reconnaissance/Surveillance/Electronic Warfare Navigator	30
12R1J	Reconnaissance/Surveillance/Electronic Warfare Navigator	16
12R1K	Reconnaissance/Surveillance/Electronic Warfare Navigator	2
12R1T	Reconnaissance/Surveillance/Electronic Warfare Navigator	1
12R1Y	Reconnaissance/Surveillance/Electronic Warfare Navigator	7
12R1Z	Reconnaissance/Surveillance/Electronic Warfare Navigator	1
12R3A	Reconnaissance/Surveillance/Electronic Warfare Navigator	102
12R3B	Reconnaissance/Surveillance/Electronic Warfare Navigator	7
12R3C	Reconnaissance/Surveillance/Electronic Warfare Navigator	35
12R3D	Reconnaissance/Surveillance/Electronic Warfare Navigator	32

12R3E	Reconnaissance/Surveillance/Electronic Warfare Navigator	8
12R3G	Reconnaissance/Surveillance/Electronic Warfare Navigator	20
12R3H	Reconnaissance/Surveillance/Electronic Warfare Navigator	219
12R3J	Reconnaissance/Surveillance/Electronic Warfare Navigator	94
12R3K	Reconnaissance/Surveillance/Electronic Warfare Navigator	7
12R3S	Reconnaissance/Surveillance/Electronic Warfare Navigator	8
12R3T	Reconnaissance/Surveillance/Electronic Warfare Navigator	9
12R3W	Reconnaissance/Surveillance/Electronic Warfare Navigator	6
12R3Y	Reconnaissance/Surveillance/Electronic Warfare Navigator	36
12R3Z	Reconnaissance/Surveillance/Electronic Warfare Navigator	3
12R4A	Reconnaissance/Surveillance/Electronic Warfare Navigator	5
12R4B	Reconnaissance/Surveillance/Electronic Warfare Navigator	5
12R4C	Reconnaissance/Surveillance/Electronic Warfare Navigator	4
12R4D	Reconnaissance/Surveillance/Electronic Warfare Navigator	1
12R4E	Reconnaissance/Surveillance/Electronic Warfare Navigator	1
12R4G	Reconnaissance/Surveillance/Electronic Warfare Navigator	1
12R4H	Reconnaissance/Surveillance/Electronic Warfare Navigator	20
12R4J	Reconnaissance/Surveillance/Electronic Warfare Navigator	18
12R4U	Reconnaissance/Surveillance/Electronic Warfare Navigator	1
12R4W	Reconnaissance/Surveillance/Electronic Warfare Navigator	23
12R4Y	Reconnaissance/Surveillance/Electronic Warfare Navigator	27
12S1A	Special Operations Navigator	2
12S1B	Special Operations Navigator	1
12S1C	Special Operations Navigator	1
12S1D	Special Operations Navigator	4
12S1F	Special Operations Navigator	1
12S1G	Special Operations Navigator	7
12S1H	Special Operations Navigator	1
12S1J	Special Operations Navigator	1
12S1K	Special Operations Navigator	2
12S1L	Special Operations Navigator	1
12S1T	Special Operations Navigator	1
12S1W	Special Operations Navigator	1
12S1Y	Special Operations Navigator	2
12S3A	Special Operations Navigator	16
12S3B	Special Operations Navigator	27
12S3C	Special Operations Navigator	24
12S3D	Special Operations Navigator	14
12S3E	Special Operations Navigator	14
12S3F	Special Operations Navigator	13
12S3G	Special Operations Navigator	83
12S3H	Special Operations Navigator	18
12S3J	Special Operations Navigator	30
12S3K	Special Operations Navigator	41
12S3L	Special Operations Navigator	42
12S3S	Special Operations Navigator	2
12S3U	Special Operations Navigator	1
12S3W	Special Operations Navigator	9

12S3Y	Special Operations Navigator	47
12S4A	Special Operations Navigator	1
12S4B	Special Operations Navigator	1
12S4C	Special Operations Navigator	2
12S4G	Special Operations Navigator	2
12S4H	Special Operations Navigator	1
12S4J	Special Operations Navigator	5
12S4L	Special Operations Navigator	4
12S4W	Special Operations Navigator	12
12S4Y	Special Operations Navigator	32
12T1A	Tanker Navigator	26
12T1Y	Tanker Navigator	1
12T3A	Tanker Navigator	418
12T3T	Tanker Navigator	16
12T3Y	Tanker Navigator	30
12T3Z	Tanker Navigator	7
12T4A	Tanker Navigator	36
12T4Y	Tanker Navigator	56

6 Communications Managers

MOC	MOC Title	Personnel
13B1D	Air Battle Management	15
13B3D	Air Battle Management	144
13B4D	Air Battle Management	183

7 Communications Operators

MOC	MOC Title	Personnel
1A300	Airborne Communications Systems Manager	5
1A311	Airborne Communications Systems	31
1A331	Airborne Communications Systems	200
1A351	Airborne Communications Systems	177
1A371	Airborne Communications Systems	324
1A391	Airborne Communications Systems	14
1A400	Airborne Warning Command and Control Systems Manager	9
1A411	Airborne Battle Management Systems	44
1A431	Airborne Battle Management Systems	88
1A451	Airborne Battle Management Systems	228
1A451D	Airborne Battle Management Systems	56
1A471	Airborne Battle Management Systems	169
1A471D	Airborne Battle Management Systems	89
1A491	Airborne Battle Management Systems	11
1C300	Command and Control Manager	18
1C311	Command and Control	112
1C331	Command and Control	265
1C351	Command and Control	700
1C371	Command and Control	791
1C391	Command and Control	66

1C400	Tactical Air Command and Control Manager	4
1C411	Tactical Air Command and Control	100
1C431	Tactical Air Command and Control	154
1C451	Tactical Air Command and Control	304
1C471	Tactical Air Command and Control	369
1C491	Tactical Air Command and Control	11
1C500	Aerospace Control and Warning System Manager	12
1C551	Aerospace Control and Warning Systems	364
1C551D	Aerospace Control and Warning Systems	35
1N200	Signals Intelligence Analysis Manager	36
1N211	Signals Intelligence Production	308
1N231	Signals Intelligence Production	220
1N251	Signals Intelligence Production	650
1N271	Signals Intelligence Production	786
1N291	Signals Intelligence Production	47
1N500	Electronic Signals Intelligence Exploitation Manager	5
1N511	Electronic Signals Intelligence Exploitation	29
1N531	Electronic Signals Intelligence Exploitation	102
1N551	Electronic Signals Intelligence Exploitation	214
1N571	Electronic Signals Intelligence Exploitation	390
1N591	Electronic Signals Intelligence Exploitation	15
1N600	Electronic Systems Security Assess Manager	1
2A413	Aircraft Command Control Communications and Navigation Systems	35
2A433	Aircraft Command Control Communications and Navigation Systems	118
2A453	Aircraft Command Control Communications and Navigation Systems	88
2A473	Aircraft Command Control Communications and Navigation Systems	129
2E000	Communications-Electronics Systems Manager	112
2E690	Telephone and Distributed Communications Systems	54
3C111	Radio Communications Systems	79
3C131	Radio Communications Systems	126
3C132	Electromagnetic Spectrum Management	2
3C151	Radio Communications Systems	379
3C171	Radio Communications Systems	555
3C172	Electromagnetic Spectrum Management	47
3C191	Radio Communications Systems	22
3C192	Electromagnetic Spectrum Management	3

8 Computer Systems Specialists

MOC	MOC Title	Personnel
1A511	Airborne Missions Systems	36
1A531	Airborne Missions Systems	94
1A551	Airborne Missions Systems	141
1A571	Airborne Missions Systems	138
1A591	Airborne Missions Systems	6

2S012	Supply Systems Analysis	29
2S032	Supply Systems Analysis	84
2S052	Supply Systems Analysis	101
2S072	Supply Systems Analysis	501
33S1	Communications and Information	515
33S1A	Communications and Information	59
33S1B	Communications and Information	19
33S1C	Communications and Information	215
33S3	Communications and Information	1,328
33S3A	Communications and Information	259
33S3B	Communications and Information	78
33S3C	Communications and Information	1,067
33S3W	Communications and Information	1
33S4	Communications and Information	1,106
33S4W	Communications and Information	1
3A000	Information Management Manager	93
3C000	Communications-Computer Systems Manager	74
3C011	Communications-Computer Systems Operations	351
3C012	Communications-Computer Systems Programming	33
3C031	Communications-Computer Systems Operations	1,127
3C032	Communications-Computer Systems Programming	222
3C051	Communications-Computer Systems Operations	2,820
3C052	Communications-Computer Systems Programming	697
3C071	Communications-Computer Systems Operations	2,946
3C072	Communications-Computer Systems Programming	924
3C090	Communications-Computer Systems	197
3C211	Communications-Computer Systems Control	91
3C231	Communications-Computer Systems Control	372
3C251	Communications-Computer Systems Control	524
3C271	Communications-Computer Systems Control	840
3C291	Communications-Computer Systems Control	43
3C311	Communications-Computer Systems Planning and Implementation	10
3C331	Communications-Computer Systems Planning and Implementation	34
3C351	Communications-Computer Systems Planning and Implementation	177
3C371	Communications-Computer Systems Planning and Implementation	306
3C391	Communications-Computer Systems Planning and Implementation	31

9 Construction and Engineering Operators

MOC	MOC Title	Personnel
1T100	Aircrew Life Support Manager	11
1T111	Aircrew Life Support	84
1T131	Aircrew Life Support	386
1T151	Aircrew Life Support	724

1T171	Aircrew Life Support	712
1T191	Aircrew Life Support	30
2A714	Survival Equipment	33
2A734	Survival Equipment	116
2A754	Survival Equipment	308
2A774	Survival Equipment	299
3E211	Pavements and Construction Equipment	110
3E231	Pavements and Construction Equipment	464
3E251	Pavements and Construction Equipment	564
3E271	Pavements and Construction Equipment	751
3E291	Pavements and Construction Equipment	43

11 Dental and Pharmacy Specialists

MOC	MOC Title	Personnel
40C0D	Medical Commander	5
47B1	Orthodontist	2
47B3	Orthodontist	20
47D3	Oral and Maxillofacial Pathologist	7
47E3	Endodontist	18
47G1A	Dentist	3
47G1C	Dentist	10
47G3A	Dentist	188
47G3B	Dentist	37
47G3C	Dentist	328
47G4A	Dentist	1
47G4B	Dentist	1
47H1	Periodontist	1
47H3	Periodontist	54
47K3	Pediatric Dentist	15
47P1	Prosthodontist	1
47P3	Prosthodontist	58
4P000	Pharmacy Manager	6
4P011	Pharmacy	64
4P031	Pharmacy	171
4P051	Pharmacy	423
4P071	Pharmacy	344
4P091	Pharmacy	12
4Y000	Dental Manager	18
4Y011	Dental Assistant	190
4Y031	Dental Assistant	540
4Y051	Dental Assistant	750
4Y071	Dental Assistant	885

13 Emergency Management and Laboratory Specialists

MOC	MOC Title	Personnel
3E900	Readiness Manager	6
3E911	Readiness	6

3E931	Readiness	52
3E951	Readiness	88
3E971	Readiness	273
3E991	Readiness	20

14 Environmental Health and Safety Specialists

MOC	MOC Title	Personnel
3E413	Environmental	7
3E433	Environmental	44
3E453	Environmental	98
3E473	Environmental	146
4B011	Bioenvironmental Engineering	43
4B031	Bioenvironmental Engineering	179
4B051	Bioenvironmental Engineering	312
4B071	Bioenvironmental Engineering	271
4B091	Bioenvironmental Engineering	11
4E011	Public Health	70
4E031	Public Health	159
4E051	Public Health	211
4E071	Public Health	252
4E091	Public Health	10

15 Finance and Accounting Managers

MOC	MOC Title	Personnel
65A3	Audit	4
65A4	Audit	9
65F1	Financial Management	113
65F3	Financial Management	424
65F4	Financial Management	226
65W1	Cost Analysis	22
65W3	Cost Analysis	112
65W4	Cost Analysis	21
87G0	Inspector General	23

16 Firefighters

MOC	MOC Title	Personnel
3E700	Fire Protection Manager	21
3E711	Fire Protection	294
3E731	Fire Protection	1,812
3E751	Fire Protection	1,043
3E771	Fire Protection	1,141
3E791	Fire Protection	37

17 Flight Engineers

MOC	MOC Title	Personnel
1A100	Flight Engineer Manager	27
1A131C	Flight Engineer	7

1A151C	Flight Engineer	195
1A171C	Flight Engineer	966
1A190	Flight Engineer	110
1A200	Aircraft Loadmaster Manager	13

18 Functional Specialty Managers

MOC	MOC Title	Personnel
10C0	Operations Commander	198
13B1F	Air Battle Management	25
13B3F	Air Battle Management	132
13B4F	Air Battle Management	4
16G1	Air Force Operations Staff Officer	28
16G3	Air Force Operations Staff Officer	20
16G4	Air Force Operations Staff Officer	88
16R1	Planning and Programming	46
16R3	Planning and Programming	63
16R4	Planning and Programming	269
20C0	Logistics Commander	250
20C0W	Logistics Commander	1
21A1	Aircraft Maintenance and Munitions	308
21A1A	Aircraft Maintenance and Munitions	18
21A3	Aircraft Maintenance and Munitions	1,202
21A3A	Aircraft Maintenance and Munitions	122
21A4	Aircraft Maintenance and Munitions	271
21G1	Logistics Plans	58
21G3	Logistics Plans	249
21G4	Logistics Plans	143
21L1	Logistician	47
21L3	Logistician	355
21L3W	Logistician	1
21L4	Logistician	277
21S1	Supply	92
21S3	Supply	353
21S4	Supply	89
21T1	Transportation	86
21T3	Transportation	379
21T4	Transportation	130
30C0	Support Commander	324
30C0W	Support Commander	4
31P1	Security Police	144
31P3	Security Police	497
31P4	Security Police	175
34M1	Services	72
34M3	Services	209
34M4	Services	81
36M1	Mission Support	19
36M3	Mission Support	141
36P1	Personnel	297

36P3	Personnel	1,010
36P4	Personnel	448
36P4W	Personnel	5
38M1	Manpower and Quality Management	69
38M3	Manpower and Quality Management	88
38M4	Manpower and Quality Management	140
3M000	Services Manager	20
3M011	Services	209
3M031	Services	828
3M051	Services	2,090
3M071	Services	1,634
3M091	Services	60
4D000	Diet Therapy Manager	4
4D011	Diet Therapy	20
4D031	Diet Therapy	118
4D051	Diet Therapy	209
4D071	Diet Therapy	232
4D091	Diet Therapy	6
60C0	Program Director	26
63A1	Acquisition Manager	290
63A1W	Acquisition Manager	20
63A3	Acquisition Manager	1,298
63A3P	Acquisition Manager	10
63A3R	Acquisition Manager	5
63A3U	Acquisition Manager	1
63A3V	Acquisition Manager	3
63A3W	Acquisition Manager	54
63A4	Acquisition Manager	570
63A4P	Acquisition Manager	5
63A4R	Acquisition Manager	2
63A4T	Acquisition Manager	1
63A4U	Acquisition Manager	1
63A4V	Acquisition Manager	2
63A4W	Acquisition Manager	25
64P1	Contracting	107
64P3	Contracting	581
64P4	Contracting	302
71S1	Special Investigations	66
71S3	Special Investigations	182
71S4	Special Investigations	89
86M0	Operations Management	115
88A0	Aide-de-Camp	9
91C0	Commander	109
91C0W	Commander	1
91W0	Wing Commander	132
97E0	Executive Officer Above Wing Level	59
9D000	Dormitory Manager	94
9G000	Airman Aide	27

20 Health, Education and Welfare Workers

MOC	MOC Title	Personnel
1N312A	Romance Cryptologic Linguist	73
1N312C	Romance Cryptologic Linguist	5
1N312E	Romance Cryptologic Linguist	1
1N313A	Slavic Cryptologic Linguist	208
1N313D	Slavic Cryptologic Linguist	71
1N313E	Slavic Cryptologic Linguist	1
1N313K	Slavic Cryptologic Linguist	4
1N313L	Slavic Cryptologic Linguist	5
1N314A	Far East Cryptologic Linguist	122
1N314B	Far East Cryptologic Linguist	32
1N314C	Far East Cryptologic Linguist	3
1N314D	Far East Cryptologic Linguist	5
1N314E	Far East Cryptologic Linguist	6
1N314G	Far East Cryptologic Linguist	210
1N314J	Far East Cryptologic Linguist	2
1N315A	Mid East Cryptologic Linguist	191
1N315C	Mid East Cryptologic Linguist	41
1N315D	Mid East Cryptologic Linguist	84
1N315E	Mid East Cryptologic Linguist	8
1N332A	Romance Cryptologic Linguist	73
1N332B	Romance Cryptologic Linguist	1
1N332F	Romance Cryptologic Linguist	3
1N333A	Slavic Cryptologic Linguist	103
1N333D	Slavic Cryptologic Linguist	24
1N333F	Slavic Cryptologic Linguist	2
1N333J	Slavic Cryptologic Linguist	1
1N333K	Slavic Cryptologic Linguist	1
1N334A	Far East Cryptologic Linguist	73
1N334B	Far East Cryptologic Linguist	31
1N334C	Far East Cryptologic Linguist	4
1N334D	Far East Cryptologic Linguist	4
1N334E	Far East Cryptologic Linguist	3
1N334G	Far East Cryptologic Linguist	84
1N335A	Mid East Cryptologic Linguist	83
1N335C	Mid East Cryptologic Linguist	12
1N335D	Mid East Cryptologic Linguist	44
1N335E	Mid East Cryptologic Linguist	6
1N335F	Mid East Cryptologic Linguist	2
1N351A	German Cryptologic Linguist	8
1N352A	Romance Cryptologic Linguist	137
1N352B	Romance Cryptologic Linguist	4
1N352C	Romance Cryptologic Linguist	5
1N352E	Romance Cryptologic Linguist	1
1N353A	Slavic Cryptologic Linguist	114
1N353D	Slavic Cryptologic Linguist	16
1N353E	Slavic Cryptologic Linguist	1

1N353F	Slavic Cryptologic Linguist	2
1N353J	Slavic Cryptologic Linguist	2
1N354A	Far East Cryptologic Linguist	84
1N354B	Far East Cryptologic Linguist	18
1N354C	Far East Cryptologic Linguist	3
1N354D	Far East Cryptologic Linguist	4
1N354E	Far East Cryptologic Linguist	3
1N354G	Far East Cryptologic Linguist	81
1N354J	Far East Cryptologic Linguist	1
1N355A	Mid East Cryptologic Linguist	201
1N355C	Mid East Cryptologic Linguist	28
1N355D	Mid East Cryptologic Linguist	30
1N355E	Mid East Cryptologic Linguist	7
1N371A	German Cryptologic Linguist	10
1N372A	Romance Cryptologic Linguist	161
1N372B	Romance Cryptologic Linguist	4
1N372C	Romance Cryptologic Linguist	3
1N372E	Romance Cryptologic Linguist	4
1N373A	Slavic Cryptologic Linguist	392
1N373B	Slavic Cryptologic Linguist	9
1N373C	Slavic Cryptologic Linguist	12
1N373D	Slavic Cryptologic Linguist	38
1N373E	Slavic Cryptologic Linguist	1
1N373F	Slavic Cryptologic Linguist	1
1N373J	Slavic Cryptologic Linguist	4
1N374A	Far East Cryptologic Linguist	83
1N374B	Far East Cryptologic Linguist	42
1N374C	Far East Cryptologic Linguist	2
1N374D	Far East Cryptologic Linguist	3
1N374G	Far East Cryptologic Linguist	153
1N374J	Far East Cryptologic Linguist	9
1N375A	Mid East Cryptologic Linguist	145
1N375C	Mid East Cryptologic Linguist	36
1N375D	Mid East Cryptologic Linguist	23
1N375E	Mid East Cryptologic Linguist	3
1N390	Cryptologic Linguist	80
1T000	Survival, Evasion, Resistance, and Escape Training Manager	4
1T011	Survival, Evasion, Resistance, and Escape Training	58
1T031	Survival, Evasion, Resistance, and Escape Training	60
1T051	Survival, Evasion, Resistance, and Escape Training	103
1T071	Survival, Evasion, Resistance, and Escape Training	157
1T091	Survival, Evasion, Resistance, and Escape Training	7
3S100	Equal Opportunity and Treatment Manager	6
3S200	Education and Training Manager	13
3S211	Education and Training	11
3S231	Education and Training	50
3S251	Education and Training	374
3S271	Education and Training	862

40C0A	Medical Commander	20
40C0C	Medical Commander	33
41A1	Health Services Administrator	251
41A3	Health Services Administrator	568
41A4	Health Services Administrator	300
42N1A	Audiology/Speech Pathologist	7
42N3A	Audiology/Speech Pathologist	31
42N3B	Audiology/Speech Pathologist	6
42N4A	Audiology/Speech Pathologist	1
42P3	Clinical Psychologist	118
42P3A	Clinical Psychologist	9
42S1	Clinical Social Worker	50
42S3	Clinical Social Worker	165
42S4	Clinical Social Worker	4
43D1	Dietitian	16
43D3	Dietitian	68
43P1	Pharmacist	78
43P3	Pharmacist	179
43P4	Pharmacist	3
4C000	Mental Health Service Manager	2
4C011	Mental Health Service	36
4C031	Mental Health Service	158
4C051	Mental Health Service	219
4C071	Mental Health Service	328
4C091	Mental Health Service	11
4M000	Aerospace Physiology Manager	2
4M011	Aerospace Physiology	19
4M031	Aerospace Physiology	69
4M051	Aerospace Physiology	127
4M071	Aerospace Physiology	170
4M091	Aerospace Physiology	9
51J1	Judge Advocate	127
51J3	Judge Advocate	722
51J4	Judge Advocate	441
52R3	Chaplain	430
52R3A	Chaplain	9
52R3C	Chaplain	1
52R4	Chaplain	145
80C0	Commander, Cadet Squadron, USAF Academy	5
80C0W	Commander, Cadet Squadron, USAF Academy	17
81C0	Training Commander, Officer Training School	2
81C0W	Training Commander, Officer Training School	1
81T0	Instructor	261
81T0U	Instructor	1
81T0W	Instructor	30
82A0	Academic Program Manager	60
82A0W	Academic Program Manager	15
8B000	Military Training Instructor	36

8B100	Military Training Manager	42
8C000	Family Support Center Superintendent	75
8D000	Linguist Debriefer/Interrogator	23
8T000	Professional Military Education Instructor	204
92J0	Nondesignated Lawyer	1
9L000	Interpreter/Translator	23

21 Intelligence Specialists

MOC	MOC Title	Personnel
14N4	Intelligence	508
1N000	Intelligence Applications and Exploitation Manager	13
1N011	Intelligence Applications	213
1N031	Intelligence Applications	444
1N051	Intelligence Applications	522
1N071	Intelligence Applications	873
1N091	Intelligence Applications	58
1N111	Imagery Analysis	143
1N131	Imagery Analysis	305
1N151	Imagery Analysis	339
1N171	Imagery Analysis	331
1N191	Imagery Analysis	20
1N411	Signals Intelligence Analysis	67
1N431	Signals Intelligence Analysis	211
1N451	Signals Intelligence Analysis	348
1N471	Signals Intelligence Analysis	722
1N491	Signals Intelligence Analysis	35
1N611	Electronic System Security Assessment	16
1N631	Electronic System Security Assessment	67
1N651	Electronic System Security Assessment	81
1N671	Electronic System Security Assessment	109
1N691	Electronic System Security Assessment	9
8P100	Defense Attaché	7
8S100	Sensor Operator	36

22 Law Enforcement Specialists

MOC	MOC Title	Personnel
1S000	Safety Manager	6
1S011	Safety	2
1S031	Safety	3
1S051	Safety	48
1S071	Safety	181
1S091	Safety	13
3P000	Security Manager	104
3P011	Security	2,053
3P031	Security	4,590
3P051	Security	7,164
3P071	Security	7,498

7S000	Special Investigations Manager	9
7S031	Special Investigations	7
7S071	Special Investigations	505
7S091	Special Investigations	22
8G000	United States Air Force Honor Guard	142
8J000	Correctional Custody Supervisor	4

23 Legal Specialists and Court Reporters

MOC	MOC Title	Personnel
5J000	Paralegal Manager	9
5J031	Paralegal	38
5J051	Paralegal	274
5J071	Paralegal	405
5J091	Paralegal	26

24 Life Scientists

MOC	MOC Title	Personnel
40C0B	Medical Commander	4
43A1	Aerospace Physiologist	9
43A3	Aerospace Physiologist	66
43A4	Aerospace Physiologist	4
43M1	Medical Entomologist	2
43M3	Medical Entomologist	14
43T1A	Biomedical Laboratory	27
43T1B	Biomedical Laboratory	1
43T1E	Biomedical Laboratory	3
43T3A	Biomedical Laboratory	147
43T3B	Biomedical Laboratory	11
43T3E	Biomedical Laboratory	11
43T3F	Biomedical Laboratory	2
43T3G	Biomedical Laboratory	1
43T4A	Biomedical Laboratory	3
43T4B	Biomedical Laboratory	2
43V3E	Veterinary Clinician	1
61S1B	Scientist	39
61S3B	Scientist	86

25 Machinists, Technicians, and Cargo Specialists

MOC	MOC Title	Personnel
1A211	Aircraft Loadmaster	152
1A231	Aircraft Loadmaster	209
1A251	Aircraft Loadmaster	484
1A271	Aircraft Loadmaster	839
1A291	Aircraft Loadmaster	73
2A711	Aircraft Metals Technology	38
2A731	Aircraft Metals Technology	145
2A751	Aircraft Metals Technology	218

2A771	Aircraft Metals Technology	270
2A790	Aircraft Fabrication	143
2F000	Fuels Manager	23
2F011	Fuels	154
2F031	Fuels	824
2F051	Fuels	1,521
2F071	Fuels	1,516
2F091	Fuels	96
3E411	Utilities Systems	62
3E412	Liquid Fuel Systems Maintenance	21
3E431	Utilities Systems	556
3E432	Liquid Fuel Systems Maintenance	83
3E451	Utilities Systems	508
3E452	Liquid Fuel Systems Maintenance	114
3E471	Utilities Systems	572
3E472	Liquid Fuel Systems Maintenance	98
3E490	Utilities Systems	37
3R000	Printing Management Manager	3
3R031	Printing Management	2
3R051	Printing Management	64
3R071	Printing Management	103
3R091	Printing Management	2
4Y032	Dental Laboratory	23
4Y052	Dental Laboratory	162
4Y072	Dental Laboratory	202

26 Medical Service and Medical Care Technicians

MOC	MOC Title	Personnel
1T200	Pararescue Manager	2
1T211	Pararescue	120
1T231	Pararescue	54
1T251	Pararescue	93
1T271	Pararescue	90
1T291	Pararescue	9
42G1D	Physician Assistant	1
42G3	Physician Assistant	320
42G3A	Physician Assistant	14
42G3B	Physician Assistant	4
42G3C	Physician Assistant	1
42G3D	Physician Assistant	1
4F000	Aeromedical Manager	3
4F011	Aeromedical	55
4F031	Aeromedical	200
4F051	Aeromedical	321
4F071	Aeromedical	339
4F091	Aeromedical	11
4H000	Cardiopulmonary Laboratory Manager	2
4H011	Cardiopulmonary Laboratory	21

4H031	Cardiopulmonary Laboratory	56
4H051	Cardiopulmonary Laboratory	174
4H071	Cardiopulmonary Laboratory	125
4H091	Cardiopulmonary Laboratory	3
4N000	Medical Service Manager	32
4N011	Medical Service	326
4N031	Medical Service	1,332
4N031A	Medical Service	2
4N051	Medical Service	2,449
4N051A	Medical Service	77
4N051B	Medical Service	12
4N071	Medical Service	2,447
4N091	Medical Service	83
4N111	Surgical Service	38
4N131	Surgical Service	283
4N151	Surgical Service	369
4N151B	Surgical Service	11
4N151C	Surgical Service	59
4N151D	Surgical Service	31
4N171	Surgical Service	296
4N171B	Surgical Service	26
4N171C	Surgical Service	45
4N171D	Surgical Service	21
4N191	Surgical Service	3
4R000	Diagnostic Imaging Manager	3
4R011	Diagnostic Imaging Helper	100
4R031	Diagnostic Imaging Apprentice	114
4R031B	Diagnostic Imaging	1
4R051	Diagnostic Imaging Journeyman	426
4R051A	Diagnostic Imaging	10
4R051B	Diagnostic Imaging	31
4R051C	Diagnostic Imaging	10
4R071	Diagnostic Imaging Craftsman	258
4R071A	Diagnostic Imaging	41
4R071B	Diagnostic Imaging	64
4R071C	Diagnostic Imaging	22
4R090	Diagnostic Imaging	17
4T000	Medical Laboratory Manager	7
4T011	Medical Laboratory	103
4T012	Histopathology	11
4T031	Medical Laboratory	272
4T032	Histopathology	23
4T051	Medical Laboratory	622
4T052	Histopathology	47
4T053	Cytotechnology	4
4T071	Medical Laboratory	462
4T072	Histopathology	37
4T073	Cytotechnology	19

4T090	Medical Laboratory	24
4U011	Orthotic	6
4U031	Orthotic	10
4U051	Orthotic	9
4U071	Orthotic	15
4U091	Orthotic	2

27 Musicians and Media Directors

MOC	MOC Title	Personnel
35B1	Band	4
35B3	Band	17
35B4	Band	5
3N100	Regional Band Manager	6
3N131A	Regional Band	16
3N131B	Regional Band	6
3N131C	Regional Band	5
3N131D	Regional Band	3
3N131E	Regional Band	7
3N131F	Regional Band	11
3N131G	Regional Band	16
3N131H	Regional Band	3
3N131J	Regional Band	11
3N131K	Regional Band	5
3N131L	Regional Band	16
3N131M	Regional Band	4
3N131N	Regional Band	8
3N131P	Regional Band	2
3N131R	Regional Band	13
3N131S	Regional Band	6
3N131V	Regional Band	2
3N151A	Regional Band	21
3N151B	Regional Band	18
3N151C	Regional Band	5
3N151D	Regional Band	5
3N151E	Regional Band	8
3N151F	Regional Band	12
3N151G	Regional Band	19
3N151H	Regional Band	1
3N151J	Regional Band	14
3N151K	Regional Band	7
3N151L	Regional Band	18
3N151M	Regional Band	6
3N151N	Regional Band	9
3N151P	Regional Band	1
3N151R	Regional Band	7
3N151S	Regional Band	13
3N151V	Regional Band	3
3N171A	Regional Band	15

3N171B	Regional Band	28
3N171C	Regional Band	5
3N171D	Regional Band	6
3N171E	Regional Band	6
3N171F	Regional Band	10
3N171G	Regional Band	33
3N171H	Regional Band	6
3N171J	Regional Band	22
3N171K	Regional Band	7
3N171L	Regional Band	13
3N171M	Regional Band	13
3N171N	Regional Band	6
3N171P	Regional Band	6
3N171R	Regional Band	16
3N171S	Regional Band	11
3N171V	Regional Band	15
3N190	Regional Band	19
3N200	Premier Band Manager	21
3N231	Premier Band	1
3N271	Premier Band	213
3N291	Premier Band	44

28 Nondestructive Testers

MOC	MOC Title	Personnel
2A712	Nondestructive Inspection	18
2A732	Nondestructive Inspection	86
2A752	Nondestructive Inspection	331
2A772	Nondestructive Inspection	192

29 Ordnance Specialists

MOC	MOC Title	Personnel
3E811	Explosive Ordnance Disposal	199
3E831	Explosive Ordnance Disposal	164
3E851	Explosive Ordnance Disposal	155
3E871	Explosive Ordnance Disposal	423
3E891	Explosive Ordnance Disposal	21

30 Nurses and Physical Therapists

MOC	MOC Title	Personnel
40C0E	Medical Commander	9
42B1	Physical Therapist	41
42B3	Physical Therapist	130
42B4	Physical Therapist	1
42T1	Occupational Therapist	10
42T3	Occupational Therapist	21
46A1	Nursing Administrator	16
46A3	Nursing Administrator	159

46A4	Nursing Administrator	29
46F1	Flight Nurse	8
46F3	Flight Nurse	78
46F4	Flight Nurse	9
46G3	Nurse-Midwife	39
46M1	Nurse Anesthetist	7
46M3	Nurse Anesthetist	244
46M4	Nurse Anesthetist	1
46N1	Clinical Nurse	160
46N1A	Clinical Nurse	2
46N1B	Clinical Nurse	2
46N1C	Clinical Nurse	1
46N1D	Clinical Nurse	5
46N1E	Clinical Nurse	50
46N1F	Clinical Nurse	19
46N1G	Clinical Nurse	52
46N1H	Clinical Nurse	1
46N3	Clinical Nurse	2,116
46N3A	Clinical Nurse	103
46N3B	Clinical Nurse	77
46N3C	Clinical Nurse	9
46N3D	Clinical Nurse	62
46N3E	Clinical Nurse	515
46N3F	Clinical Nurse	79
46N3G	Clinical Nurse	375
46N3H	Clinical Nurse	18
46N4B	Clinical Nurse	1
46P3A	Mental Health Nurse	14
46S1	Operating Room Nurse	22
46S3	Operating Room Nurse	307
4J000	Biomedical Therapy Manager	1
4J011	Occupational Therapy	8
4J012	Physical Therapy	24
4J031	Occupational Therapy	1
4J032	Physical Therapy	70
4J051	Occupational Therapy	8
4J052	Physical Therapy	124
4J071	Occupational Therapy	18
4J072	Physical Therapy	125
4J091	Occupational Therapy	3
4J092	Physical Therapy	4

31 Optometric Technicians

MOC	MOC Title	Personnel
4V000	Optometry Manager	1
4V011	Optometry	8
4V031	Optometry	38
4V031A	Optometry	1

4V051	Optometry	81
4V051A	Optometry	11
4V071	Optometry	89
4V071A	Optometry	36
4V090	Optometry	6

32 Photographic and Audiovisual Specialists

MOC	MOC Title	Personnel
3V000	Visual Information Manager	13
3V011	Visual Information	31
3V012	Still Photographic	32
3V013	Visual Information Production-Documentation	13
3V031	Visual Information	114
3V032	Still Photographic	107
3V033	Visual Information Production-Documentation	52
3V051	Visual Information	203
3V052	Still Photographic	304
3V053	Visual Information Production-Documentation	120
3V071	Visual Information	208
3V072	Still Photographic	279
3V073	Visual Information Production-Documentation	88
3V090	Visual Information Services	28

33 Physicians, Surgeons, and Optometrists

MOC	MOC Title	Personnel
42E1	Optometrist	30
42E3	Optometrist	121
42E4	Optometrist	2
42F1	Podiatrist	3
42F3	Podiatrist	22
43Y3A	Health Physicist	4
43Y4A	Health Physicist	1
44A1	Chief, Hospital/Clinic Services	2
44A3	Chief, Hospital/Clinic Services	39
44D1B	Pathologist	1
44D3A	Pathologist	1
44D3B	Pathologist	7
44D3C	Pathologist	1
44D3D	Pathologist	4
44D3F	Pathologist	1
44D3G	Pathologist	1
44D3H	Pathologist	1
44D3K	Pathologist	1
44E1A	Emergency Services Physician	14
44E3A	Emergency Services Physician	110
44E4A	Emergency Services Physician	1
44F1	Family Physician	168

44F3	Family Physician	520
44F4	Family Physician	2
44G1	General Practice Physician	57
44G3	General Practice Physician	83
44H3	Nuclear Medicine Physician	7
44H4	Nuclear Medicine Physician	1
44K1C	Pediatrician	1
44K1E	Pediatrician	4
44K3	Pediatrician	175
44K3A	Pediatrician	8
44K3B	Pediatrician	5
44K3C	Pediatrician	7
44K3D	Pediatrician	4
44K3E	Pediatrician	14
44K3F	Pediatrician	4
44K3G	Pediatrician	6
44K3H	Pediatrician	3
44K3J	Pediatrician	1
44K3K	Pediatrician	3
44K3M	Pediatrician	2
44K4F	Pediatrician	1
44M1	Internist	164
44M1B	Internist	15
44M1D	Internist	3
44M1E	Internist	1
44M1F	Internist	1
44M1G	Internist	3
44M1H	Internist	2
44M1J	Internist	3
44M3	Internist	252
44M3A	Internist	7
44M3B	Internist	22
44M3C	Internist	8
44M3D	Internist	11
44M3E	Internist	9
44M3F	Internist	9
44M3G	Internist	17
44M3H	Internist	15
44M3J	Internist	6
44N1	Neurologist	8
44N3	Neurologist	25
44N4	Neurologist	1
44P1A	Psychiatrist	1
44P3A	Psychiatrist	9
44R1A	Diagnostic Radiologist	1
44R3	Diagnostic Radiologist	150
44R3A	Diagnostic Radiologist	6
44R3B	Diagnostic Radiologist	8

44R3E	Diagnostic Radiologist	2
44S3A	Dermatologist	4
44S3B	Dermatologist	2
44T1	Radiotherapist	1
44T3	Radiotherapist	10
44Y3A	Critical Care Medicine	3
44Z1	Allergist	3
44Z3	Allergist	18
44Z4	Allergist	1
45A1	Anesthesiologist	19
45A3	Anesthesiologist	117
45B3	Orthopedic Surgeon	101
45B3A	Orthopedic Surgeon	6
45B3B	Orthopedic Surgeon	3
45B3D	Orthopedic Surgeon	4
45B3E	Orthopedic Surgeon	4
45B3F	Orthopedic Surgeon	1
45B3G	Orthopedic Surgeon	2
45E3A	Ophthalmologist	1
45E3B	Ophthalmologist	3
45E3C	Ophthalmologist	1
45E3D	Ophthalmologist	1
45E3E	Ophthalmologist	1
45E3G	Ophthalmologist	4
45G1D	Obstetrician and Gynecologist	1
45G3	Obstetrician and Gynecologist	163
45G3A	Obstetrician and Gynecologist	3
45G3B	Obstetrician and Gynecologist	3
45G3C	Obstetrician and Gynecologist	2
45G3D	Obstetrician and Gynecologist	8
45N1	Otorhinolaryngologist	4
45N3	Otorhinolaryngologist	47
45P3	Physical Medicine Physician	1
45S1	Surgeon	126
45S1A	Surgeon	1
45S1C	Surgeon	1
45S1F	Surgeon	1
45S1G	Surgeon	4
45S1H	Surgeon	1
45S3	Surgeon	173
45S3A	Surgeon	8
45S3B	Surgeon	5
45S3C	Surgeon	9
45S3D	Surgeon	5
45S3E	Surgeon	8
45S3F	Surgeon	13
45S3G	Surgeon	8
45S3H	Surgeon	3

45S3J	Surgeon	1
45U3A	Urologist	1
45U3B	Urologist	1
47S1	Oral and Maxillofacial Surgeon	1
47S3	Oral and Maxillofacial Surgeon	36
47S4	Oral and Maxillofacial Surgeon	1
48A1	Aerospace Medicine Specialist	2
48A3	Aerospace Medicine Specialist	106
48A4	Aerospace Medicine Specialist	17
48E3	Occupational Medicine Specialist	5
48E4	Occupational Medicine Specialist	2
48F1	Family Practice Specialist	10
48F3	Family Practice Specialist	42
48F4	Family Practice Specialist	1
48G1	Aerospace Medicine Physician	59
48G3	Aerospace Medicine Physician	305
48G3P	Aerospace Medicine Physician	1
48G3R	Aerospace Medicine Physician	1
48G4	Aerospace Medicine Physician	23
48P1	Preventive Medicine Specialist	2
48P3	Preventive Medicine Specialist	9
48P4	Preventive Medicine Specialist	1

34 Pilots and Ship/Submarine Operators

MOC	MOC Title	Personnel
10C0P	Operations Commander	13
10C0S	Operations Commander	1
10C0U	Operations Commander	1
10C0W	Operations Commander	52
11A1A	Airlift Pilot	12
11A1B	Airlift Pilot	9
11A1C	Airlift Pilot	1
11A1D	Airlift Pilot	8
11A1E	Airlift Pilot	2
11A1F	Airlift Pilot	17
11A1K	Airlift Pilot	61
11A1L	Airlift Pilot	3
11A1M	Airlift Pilot	35
11A1R	Airlift Pilot	1
11A1S	Airlift Pilot	5
11A1T	Airlift Pilot	5
11A1V	Airlift Pilot	3
11A1W	Airlift Pilot	2
11A1Y	Airlift Pilot	25
11A1Z	Airlift Pilot	4
11A2A	Airlift Pilot	77
11A2B	Airlift Pilot	38
11A2C	Airlift Pilot	1

11A2D	Airlift Pilot	49
11A2E	Airlift Pilot	22
11A2F	Airlift Pilot	41
11A2H	Airlift Pilot	3
11A2J	Airlift Pilot	2
11A2K	Airlift Pilot	217
11A2L	Airlift Pilot	1
11A2M	Airlift Pilot	87
11A2N	Airlift Pilot	1
11A2Z	Airlift Pilot	4
11A3A	Airlift Pilot	302
11A3B	Airlift Pilot	98
11A3C	Airlift Pilot	33
11A3D	Airlift Pilot	137
11A3E	Airlift Pilot	42
11A3F	Airlift Pilot	279
11A3G	Airlift Pilot	7
11A3H	Airlift Pilot	4
11A3J	Airlift Pilot	21
11A3K	Airlift Pilot	656
11A3L	Airlift Pilot	63
11A3M	Airlift Pilot	532
11A3N	Airlift Pilot	21
11A3P	Airlift Pilot	18
11A3R	Airlift Pilot	8
11A3S	Airlift Pilot	177
11A3T	Airlift Pilot	162
11A3U	Airlift Pilot	6
11A3V	Airlift Pilot	30
11A3W	Airlift Pilot	5
11A3Y	Airlift Pilot	111
11A3Z	Airlift Pilot	64
11A4A	Airlift Pilot	6
11A4D	Airlift Pilot	3
11A4F	Airlift Pilot	2
11A4K	Airlift Pilot	55
11A4M	Airlift Pilot	17
11A4R	Airlift Pilot	1
11A4T	Airlift Pilot	1
11A4U	Airlift Pilot	1
11A4V	Airlift Pilot	15
11A4W	Airlift Pilot	9
11A4Y	Airlift Pilot	196
11A4Z	Airlift Pilot	2
11B1A	Bomber Pilot	21
11B1B	Bomber Pilot	7
11B1C	Bomber Pilot	34
11B1N	Bomber Pilot	5

11B1S	Bomber Pilot	3
11B1Y	Bomber Pilot	12
11B2A	Bomber Pilot	43
11B2C	Bomber Pilot	44
11B3A	Bomber Pilot	204
11B3B	Bomber Pilot	42
11B3C	Bomber Pilot	209
11B3N	Bomber Pilot	18
11B3P	Bomber Pilot	3
11B3R	Bomber Pilot	4
11B3S	Bomber Pilot	43
11B3T	Bomber Pilot	52
11B3U	Bomber Pilot	1
11B3Y	Bomber Pilot	36
11B3Z	Bomber Pilot	2
11B4A	Bomber Pilot	8
11B4B	Bomber Pilot	3
11B4C	Bomber Pilot	11
11B4S	Bomber Pilot	1
11B4U	Bomber Pilot	2
11B4Y	Bomber Pilot	76
11E1A	Experimental Test Pilot	1
11E1B	Experimental Test Pilot	7
11E1Z	Experimental Test Pilot	2
11E3A	Experimental Test Pilot	32
11E3B	Experimental Test Pilot	57
11E3C	Experimental Test Pilot	4
11E3Q	Experimental Test Pilot	1
11E3Z	Experimental Test Pilot	6
11E4A	Experimental Test Pilot	2
11E4B	Experimental Test Pilot	1
11E4C	Experimental Test Pilot	1
11F1A	Fighter Pilot	1
11F1B	Fighter Pilot	24
11F1C	Fighter Pilot	2
11F1D	Fighter Pilot	2
11F1E	Fighter Pilot	2
11F1F	Fighter Pilot	56
11F1G	Fighter Pilot	38
11F1H	Fighter Pilot	231
11F1K	Fighter Pilot	9
11F1L	Fighter Pilot	1
11F1M	Fighter Pilot	2
11F1N	Fighter Pilot	2
11F1Q	Fighter Pilot	3
11F1R	Fighter Pilot	1
11F1S	Fighter Pilot	3
11F1T	Fighter Pilot	3

11F1U	Fighter Pilot	3
11F1Y	Fighter Pilot	22
11F1Z	Fighter Pilot	5
11F3B	Fighter Pilot	323
11F3C	Fighter Pilot	27
11F3D	Fighter Pilot	10
11F3E	Fighter Pilot	3
11F3F	Fighter Pilot	639
11F3G	Fighter Pilot	347
11F3H	Fighter Pilot	1,187
11F3K	Fighter Pilot	42
11F3L	Fighter Pilot	25
11F3M	Fighter Pilot	110
11F3N	Fighter Pilot	63
11F3P	Fighter Pilot	3
11F3Q	Fighter Pilot	105
11F3R	Fighter Pilot	4
11F3S	Fighter Pilot	68
11F3T	Fighter Pilot	258
11F3U	Fighter Pilot	14
11F3Y	Fighter Pilot	130
11F3Z	Fighter Pilot	25
11F4B	Fighter Pilot	19
11F4C	Fighter Pilot	3
11F4E	Fighter Pilot	3
11F4F	Fighter Pilot	51
11F4G	Fighter Pilot	9
11F4H	Fighter Pilot	56
11F4K	Fighter Pilot	6
11F4L	Fighter Pilot	1
11F4M	Fighter Pilot	4
11F4N	Fighter Pilot	1
11F4Q	Fighter Pilot	2
11F4U	Fighter Pilot	26
11F4Y	Fighter Pilot	311
11F4Z	Fighter Pilot	2
11G3	Generalist Pilot	26
11G4	Generalist Pilot	82
11H1B	Helicopter Pilot	1
11H1C	Helicopter Pilot	4
11H1D	Helicopter Pilot	3
11H1E	Helicopter Pilot	2
11H1Y	Helicopter Pilot	2
11H2A	Helicopter Pilot	1
11H2B	Helicopter Pilot	1
11H2C	Helicopter Pilot	32
11H2E	Helicopter Pilot	50
11H3A	Helicopter Pilot	14

11H3C	Helicopter Pilot	134
11H3D	Helicopter Pilot	3
11H3E	Helicopter Pilot	118
11H3T	Helicopter Pilot	7
11H3Y	Helicopter Pilot	7
11H3Z	Helicopter Pilot	5
11H4C	Helicopter Pilot	7
11H4D	Helicopter Pilot	3
11H4E	Helicopter Pilot	4
11H4Y	Helicopter Pilot	29
11K1A	Trainer Pilot	2
11K1C	Trainer Pilot	15
11K1D	Trainer Pilot	4
11K1Y	Trainer Pilot	1
11K1Z	Trainer Pilot	1
11K3A	Trainer Pilot	10
11K3B	Trainer Pilot	1
11K3C	Trainer Pilot	174
11K3D	Trainer Pilot	49
11K3N	Trainer Pilot	4
11K3Y	Trainer Pilot	3
11K3Z	Trainer Pilot	5
11K4C	Trainer Pilot	1
11K4D	Trainer Pilot	3
11K4U	Trainer Pilot	1
11K4Y	Trainer Pilot	7
11R1A	Reconnaissance/Surveillance/Electronic Warfare Pilot	8
11R1B	Reconnaissance/Surveillance/Electronic Warfare Pilot	2
11R1C	Reconnaissance/Surveillance/Electronic Warfare Pilot	7
11R1D	Reconnaissance/Surveillance/Electronic Warfare Pilot	1
11R1G	Reconnaissance/Surveillance/Electronic Warfare Pilot	11
11R1H	Reconnaissance/Surveillance/Electronic Warfare Pilot	1
11R1J	Reconnaissance/Surveillance/Electronic Warfare Pilot	4
11R1Y	Reconnaissance/Surveillance/Electronic Warfare Pilot	1
11R2A	Reconnaissance/Surveillance/Electronic Warfare Pilot	40
11R2C	Reconnaissance/Surveillance/Electronic Warfare Pilot	31
11R2D	Reconnaissance/Surveillance/Electronic Warfare Pilot	7
11R2F	Reconnaissance/Surveillance/Electronic Warfare Pilot	10
11R2G	Reconnaissance/Surveillance/Electronic Warfare Pilot	18
11R2H	Reconnaissance/Surveillance/Electronic Warfare Pilot	3
11R3A	Reconnaissance/Surveillance/Electronic Warfare Pilot	142
11R3B	Reconnaissance/Surveillance/Electronic Warfare Pilot	17
11R3C	Reconnaissance/Surveillance/Electronic Warfare Pilot	55
11R3D	Reconnaissance/Surveillance/Electronic Warfare Pilot	21
11R3F	Reconnaissance/Surveillance/Electronic Warfare Pilot	36
11R3G	Reconnaissance/Surveillance/Electronic Warfare Pilot	70
11R3H	Reconnaissance/Surveillance/Electronic Warfare Pilot	3
11R3J	Reconnaissance/Surveillance/Electronic Warfare Pilot	91

11R3L	Reconnaissance/Surveillance/Electronic Warfare Pilot	15
11R3P	Reconnaissance/Surveillance/Electronic Warfare Pilot	1
11R3R	Reconnaissance/Surveillance/Electronic Warfare Pilot	1
11R3S	Reconnaissance/Surveillance/Electronic Warfare Pilot	18
11R3T	Reconnaissance/Surveillance/Electronic Warfare Pilot	22
11R3Y	Reconnaissance/Surveillance/Electronic Warfare Pilot	5
11R3Z	Reconnaissance/Surveillance/Electronic Warfare Pilot	5
11R4A	Reconnaissance/Surveillance/Electronic Warfare Pilot	4
11R4D	Reconnaissance/Surveillance/Electronic Warfare Pilot	3
11R4G	Reconnaissance/Surveillance/Electronic Warfare Pilot	5
11R4J	Reconnaissance/Surveillance/Electronic Warfare Pilot	6
11R4T	Reconnaissance/Surveillance/Electronic Warfare Pilot	1
11R4Y	Reconnaissance/Surveillance/Electronic Warfare Pilot	17
11R4Z	Reconnaissance/Surveillance/Electronic Warfare Pilot	1
11S1C	Special Operations Pilot	2
11S1D	Special Operations Pilot	1
11S1E	Special Operations Pilot	3
11S1F	Special Operations Pilot	1
11S1Y	Special Operations Pilot	3
11S2C	Special Operations Pilot	12
11S2D	Special Operations Pilot	8
11S2E	Special Operations Pilot	10
11S2F	Special Operations Pilot	4
11S3C	Special Operations Pilot	30
11S3D	Special Operations Pilot	18
11S3E	Special Operations Pilot	74
11S3F	Special Operations Pilot	29
11S3S	Special Operations Pilot	2
11S3T	Special Operations Pilot	3
11S3W	Special Operations Pilot	18
11S3Y	Special Operations Pilot	43
11S4E	Special Operations Pilot	1
11S4U	Special Operations Pilot	1
11S4W	Special Operations Pilot	8
11S4Y	Special Operations Pilot	46
11T1A	Tanker Pilot	11
11T1B	Tanker Pilot	45
11T1L	Tanker Pilot	1
11T1R	Tanker Pilot	1
11T1S	Tanker Pilot	5
11T1T	Tanker Pilot	3
11T1Y	Tanker Pilot	3
11T1Z	Tanker Pilot	1
11T2A	Tanker Pilot	80
11T2B	Tanker Pilot	263
11T2Z	Tanker Pilot	1
11T3A	Tanker Pilot	272
11T3B	Tanker Pilot	775

11T3L	Tanker Pilot	3
11T3N	Tanker Pilot	4
11T3P	Tanker Pilot	8
11T3R	Tanker Pilot	6
11T3S	Tanker Pilot	118
11T3T	Tanker Pilot	131
11T3Y	Tanker Pilot	44
11T3Z	Tanker Pilot	1
11T4A	Tanker Pilot	12
11T4B	Tanker Pilot	32
11T4Y	Tanker Pilot	74
12R3L	Reconnaissance/Surveillance/Electronic Warfare Navigator	6

36 Precision Equipment Repairers

MOC	MOC Title	Personnel
1A500	Airborne Missions System Manager	2
1C600	Space Systems Operations Manager	7
1C611	Space Systems Operations	72
1C631	Space Systems Operations	176
1C651	Space Systems Operations	302
1C671	Space Systems Operations	364
1C691	Space Systems Operations	16
2A000	Avionics Systems Manager	64
2A011A	Avionics Test Station and Components	81
2A011B	Avionics Test Station and Components	51
2A031A	Avionics Test Station and Components	112
2A031B	Avionics Test Station and Components	142
2A051A	Avionics Test Station and Components	299
2A051B	Avionics Test Station and Components	147
2A071A	Avionics Test Station and Components	405
2A071B	Avionics Test Station and Components	225
2A090	Avionics Test Station and Components	73
2A113	Communication and Navigation Systems	34
2A114	Airborne Surveillance Radar Systems	22
2A117	Electronic Warfare Systems	206
2A133	Communication and Navigation Systems	100
2A134	Airborne Surveillance Radar Systems	29
2A137	Electronic Warfare Systems	394
2A153	Communication and Navigation Systems	172
2A154	Airborne Surveillance Radar Systems	94
2A157	Electronic Warfare Systems	535
2A173	Communication and Navigation Systems	277
2A174	Airborne Surveillance Radar Systems	85
2A177	Electronic Warfare Systems	897
2A190	Conventional Avionics	150
2A300	Aircraft Manager	274
2A311A	F-15/F-111 Avionic Systems	55
2A311B	F-15/F-111 Avionic Systems	28

2A311C	F-15/F-111 Avionic Systems	36
2A312A	F-16 Avionic Systems	48
2A312B	F-16 Avionic Systems	66
2A312C	F-16 Avionic Systems	53
2A313A	Tactical Aircraft Maintenance	309
2A331A	F-15/F-111 Avionic Systems	136
2A331B	F-15/F-111 Avionic Systems	104
2A331C	F-15/F-111 Avionic Systems	108
2A332A	F-16 Avionic Systems	147
2A332B	F-16 Avionic Systems	144
2A332C	F-16 Avionic Systems	164
2A333A	Tactical Aircraft Maintenance	810
2A351A	F-15/F-111 Avionic Systems	249
2A351B	F-15/F-111 Avionic Systems	183
2A351C	F-15/F-111 Avionic Systems	192
2A352A	F-16 Avionic Systems	194
2A352B	F-16 Avionic Systems	112
2A352C	F-16 Avionic Systems	159
2A353A	Tactical Aircraft Maintenance	1,223
2A371	F-15/F-111 Avionic Systems	717
2A372	F-16 Avionic Systems	628
2A373A	Tactical Aircraft Maintenance	1,625
2A390	Tactical Aircraft	586
2A411	Aircraft Guidance and Control Systems	138
2A412	Aircraft Communication and Navigation Systems	133
2A431	Aircraft Guidance and Control Systems	413
2A432	Aircraft Communication and Navigation Systems	453
2A451	Aircraft Guidance and Control Systems	603
2A452	Aircraft Communication and Navigation Systems	447
2A471	Aircraft Guidance and Control Systems	960
2A472	Aircraft Communication and Navigation Systems	908
2A490	Aircraft Avionics	87
2A513A	Bomber Avionics Systems	42
2A513B	Bomber Avionics Systems	29
2A513C	Bomber Avionics Systems	38
2A533A	Bomber Avionics Systems	75
2A533B	Bomber Avionics Systems	63
2A533C	Bomber Avionics Systems	45
2A553A	Bomber Avionics Systems	106
2A553B	Bomber Avionics Systems	78
2A553C	Bomber Avionics Systems	49
2A573A	Bomber Avionics Systems	187
2A573B	Bomber Avionics Systems	70
2A573C	Bomber Avionics Systems	89
2A590	Aerospace Maintenance	477
2E011	Ground Radar Systems	95
2E031	Ground Radar Systems	158
2E051	Ground Radar Systems	454

2E071	Ground Radar Systems	642
2E091	Ground Radar Systems	38
2E111	Satellite and Wideband Communications Equipment	193
2E112	Meteorological and Navigation Systems	64
2E113	Ground Radio Communications	275
2E114	Visual Imagery and Intrusion Detection Systems	72
2E131	Satellite and Wideband Communications Equipment	384
2E132	Meteorological and Navigation Systems	117
2E133	Ground Radio Communications	548
2E134	Visual Imagery and Intrusion Detection Systems	75
2E151	Satellite and Wideband Communications Equipment	717
2E152	Meteorological and Navigation Systems	192
2E153	Ground Radio Communications	934
2E154	Visual Imagery and Intrusion Detection Systems	183
2E171	Satellite and Wideband Communications Equipment	1,030
2E172	Meteorological and Navigation Systems	300
2E173	Ground Radio Communications	1,507
2E174	Visual Imagery and Intrusion Detection Systems	332
2E190	Communications Systems	199
2E211	Electronic Computer and Switching Systems	91
2E211A	Electronic Computer and Switching Systems	45
2E211B	Electronic Computer and Switching Systems	5
2E211C	Electronic Computer and Switching Systems	17
2E231	Electronic Computer and Switching Systems	296
2E231A	Electronic Computer and Switching Systems	36
2E231B	Electronic Computer and Switching Systems	33
2E231C	Electronic Computer and Switching Systems	37
2E251	Electronic Computer and Switching Systems	503
2E251A	Electronic Computer and Switching Systems	49
2E251B	Electronic Computer and Switching Systems	108
2E251C	Electronic Computer and Switching Systems	89
2E271	Electronic Computer and Switching Systems	986
2E291	Electronic Computer and Switching Systems	53
2E311	Secure Communications Systems	82
2E331	Secure Communications Systems	208
2E351	Secure Communications Systems	531
2E371	Secure Communications Systems	716
2E391	Secure Communications Systems	50
2E411	Space Systems	13
2E431	Space Systems	15
2E451	Space Systems	130
2E471	Space Systems	145
2E491	Space Systems	6
2E611	Communications Antenna Systems	18
2E612	Communications Cable Systems	48
2E613	Telephone Systems	73
2E631	Communications Antenna Systems	67
2E632	Communications Cable Systems	176

2E633	Telephone Systems	336
2E651	Communications Antenna Systems	146
2E652	Communications Cable Systems	278
2E653	Telephone Systems	498
2E671	Communications Antenna Systems	181
2E672	Communications Cable Systems	315
2E673	Telephone Systems	553
2E800	Instrumentation and Telemetry Systems Manager	2
2E811	Instrumentation and Telemetry Systems	28
2E831	Instrumentation and Telemetry Systems	63
2E851	Instrumentation and Telemetry Systems	132
2E871	Instrumentation and Telemetry Systems	163
2E891	Instrumentation and Telemetry Systems	12
2M000	Missile and Space Systems Maintenance Manager	30
2M011A	Missile and Space Systems Electronic Maintenance	43
2M011B	Missile and Space Systems Electronic Maintenance	35
2M012A	Missile and Space Systems Maintenance	42
2M013	Missile and Space Facilities	1
2M013A	Missile and Space Facilities	32
2M031	Missile and Space Systems Electronic Maintenance	5
2M031A	Missile and Space Systems Electronic Maintenance	169
2M031B	Missile and Space Systems Electronic Maintenance	99
2M032	Missile and Space Systems Maintenance	6
2M032A	Missile and Space Systems Maintenance	73
2M033	Missile and Space Facilities	5
2M033A	Missile and Space Facilities	97
2M051	Missile and Space Systems Electronic Maintenance	377
2M052	Missile and Space Systems Maintenance	333
2M053	Missile and Space Facilities	208
2M071	Missile and Space Systems Electronic Maintenance	537
2M072	Missile and Space Systems Maintenance	445
2M073	Missile and Space Facilities	211
2M090	Missile and Space Systems Maintenance	101
2P000	Precision Measurement Equipment Laboratory Manager	14
2P011	Precision Measurement Equipment Laboratory	181
2P031	Precision Measurement Equipment Laboratory	255
2P051	Precision Measurement Equipment Laboratory	427
2P071	Precision Measurement Equipment Laboratory	633
2P091	Precision Measurement Equipment Laboratory	30
2W000	Munitions Maintenance Manager	40
2W011	Munitions Systems	262
2W031	Munitions Systems	1,568
2W051	Munitions Systems	2,223
2W071	Munitions Systems	2,537
2W091	Munitions Systems	149
2W100	Aircraft Armament Manager	62
2W111C	Aircraft Armament Systems	35
2W111E	Aircraft Armament Systems	88

2W111F	Aircraft Armament Systems	144
2W111K	Aircraft Armament Systems	32
2W111L	Aircraft Armament Systems	19
2W111Z	Aircraft Armament Systems	17
2W131C	Aircraft Armament Systems	202
2W131E	Aircraft Armament Systems	535
2W131F	Aircraft Armament Systems	661
2W131K	Aircraft Armament Systems	96
2W131L	Aircraft Armament Systems	98
2W131Z	Aircraft Armament Systems	45
2W151	Aircraft Armament Systems	2,599
2W171	Aircraft Armament Systems	3,274
2W191	Aircraft Armament Systems	277
2W200	Nuclear Weapons Manager	7
2W211	Nuclear Weapons	58
2W231	Nuclear Weapons	243
2W251	Nuclear Weapons	257
2W271	Nuclear Weapons	326
2W291	Nuclear Weapons	29
3E800	Explosive Ordnance Disposal Manager	7
4A200	Biomedical Equipment Manager	3
4A211	Biomedical Equipment	34
4A231	Biomedical Equipment	87
4A251	Biomedical Equipment	180
4A271	Biomedical Equipment	228
4A291	Biomedical Equipment	13
8S000	Missile Facility Manager	22

37 Preventive Maintenance Analysts

MOC	MOC Title	Personnel
2A531A	Aerospace Maintenance	184
2A531B	Aerospace Maintenance	188
2A531C	Aerospace Maintenance	167
2A531D	Aerospace Maintenance	156
2A531E	Aerospace Maintenance	167
2A531F	Aerospace Maintenance	161
2A531G	Aerospace Maintenance	442
2A531H	Aerospace Maintenance	196
2A551J	Aerospace Maintenance	2,329
2A551K	Aerospace Maintenance	562
2A551L	Aerospace Maintenance	986
2R000	Maintenance Data Systems Analysis Manager	7
2R011	Maintenance Data Systems Analysis	33
2R031	Maintenance Data Systems Analysis	96
2R051	Maintenance Data Systems Analysis	190
2R071	Maintenance Data Systems Analysis	298
2R091	Maintenance Data Systems Analysis	17
2R100	Maintenance Scheduling Manager	8

2R111	Maintenance Scheduling	34
2R131	Maintenance Scheduling	121
2R151	Maintenance Scheduling	417
2R171	Maintenance Scheduling	487
2R191	Maintenance Scheduling	24
2T111	Vehicle Operations	114
2T131	Vehicle Operations	463
2T151	Vehicle Operations	1,314
2T171	Vehicle Operations	749
2T191	Vehicle Operations	44
3E611	Operations	1
3E631	Operations	65
3E671	Operations	233
3E691	Operations	21

38 Public Information Managers and Journalists

MOC	MOC Title	Personnel
16A1	Air Attaché	1
16A4	Air Attaché	22
16A4W	Air Attaché	11
16P1	International Politico-Military Affairs	42
16P3	International Politico-Military Affairs	43
16P4	International Politico-Military Affairs	135
35P1	Public Affairs	46
35P3	Public Affairs	204
35P4	Public Affairs	123
3H000	Historian Manager	8
3H031	Historian	2
3H051	Historian	14
3H071	Historian	43
3H091	Historian	3
3N000	Public Affairs Manager	7
3N090	Public Affairs	13
84H0	Historian	2
86P0	Command and Control	225
88P0	Protocol	39

39 Radar and Sonar Operators

MOC	MOC Title	Personnel
1C511A	Aerospace Control and Warning Systems	5
1C511C	Aerospace Control and Warning Systems	19
1C531A	Aerospace Control and Warning Systems	1
1C531B	Aerospace Control and Warning Systems	14
1C531C	Aerospace Control and Warning Systems	78
1C571D	Aerospace Control and Warning Systems	100
1C591	Aerospace Control and Warning Systems	27

40 Recruiting Specialists

MOC	MOC Title	Personnel
3S291	Education and Training	52
83R0	Recruiting Service	16
8R000	Recruiter	627

41 Scientists and Engineers

MOC	MOC Title	Personnel
13A3W	Astronaut	8
13S1A	Space and Missile Operations	58
13S1B	Space and Missile Operations	12
13S1C	Space and Missile Operations	167
13S1D	Space and Missile Operations	10
13S1E	Space and Missile Operations	18
13S1S	Space and Missile Operations	1
13S2C	Space and Missile Operations	317
13S3A	Space and Missile Operations	444
13S3B	Space and Missile Operations	119
13S3C	Space and Missile Operations	1,504
13S3D	Space and Missile Operations	149
13S3E	Space and Missile Operations	232
13S4	Space and Missile Operations	578
21M1A	Space and Missile Maintenance	25
21M1B	Space and Missile Maintenance	5
21M3	Space and Missile Maintenance	6
21M3A	Space and Missile Maintenance	99
21M3B	Space and Missile Maintenance	2
21M4	Space and Missile Maintenance	29
32E1A	Civil Engineer	17
32E1B	Civil Engineer	2
32E1C	Civil Engineer	46
32E1E	Civil Engineer	5
32E1F	Civil Engineer	27
32E1G	Civil Engineer	128
32E1H	Civil Engineer	2
32E1J	Civil Engineer	19
32E1K	Civil Engineer	1
32E1V	Civil Engineer	1
32E1W	Civil Engineer	1
32E3A	Civil Engineer	50
32E3B	Civil Engineer	9
32E3C	Civil Engineer	191
32E3D	Civil Engineer	15
32E3E	Civil Engineer	69
32E3F	Civil Engineer	71
32E3G	Civil Engineer	529
32E3H	Civil Engineer	8

32E3J	Civil Engineer	33
32E3K	Civil Engineer	8
32E4	Civil Engineer	309
43E1A	Bioenvironmental Engineer	51
43E1B	Bioenvironmental Engineer	1
43E1D	Bioenvironmental Engineer	1
43E1E	Bioenvironmental Engineer	4
43E1F	Bioenvironmental Engineer	2
43E3A	Bioenvironmental Engineer	179
43E3B	Bioenvironmental Engineer	22
43E3C	Bioenvironmental Engineer	2
43E3D	Bioenvironmental Engineer	24
43E3E	Bioenvironmental Engineer	7
43E3F	Bioenvironmental Engineer	6
43E3G	Bioenvironmental Engineer	3
43E4A	Bioenvironmental Engineer	15
43E4C	Bioenvironmental Engineer	2
43E4E	Bioenvironmental Engineer	4
43E4F	Bioenvironmental Engineer	1
43H1	Public Health	36
43H3	Public Health	119
43H4	Public Health	13
43T3C	Biomedical Laboratory	6
43T3D	Biomedical Laboratory	3
43T4D	Biomedical Laboratory	1
4B000	Bioenvironmental Engineering Manager	4
61S1A	Scientist	103
61S1C	Scientist	27
61S1D	Scientist	40
61S1E	Scientist	1
61S3A	Scientist	275
61S3C	Scientist	67
61S3D	Scientist	212
61S3E	Scientist	4
61S3W	Scientist	10
61S4	Scientist	134
61S4W	Scientist	7
62E1A	Developmental Engineer	70
62E1B	Developmental Engineer	46
62E1C	Developmental Engineer	43
62E1E	Developmental Engineer	216
62E1F	Developmental Engineer	2
62E1G	Developmental Engineer	78
62E1H	Developmental Engineer	54
62E1P	Developmental Engineer	2
62E1W	Developmental Engineer	2
62E3A	Developmental Engineer	384
62E3B	Developmental Engineer	292

62E3C	Developmental Engineer	142
62E3E	Developmental Engineer	967
62E3F	Developmental Engineer	38
62E3G	Developmental Engineer	278
62E3H	Developmental Engineer	271
62E3P	Developmental Engineer	3
62E3V	Developmental Engineer	1
62E3W	Developmental Engineer	11
62E4	Developmental Engineer	300
62E4W	Developmental Engineer	2

42 Ship Engineers and Air Crew Members

MOC	MOC Title	Personnel
1A000	In-Flight Refueling Manager	8
1A011	In-Flight Refueling	48
1A031	In-Flight Refueling	98
1A051	In-Flight Refueling	156
1A071	In-Flight Refueling	325
1A091	In-Flight Refueling	29
1A111B	Flight Engineer	1
1A131B	Flight Engineer	4
1A151B	Flight Engineer	52
1A171B	Flight Engineer	153

43 Surveyors and Mappers

MOC	MOC Title	Personnel
3E000	Civil Engineer Manager	110
3E511	Engineering	63
3E531	Engineering	251
3E551	Engineering	261
3E571	Engineering	426
3E591	Engineering	32

44 Transportation Specialists

MOC	MOC Title	Personnel
8A000	In-Flight Passenger Service Specialist	94

45 Vehicle Drivers

MOC	MOC Title	Personnel
2T100	Vehicle Operations Manager	12

46 Weather Personnel

MOC	MOC Title	Personnel
15W1A	Weather	6
15W3A	Weather	169
15W4	Weather	132

1W000	Weather Manager	12
1W011	Weather	171
1W031	Weather	396
1W031A	Weather	14
1W051	Weather	502
1W051A	Weather	253
1W071A	Weather	1,028
1W091	Weather	65

MARINE CORPS OCCUPATIONS BY OCCUPATIONAL CLUSTER

2 Administrative, Personnel, and Supply Specialists

MOC	MOC Title	Personnel
0100	Basic Administrative Marine	161
0121	Personnel Clerk	1,398
0131	Unit Diary Clerk	1,436
0151	Administrative Clerk	3,893
0161	Postal Clerk	365
0193	Personnel/Administrative Chief	1,864
0400	Basic Logistics Marine	62
0431	Embarkation/Logistics and Combat Service Support (CSS) Specialist	1,023
0451	Air Delivery Specialist	150
0481	Landing Support Specialist	786
3000	Basic Supply Administration and Operations Marine	108
3043	Supply Administration and Operations Clerk	4,241
3044	Purchasing and Contracting Specialist	107
3051	Warehouse Clerk	2,808
3052	Packaging Specialist	190
3361	Subsistence Supply Clerk	348
3400	Basic Auditing, Finance, and Accounting Marine	17
3441	NAF Audit Technician	39
3451	Fiscal/Budget Technician	368
4100	Basic Marine Corps Exchange Marine	11
4133	Morale, Welfare, Recreation (MWR) Specialist	124
6042	Support Equipment Asset Manager	267
6600	Basic Aviation Supply Marine	34
6672	Aviation Supply Clerk	1,461
7041	Aviation Operations Specialist	748
7300	Basic Air Traffic Controller/Enlisted Flight Crew Marine	6
9991	Sergeant Major of the Marine Corps	1
9999	Sergeant Major-First Sergeant	1,220

3 Aircraft, Automotive, and Electrical Maintenance Specialists

MOC	MOC Title	Personnel
1141	Electrician	598
1142	Electrical Equipment Repair Specialist	618
1161	Refrigeration Mechanic	367
1341	Engineer Equipment Mechanic	1,145
1349	Engineer Equipment Chief	183
2141	Assault Amphibious Vehicle (AAV) Repairer/Technician	601
2146	Main Battle Tank (MBT) Repairer/Technician	294
2147	Light Armored Vehicle (LAV) Repairer/Technician	399
2147	Light Armored Vehicle (LAV) Repairer/Technician	399
2149	Ordnance Vehicle Maintenance Chief	60
3513	Body Repair Mechanic	5
3521	Organizational Automotive Mechanic	3,037
3523	Vehicle Recovery Mechanic	1
3529	Motor Transport Maintenance Chief	679
6000	Basic Aircraft Maintenance Marine	123
6011	Aircraft Mechanic-Trainee	220
6013	Aircraft Mechanic, EA-6	81
6014	Unmanned Aerial Vehicle (UAV) Mechanic	42
6015	Aircraft Mechanic, AV-8/TAV-8	505
6016	Aircraft Mechanic, KC-130	180
6017	Aircraft Mechanic, F/A-18	605
6019	Aircraft Maintenance Chief	115
6022	Aircraft Power Plants Mechanic, J-52	36
6025	Aircraft Power Plants Mechanic, Rolls Royce Pegasus	88
6026	Aircraft Power Plants Mechanic, T-56	76
6027	Aircraft Power Plants Mechanic, F-404	130
6035	Aircraft Power Plants Test Cell Operator Fixed-Wing	24
6051	Aircraft Airframe Mechanic-Trainee	226
6053	Aircraft Airframe, EA-6	75
6055	Aircraft Airframe Mechanic, AV-8/TAV-8	274
6056	Aircraft Airframe Mechanic, KC-130	168
6057	Aircraft Airframe Mechanic, F/A-18	376
6071	Aircraft Maintenance Support Equipment (SE) Mechanic-Trainee	142
6072	Aircraft Maintenance Support Equipment Hydraulic/Pneumatic/Structures Mechanic	599
6073	Aircraft Maintenance Support Equipment Electrician/Refrigeration Mechanic	399
6081	Aircraft Safety Equipment Mechanic-Trainee	24
6083	Aircraft Safety Equipment Mechanic, A-6/EA-6	44
6085	Aircraft Safety Equipment Mechanic, AV-8/TAV-8	106
6086	Aircraft Safety Equipment Mechanic, KC-130	58
6087	Aircraft Safety Equipment Mechanic, F/A-18	151
6091	Aircraft Structures Mechanic-Trainee	1
6092	Aircraft Structures Mechanic, A-4/TA-4	533
6094	Aircraft Intermediate Level Hydraulic/Pneumatic Mechanic	312

6112	Helicopter Mechanic, CH-46	601
6113	Helicopter Mechanic, CH-53	546
6114	Helicopter Mechanic, U/AH-1	546
6122	Helicopter Power Plants Mechanic, T-58	153
6123	Helicopter Power Plants Mechanic, T-64	165
6124	Helicopter Power Plants Mechanic, T-400/T-700	141
6152	Helicopter Airframe Mechanic, CH-46	289
6153	Helicopter Airframe Mechanic, CH-53	422
6154	Helicopter Airframe Mechanic, A/UH-1	508
6331	Aircraft Electrical Systems Technician-Trainee	53
6333	Aircraft Electrical Systems Technician, EA-6	78
6335	Aircraft Electrical Systems Technician, AV-8	205
6336	Aircraft Electrical Systems Technician, KC-130	103
6337	Aircraft Electrical Systems Technician, F/A-18	320
6431	Aircraft Electrical Systems Technician-Trainee	21
6432	Aircraft Electrical/Instrument/Flight Control Systems Technician, Fixed Wing, IMA	204
6433	Aircraft Electrical/Instrument/Flight Control Systems Technician, Helicopter/OV-10, IMA	199
6434	Advanced Aircraft Electrical/Instrument/Flight Control Systems Technician IMA	80

4 Air Traffic Controllers

MOC	MOC Title	Personnel
5950	Air Traffic Control Systems Maintenance Officer	21
7251	Air Traffic Controller-Trainee	198
7252	Air Traffic Controller-Tower	117
7253	Air Traffic Controller-Radar	224
7291	Senior Air Traffic Controller	158

5 Airplane Navigators

MOC	MOC Title	Personnel
7380	Mission Specialist/Navigation Officer	18
7524	Naval Flight Officer (NFO)	24
7525	Naval Flight Officer (NFO)	185
7574	Naval Flight Officer (NFO)	2
7580	Naval Flight Officer (NFO)	33
7582	Naval Flight Officer (NFO)	13
7583	Naval Flight Officer (NFO)	19
7585	Naval Flight Officer (NFO)	2
7587	Naval Flight Officer (NFO)	7
7588	Naval Flight Officer (NFO)	148
9907	Colonel, Naval Aviator/Naval Flight Officer	171

6 Communications Managers

MOC	MOC Title	Personnel
2510	Network Management Officer	19

2802	Electronics Maintenance Officer (Ground)	50
2805	Data/Communications Maintenance Officer	56
2810	Telephone Systems Officer	35

7 Communications Operators

MOC	MOC Title	Personnel
2500	Basic Operational Communicator	211
2512	Field Wireman	1,309
2513	Construction Wireman	178
2531	Field Radio Operator	3,673
2532	Multichannel Equipment Operator	679
2534	High Frequency Communication Central Operator	67
2535	Fleet SATCOM Terminal Operator	17
2536	Ground Mobile Forces SATCOM Operator	135
2537	Radio Chief	679
2542	Communication Center Operator	925
2549	Communication Center Chief	173
2591	Operational Communication Chief	404
2621	Communications Intelligence Intercept Operator/Analyst	629
2629	Signals Intelligence Analyst	2
2631	Electronic Intelligence (ELINT) Intercept Operator/Analyst	168
7381	Airborne Radio Operator/Inflight Refueling Observer/Loadmaster-Trainee (ARO/IRO/LM)	15

8 Computer Systems Specialists

MOC	MOC Title	Personnel
4000	Basic Data Systems Marine	109
4010	Data Systems Software Officer	13
4010	Data Systems Software Officer	28
4066	Small Computer Systems Specialist (SCSS)	1,238
4067	Programmer, ADA	370
4099	Data Processing Chief	14
5970	Data Systems Maintenance Officer	14
6673	Automated Information Systems (AIS) Computer Operator	148

9 Construction and Engineering Operators

MOC	MOC Title	Personnel
1171	Hygiene Equipment Operator	771
1181	Fabric Repair Specialist	108
1300	Basic Engineer, Construction, and Equipment Marine	217
1345	Engineer Equipment Operator	1,336
1371	Combat Engineer	2,534
6060	Flight Equipment Marine	746

10 Combat Arms

MOC	MOC Title	Personnel
0300	Basic Infantryman	867

0301	Basic Infantry Officer	33
0302	Infantry Officer	2,046
0311	Rifleman	12,148
0313	LAV Crewman	681
0321	Reconnaissance Man	280
0331	Machinegunner	2,925
0341	Mortarman	2,937
0351	Assaultman	2,019
0352	Antitank Assault Guided Missileman	1,379
0369	Infantry Unit Leader	2,549
0800	Basic Field Artillery Man	64
0801	Basic Field Artillery Officer	28
0802	Field Artillery Officer	834
0811	Field Artillery Cannoneer	2,007
0844	Field Artillery Fire Control Man	489
0848	Field Artillery Operations Man	181
0861	Fire Support Man	437
1800	Basic Tank and Amphibious Vehicle Crewman	62
1801	Basic Tank and Amphibious Vehicle Officer	7
1801	Basic Tank and Assault Amphibious Vehicle Officer	7
1802	Tank Officer	190
1803	Assault Amphibious Vehicle (AAV) Officer	147
1812	M1A1 Tank Crewman	525
2120	Weapons Repair Officer	45
2305	Explosive Ordnance Disposal Officer	14
2305	Explosive Ordnance Disposal Officer	22
7200	Basic Air Control/Air Support/Anti-Air Warfare Marine	59
7201	Basic Air Control/Anti-Air Warfare Officer	2
7201	Basic Air Control/Anti-Air Warfare Officer	2
7204	Surface-to-Air Weapons Officer	81
7212	Low Altitude Air Defense (LAAD) Gunner	548
9901	Basic Officer	777
9906	Colonel, Ground	305

13 Emergency Management and Laboratory Specialists

MOC	MOC Title	Personnel
5700	Basic Nuclear, Biological, and Chemical Marine	2
5711	Nuclear Biological and Chemical Defense Specialist	629

15 Finance and Accounting Managers

MOC	MOC Title	Personnel
3401	Basic Auditing, Finance, and Accounting Officer	16
3404	Financial Management Officer	259
3410	NAF Auditing Officer	10
3410	NAF Auditing Officer	17

16 Firefighters

MOC	MOC Title	Personnel
7051	Aircraft Firefighting and Rescue Specialist	968

17 Flight Engineers

MOC	MOC Title	Personnel
6030	Aircraft Flight Mechanic, KC-130	87
6031	Aircraft Flight Engineer, KC-130-Trainee	25
6032	Aircraft Flight Engineer, KC-130	85
6172	Helicopter Crew Chief, CH-46	500
6173	Helicopter Crew Chief, CH-53	289
7314	Unmanned Aerial Vehicle (UAV) Air Vehicle Operator	40

18 Functional Specialty Managers

MOC	MOC Title	Personnel
0180	Adjutant	323
0401	Basic Logistics Officer	21
0402	Logistics Officer	879
0430	Embarkation Officer	69
1390	Bulk Fuel Officer	31
2102	Ordnance Officer	31
2340	Ammunition Officer	26
2340	Ammunition Officer	37
3001	Basic Supply Administration and Operations Officer	24
3002	Ground Supply Officer	567
3010	Ground Supply Operations Officer	29
3102	Traffic Management Officer	12
3102	Traffic Management Officer	21
3300	Basic Food Service Marine	109
3302	Food Service Officer	18
3302	Food Service Officer	27
3381	Food Service Specialist	2,848
3501	Basic Motor Transport Officer	11
3502	Motor Transport Officer	230
3510	Motor Transport Maintenance Officer	90
4130	Marine Corps Exchange Officer	13
5801	Basic Military Police and Corrections Officer	7
5803	Military Police Officer	159
5804	Corrections Officer	16
5805	Criminal Investigation Officer	17
6001	Basic Aircraft Maintenance Officer	2
6002	Aircraft Maintenance Officer	228
6004	Aircraft Maintenance Engineer Officer	50
6004	Aircraft Maintenance Engineer Officer	81
6302	Avionics Officer	47
6302	Avionics Officer	80

6601	Basic Aviation Supply Officer	3
6602	Aviation Supply Officer	168
6604	Aviation Supply Operations Officer	21
6604	Aviation Supply Operations Officer	33
9904	Colonel, Logistician	98

20 Health, Education and Welfare Workers

MOC	MOC Title	Personnel
0251	Interrogation/Translation Specialist	109
2671	Cryptologic Linguist, Arabic	97
2673	Cryptologic Linguist, Korean	50
2674	Cryptologic Linguist, Spanish	142
2675	Cryptologic Linguist, Russian	83
4401	Student Judge Advocate	50
4402	Judge Advocate	353
4430	Legal Administrative Officer	19
9914	Colonel, Judge Advocate	26
9925	Range Officer	30

21 Intelligence Specialists

MOC	MOC Title	Personnel
0200	Basic Intelligence Marine	144
0201	Basic Intelligence Officer	30
0202	Marine Air/Ground Task Force (MAGTF) Intelligence Officer	394
0203	Ground Intelligence Officer	83
0204	Human Source Intelligence Officer	21
0206	Signals Intelligence/Ground Electronic Warfare Officer	93
0207	Air Intelligence Officer	61
0210	Counterintelligence Officer	22
0211	Counterintelligence (CI) Specialist	127
0231	Intelligence Specialist	920
0241	Imagery Interpretation Specialist	196
0291	Intelligence Chief	18
2600	Basic Signals Intelligence/Ground Electronic Warfare Operator	438
2602	Signals Intelligence/Electronic Warfare Officer	27
2651	Special Intelligence Communicator	361
2691	Signals Intelligence/Electronic Warfare Chief	51

22 Law Enforcement Specialists

MOC	MOC Title	Personnel
5800	Basic Military Police and Corrections Marine	171
5811	Military Police	2,941
5821	Criminal Investigator	174
5831	Correctional Specialist	670

23 Legal Specialists and Court Reporters

MOC	MOC Title	Personnel
4400	Basic Legal Services Marine	22
4421	Legal Services Specialist	507
4429	Legal Services Reporter (Stenotype)	36

25 Machinists, Technicians, and Cargo Specialists

MOC	MOC Title	Personnel
1100	Basic Utilities Marine	153
1169	Utilities Chief	146
1316	Metal Worker	276
1391	Bulk Fuel Specialist	1,248
2161	Machinist	142
4615	Combat Lithographer	106
6075	Cryogenics Equipment Operator	163

27 Musicians and Media Directors

MOC	MOC Title	Personnel
4602	Training and Visual Information Support Officer	5
4602	Training and Visual Information Support Officer	14
5500	Basic Musician	51
5502	Band Officer	12
5519	Enlisted Bandleader	12
5519	Enlisted Bandleader	12
5521	Band Drum Major	11
5523	Instrument Repair Specialist	11
5526	Musician, Oboe/English Horn	7
5528	Musician, Bassoon	8
5534	Musician, Clarinet	80
5536	Musician, Flute and Piccolo	49
5537	Musician, Saxophone	59
5541	Musician, Cornet/Trumpet	123
5543	Musician, Baritone Horn/Euphonium	33
5544	Musician, French Horn	52
5546	Musician, Trombone	75
5547	Musician, Tuba and String Bass/Electric Bass	46
5548	Musician, String Bass/Electric Bass	19
5563	Musician, Percussion (Drums, Tympani, and Mallets)	63
5565	Musician, Piano or Guitar	11
5566	Musician, Guitar	9
9802	Director/Assistant Director, The President's Own, U.S. Marine Band	2
9803	Staff Officer, The President's Own, U.S. Marine Band	1
9803	Staff Officer, The President's Own, U.S. Marine Band	1
9805	U.S. Marine Drum & Bugle Corps Officer	1
9805	U.S. Marine Drum & Bugle Corps Officer	1

| 9811 | Member, The President's Own, United States Marine Band | 144 |
| 9812 | U.S. Marine Drum & Bugle Corps Member | 78 |

29 Ordnance Specialists

MOC	MOC Title	Personnel
2100	Basic Ordnance Marine	167
2131	Towed Artillery Systems Technician	201
2181	Senior Ground Ordnance Weapons Chief	36
2300	Basic Ammunition and Explosive Ordnance Disposal Marine	91
2311	Ammunition Technician	1,159
2336	Explosive Ordnance Disposal Technician	284
6500	Basic Aviation Ordnance Marine	9
6511	Aviation Ordnance Trainee	260
6531	Aircraft Ordnance Technician	1,246
6541	Aviation Ordnance Systems Technician	916
6591	Aviation Ordnance Chief	59

32 Photographic and Audiovisual Specialists

MOC	MOC Title	Personnel
4600	Basic Training and Visual Support Marine	32
4611	Graphics Specialist	75
4641	Combat Photographic Specialist	177
4671	Combat Motion Media Photographer	120
4691	Visual Information Chief	17

34 Pilots and Ship/Submarine Operators

MOC	MOC Title	Personnel
7208	Air Support Control Officer	139
7210	Air Defense Control Officer	122
7501	Pilot VMA	1
7507	Pilot VMA	53
7509	Pilot VMA	334
7521	Pilot VMFA	63
7522	Pilot VMFA	1
7523	Pilot VMFA	468
7541	Pilot VMAQ/VMFP	4
7543	Pilot VMAQ/VMFP	56
7545	Pilot VMAQ/VMFP	1
7556	Pilot VMGR	123
7557	Pilot VMGR	141
7558	Pilot HMH/M/L/A	9
7560	Pilot HMH/M/L/A	21
7561	Pilot HMH/M/L/A	33
7562	Pilot HMH/M/L/A	784
7563	Pilot HMH/M/L/A	259
7564	Pilot HMH/M/L/A	155
7565	Pilot HMH/M/L/A	416

7566	Pilot HMH/M/L/A	414
7567	Pilot HMH/M/L/A	17
7568	Pilot HMH/M/L/A	27
7598	Basic Fixed Wing Pilot	10
7599	Flight Student (TBS)	1,087

36 Precision Equipment Repairers

MOC	MOC Title	Personnel
2111	Small Arms Repairer/Technician	1,247
2171	Electro-Optical Ordnance Repairer	397
2515	ULS Central Office Operator/Maintainer	273
2519	Wire Chief	256
2800	Basic Data/Communications Maintenance Marine	656
2811	Telephone Technician	339
2813	Cable Systems Technician	74
2818	Personal Computer (PC)/Tactical Office Machine Repairer	370
2821	Computer Technician	158
2822	Electronic Switching Equipment Technician	116
2823	Technical Controller	57
2826	AN/MSC-63A Maintenance Technician	1
2831	Multichannel Equipment Repairer	216
2832	Multichannel Equipment Technician	56
2834	Ground Mobile Forces SATCOM Technician	49
2841	Ground Radio Repairer	1,124
2861	Radio Technician	356
2871	Test Measurement and Diagnostic Equipment Technician	56
2874	Metrology Technician	44
2881	Communication Security Equipment Technician	252
2885	Artillery Electronic System Repairer	19
2887	Counter Mortar Radar Repairer	15
2889	Ground Radar Technician	23
2891	Data/Communications Maintenance Chief	112
5900	Basic Electronics Maintenance Marine	240
5942	Aviation Radar Repairer	130
5948	Aviation Radar Technician	72
5952	Air Traffic Control Navigational Aids Technician	141
5953	Air Traffic Control Radar Technician	158
5954	Air Traffic Control Communications Technician	162
5959	Air Traffic Control Systems Maintenance Chief	22
5962	Tactical Air Command Central Repairer	56
5963	Tactical Air Operations Central Repairer	85
5974	Tactical Air Command Central Technician/Systems Administrator	36
5979	Tactical Air Operations Central Technician	39
5993	Electronics Maintenance Chief	8
6300	Basic Avionics Marine	440
6311	Aircraft Communications/Navigation/Electrical/Weapon Systems Technician-Trainee, OMA	191

| 6494 | Aviation Logistics Tactical Information Systems (ALTIS) Specialist | 92 |

37 Preventive Maintenance Analysts

MOC	MOC Title	Personnel
0411	Maintenance Management Specialist	918
6046	Aircraft Maintenance Administration Clerk	491
6047	Aircraft Maintenance Data Analyst/Administrator	526
6411	Aircraft Communications/Navigation Systems Technician-Trainee, IMA	128
6414	Advanced Aircraft Communications/Navigation Systems Technician, IMA	185

38 Public Information Managers and Journalists

MOC	MOC Title	Personnel
4300	Basic Public Affairs Marine	42
4301	Basic Public Affairs Officer	3
4302	Public Affairs Officer	108
4341	Combat Correspondent	356
5702	Nuclear, Biological, and Chemical (NBC) Officer	103
7002	Expeditionary Airfield and Emergency Services Officer	37

39 Radar and Sonar Operators

MOC	MOC Title	Personnel
0842	Field Artillery Radar Operator	78
7234	Air Command and Control Electronics Operator	132
7236	Tactical Air Defense Controller	106
7242	Air Support Operations Operator	220

40 Recruiting Specialists

MOC	MOC Title	Personnel
8412	Career Recruiter	397

41 Scientists and Engineers

MOC	MOC Title	Personnel
1120	Utilities Officer	38
1301	Basic Engineer, Construction, and Equipment Officer	9
1302	Engineer Officer	370
1310	Engineer Equipment Officer	61
2110	Ordnance Vehicle Maintenance Officer	42
2125	Electro-Optic Instrument Repair Officer	4
5902	Electronics Maintenance Officer (Aviation)	29
5910	Aviation Radar Maintenance Officer	9
6502	Aviation Ordnance Officer	40
6502	Aviation Ordnance Officer	54

42 Ship Engineers and Air Crew Members

MOC	MOC Title	Personnel
7000	Basic Airfield Services Marines	119
7372	First Navigator	71
7382	Airborne Radio Operator/Inflight Refueling Observer/Loadmaster ARO/IRO/LM	92

43 Surveyors and Mappers

MOC	MOC Title	Personnel
0261	Topographic Intelligence Specialist	125
1361	Engineer Assistant	139

44 Transportation Specialists

MOC	MOC Title	Personnel
0491	Combat Service Support Chief	331
3100	Basic Traffic Management Marine	14
3112	Traffic Management Specialist	545

45 Vehicle Drivers

MOC	MOC Title	Personnel
3500	Basic Motor Transport Marine	376
3531	Motor Vehicle Operator	5,176
3533	Logistics Vehicle System Operator	1,365
3537	Motor Transport Operations Chief	789

46 Weather Personnel

MOC	MOC Title	Personnel
0847	Artillery Meteorological Man	59
6800	Basic Weather Service Marine	8
6802	Weather Service Officer	9
6802	Weather Service Officer	9
6802	Weather Service Officer	19
6802	Weather Service Officer	19
6821	Weather Observer	204
6842	Weather Forecaster	104

DEFENSE CIVIL SERVICE OCCUPATIONS BY
OCCUPATIONAL CLUSTER

2 Administrative, Personnel, and Supply Specialists

MOC	MOC Title	Personnel
21	Community Planning Technician Series	11
119	Economics Assistant Series	3
203	Personnel Clerical and Assistance Series	3,505
204	Military Personnel Clerical and Technician Series	7,325
299	Personnel Management Student Trainee Series	30
302	Messenger Series	22
303	Miscellaneous Clerk and Assistant Series	21,242
304	Information Receptionist Series	197
305	Mail and File Series	2,708
309	Correspondence Clerk Series	52
312	Clerk-Stenographer and Reporter Series	41
313	Work Unit Supervising Series	9
318	Secretary Series	26,739
319	Closed Microphone Reporting Series	128
322	Clerk-Typist Series	383
326	Office Automation Clerical and Assistance Series	8,147
342	Support Services Administration Series	1,311
344	Management and Program Clerical and Assistance Series	4,069
350	Equipment Operator Series	349
356	Data Transcriber Series	140
357	Coding Series	52
359	Electric Accounting Machine Operation Series	1
361	Equal Opportunity Assistance Series	166
503	Financial Clerical and Assistance Series	2,173
525	Accounting Technician Series	10,850
530	Cash Processing Series	730
540	Voucher Examining Series	1,460
544	Civilian Pay Series	829
545	Military Pay Series	2,257

561	Budget Clerical and Assistance Series	2,790
669	Medical Records Administration Series	122
675	Medical Records Technician Series	1,186
679	Medical Clerk Series	3,629
1101	General Business and Industry Series	6,375
1106	Procurement Clerical and Technician Series	3,884
1107	Property Disposal Clerical and Technician Series	316
1152	Production Control Series	4,469
1521	Mathematics Technician Series	16
1530	Statistician Series	123
1670	Equipment Specialist Series	6,428
2001	General Supply Series	3,237
2005	Supply Clerical and Technician Series	12,906
2010	Inventory Management Series	4,554
2032	Packaging Series	259
2050	Supply Cataloging Series	118
2091	Sales Store Clerical Series	6,155
4754	Cemetery Caretaking	23
6902	Lumber Handling	2
6903	Coal Handling	16
6904	Tools and Parts Attending	2,224
6907	Materials Handling	10,810
6910	Materials Expediting	822
6912	Materials Examining and Identifying	2,493
6914	Store Working	4,715
6941	Bulk Money Handling	1
7304	Laundry Working	97
7305	Laundry Machine Operating	21
7306	Pressing	27
7307	Dry Cleaning	5
7603	Barbering	34
7641	Beautician	2

3 Aircraft, Automotive, and Electrical Maintanence Specialists

MOC	MOC Title	Personnel
1601	General Facilities and Equipment Series	2,155
2805	Electrician	3,840
2810	High Voltage Electrician	1,294
2854	Electrical Equipment Repairing	718
2892	Aircraft Electrician	2,336
3725	Battery Repairing	64
4371	Plaster Pattern Casting	3
4716	Railroad Car Repairing	13
4737	General Equipment Mechanic	164
4742	Utility Systems Repairing-Operating	861
4805	Medical Equipment Repairing	149
4806	Office Appliance Repairing	14
4808	Custodial Equipment Servicing	2

4812	Saw Reconditioning	8
4819	Bowling Equipment Repairing	22
4840	Tool and Equipment Repairing	131
4844	Bicycle Repairing	3
4851	Reclamation Working	4
4855	Domestic Appliance Repairing	19
5306	Air Conditioning Equipment Mechanic	1,777
5309	Heating and Boiler Plant Equipment Mechanic	583
5310	Kitchen/Bakery Equipment Repairing	64
5312	Sewing Machine Repairing	7
5313	Elevator Mechanic	22
5323	Oiling and Greasing	59
5330	Printing Equipment Repairing	4
5334	Marine Machinery Mechanic	1,658
5335	Wind Tunnel Mechanic	2
5350	Production Machinery Mechanic	556
5352	Industrial Equipment Mechanic	1,071
5364	Door Systems Mechanic	34
5365	Physiological Trainer Mechanic	15
5378	Powered Support Systems Mechanic	2,079
5803	Heavy Mobile Equipment Mechanic	9,505
5806	Mobile Equipment Servicing	165
5823	Automotive Mechanic	4,653
5876	Electromotive Equipment Mechanic	83
7006	Preservation Servicing	174
7009	Equipment Cleaning	342
8255	Pneudraulic Systems Mechanic	1,552
8268	Aircraft Pneudraulic Systems Mechanic	1,466
8602	Aircraft Engine Mechanic	4,102
8610	Small Engine Mechanic	67
8675	Liquid Fuel Rocket Engine Mechanic	27
8810	Aircraft Propeller Mechanic	142
8840	Aircraft Mechanical Parts Repairing	705
8852	Aircraft Mechanic	11,554
8862	Aircraft Attending	327
8863	Aircraft Tire Mounting	14

4 Air Traffic Controllers

MOC	MOC Title	Personnel
2152	Air Traffic Control Series	997
2154	Air Traffic Assistance Series	219

5 Airplane Navigators

MOC	MOC Title	Personnel
2183	Air Navigation Series	342

6 Communications Managers

MOC	MOC Title	Personnel
391	Telecommunications Series	3,975

7 Communications Operators

MOC	MOC Title	Personnel
382	Telephone Operating Series	684
390	Telecommunications Processing Series	463
392	General Telecommunications Series	556
394	Communications Clerical Series	172

8 Computer Systems Specialists

MOC	MOC Title	Personnel
332	Computer Operation Series	1,591
334	Computer Specialist Series	24,321
335	Computer Clerk and Assistant Series	3,072
1550	Computer Science Series	2,536

9 Construction and Engineering Operators

MOC	MOC Title	Personnel
3103	Shoe Repairing	6
3105	Fabric Working	1,005
3106	Upholstering	70
3111	Sewing Machine Operating	89
3422	Power Saw Operating	4
3502	Laboring	2,757
3508	Pipeline Working	9
3546	Railroad Repairing	36
3602	Cement Finishing	99
3603	Masonry	300
3604	Tile Setting	59
3605	Plastering	39
3606	Roofing	124
3609	Floor Covering Installing	34
3610	Insulating	794
3611	Glazing	27
3653	Asphalt Working	33
3872	Metal Tube Making, Installing, and Repairing	53
4102	Painting	3,052
4103	Paperhanging	6
4104	Sign Painting	111
4204	Pipefitting	3,059
4206	Plumbing	974
4351	Plastic Molding Equipment Operating	14
4352	Plastic Fabricating	355
4360	Rubber Products Molding	39
4361	Rubber Equipment Repairing	39

4604	Wood Working	745
4605	Wood Crafting	309
4607	Carpentry	1,548
4616	Patternmaking	49
4618	Woodworking Machine Operating	4
4639	Timber Working	43
4654	Form Block Making	10
4717	Boat Building and Repairing	51
4741	General Equipment Operating	14
4749	Maintenance Mechanic	4,946
4816	Protective and Safety Equipment Fabricating and Repair	86
4818	Aircraft Survival Flight Equipment Repairing	583
5210	Rigging	1,621
5220	Shipwright	327
5221	Lofting	42
5317	Laundry and Dry Cleaning Equipment Repairing	7
5318	Lock and Dam Repairing	468
5423	Sandblasting	381
5704	Fork Lift Operating	620
5716	Engineering Equipment Operating	1,441
5725	Crane Operating	893
5729	Drill Rig Operating	99
5738	Railroad Maintenance Vehicle Operating	26
5767	Airfield Clearing Equipment Operating	201
5788	Deckhand	271
7010	Parachute Packing	7

11 Dental and Pharmacy Specialists

MOC	MOC Title	Personnel
661	Pharmacy Technician Series	457
680	Dental Officer Series	49
681	Dental Assistant Series	1,438
682	Dental Hygiene Series	205
683	Dental Laboratory Aide and Technician Series	180

13 Emergency Management and Laboratory Specialists

MOC	MOC Title	Personnel
458	Soil Conservation Technician Series	2
1311	Physical Science Technician Series	1,147
5427	Chemical Plant Operating	70
5454	Solvent Still Operating	7

14 Environmental Health and Safety Specialists

MOC	MOC Title	Personnel
29	Environmental Protection Assistant Series	320
640	Health Aide and Technician Series	2,077
698	Environmental Health Technician Series	82

| 895 | Industrial Engineering Technician Series | 1,253 |
| 5026 | Pest Controlling | 367 |

15 Finance and Accounting Managers

MOC	MOC Title	Personnel
110	Economist Series	276
501	Financial Administration and Program Series	4,586
505	Financial Management Series	593
510	Accounting Series	5,427
511	Auditing Series	6,628
560	Budget Analysis Series	8,883
1160	Financial Analysis Series	6
1163	Insurance Examining Series	27

16 Firefighters

MOC	MOC Title	Personnel
81	Fire Protection and Prevention Series	8,877

18 Functional Specialty Managers

MOC	MOC Title	Personnel
25	Park Ranger Series	1,628
80	Security Administration Series	3,617
105	Social Insurance Administration Series	1
142	Manpower Development Series	6
201	Personnel Management Series	4,344
205	Military Personnel Management Series	1,838
212	Personnel Staffing Series	1,048
221	Position Classification Series	579
222	Occupational Analysis Series	29
223	Salary and Wage Administration Series	52
230	Employee Relations Series	702
233	Labor Relations Series	338
235	Employee Development Series	513
246	Contractor Industrial Relations Series	31
260	Equal Employment Opportunity Series	993
340	Program Management Series	1,555
341	Administrative Officer Series	2,036
343	Management and Program Analysis Series	17,138
346	Logistics Management Series	10,946
360	Equal Opportunity Compliance Series	16
1102	Contracting Series	19,498
1103	Industrial Property Management Series	576
1104	Property Disposal Series	684
1105	Purchasing Series	2,114
1130	Public Utilities Specialist Series	29
1144	Commissary Store Management Series	1,421
1170	Realty Series	1,151

1171	Appraising Series	140
1173	Housing Management Series	2,313
1176	Building Management Series	115
1382	Food Technology Series	38
1510	Actuary Series	13
1630	Cemetery Administration Series	5
1640	Facility Management Series	716
1658	Laundry and Dry Cleaning Plant Management Series	14
1667	Steward Series	54
1811	Criminal Investigating Series	1,640
2003	Supply Program Management Series	4,094
2030	Distribution Facilities and Storage Management Series	556
2130	Traffic Management Series	1,516
2150	Transportation Operations Series	544
7402	Baking	56
7404	Cooking	960
7405	Bartending	1
7407	Meatcutting	1,522
7408	Food Service Working	1,924
7420	Waiter	16

20 Health, Education and Welfare Workers

MOC	MOC Title	Personnel
60	Chaplain Series	53
101	Social Science Series	2,122
102	Social Science Aide and Technician Series	103
160	Civil Rights Analysis Series	1
180	Psychology Series	975
181	Psychology Aide and Technician Series	26
184	Sociology Series	8
185	Social Work Series	877
186	Social Services Aide and Assistant Series	400
187	Social Services Series	282
190	General Anthropology Series	31
405	Pharmacology Series	32
630	Dietitian and Nutritionist Series	70
660	Pharmacist Series	494
665	Speech Pathology and Audiology Series	132
670	Health System Administration Series	15
671	Health System Specialist Series	729
673	Hospital Housekeeping Management Series	35
904	Law Clerk Series	7
905	General Attorney Series	2,339
1040	Language Specialist Series	116
1046	Language Clerical Series	23
1221	Patent Adviser Series	11
1222	Patent Attorney Series	78
1410	Librarian Series	775

1411	Library Technician Series	1,385
1412	Technical Information Services Series	354
1420	Archivist Series	41
1421	Archives Technician Series	48
1701	General Education and Training Series	16,615
1702	Education and Training Technician Series	8,281
1710	Education and Vocational Training Series	3,290
1712	Training Instruction Series	4,092
1720	Education Program Series	33
1740	Education Services Series	1,149
1750	Instructional Systems Series	1,465

21 Intelligence Specialists

MOC	MOC Title	Personnel
132	Intelligence Series	2,806
134	Intelligence Aide and Clerk Series	224

22 Law Enforcement Specialists

MOC	MOC Title	Personnel
19	Safety Technician Series	172
83	Police Series	3,267
85	Security Guard Series	2,301
86	Security Clerical and Assistance Series	1,166
1801	General Inspection, Investigation, and Compliance Series	434
1802	Compliance Inspection and Support Series	391
1810	General Investigating Series	1,291
1812	Game Law Enforcement Series	21
1890	Customs Inspection Series	8
1897	Customs Aid Series	8

23 Legal Specialists and Court Reporters

MOC	MOC Title	Personnel
945	Clerk of Court Series	3
950	Paralegal Specialist Series	554
962	Contact Representative Series	813
963	Legal Instruments Examining Series	75
967	Passport and Visa Examining Series	8
986	Legal Clerical and Assistance Series	743
990	General Claims Examining Series	219
992	Loss and Damage Claims Examining Series	116
995	Dependents and Estates Claims Examining Series	26
998	Claims Clerical Series	222
999	Legal Occupations Student Trainee Series	6
1202	Patent Technician Series	1

24 Life Scientists

MOC	MOC Title	Personnel
401	General Biological Science Series	1,666
403	Microbiology Series	240
408	Ecology Series	139
410	Zoology Series	7
413	Physiology Series	109
414	Entomology Series	45
415	Toxicology Series	36
430	Botany Series	17
435	Plant Physiology Series	1
437	Horticulture Series	4
454	Rangeland Management Series	11
455	Range Technician Series	2
457	Soil Conservation Series	14
460	Forestry Series	112
462	Forestry Technician Series	113
470	Soil Science Series	7
471	Agronomy Series	32
480	General Fish and Wildlife Administration Series	14
482	Fishery Biology Series	59
486	Wildlife Biology Series	121
487	Animal Science Series	2
701	Veterinary Medical Science Series	15
1306	Health Physics Series	310

25 Machinists, Technicians, and Cargo Specialists

MOC	MOC Title	Personnel
351	Printing Clerical Series	68
2144	Cargo Scheduling Series	50
2161	Marine Cargo Series	40
3414	Machining	3,623
3416	Toolmaking	480
3417	Tool Grinding	31
3428	Die Sinking	5
3431	Machine Tool Operating	507
3543	Stevedoring	99
3702	Flame/Arc Cutting	9
3703	Welding	2,757
3707	Metalizing	114
3708	Metal Process Working	12
3711	Electroplating	465
3712	Heat Treating	92
3720	Brazing and Soldering	3
3722	Cold Working	2
3727	Buffing and Polishing	11
3735	Metal Phototransferring	14

3741	Furnace Operating	6
3769	Shot Peening Machine Operating	74
3802	Metal Forging	39
3806	Sheet Metal Mechanic	6,668
3807	Structural/Ornamental Iron Working	68
3808	Boilermaking	298
3809	Mobile Equipment Metal Mechanic	398
3816	Engraving	12
3818	Springmaking	3
3819	Airframe Jig Fitting	3
3820	Shipfitting	1,032
3830	Blacksmithing	1
3858	Metal Tank and Radiator Repairing	61
3869	Metal Forming Machine Operating	20
4005	Optical Element Working	4
4010	Prescription Eyeglass Making	24
4255	Fuel Distribution Systems Mechanic	190
4402	Bindery Working	166
4405	Film Assembly-Stripping	10
4406	Letterpress Operating	2
4413	Negative Engraving	1
4414	Offset Photography	40
4416	Offset Platemaking	5
4417	Offset Press Operating	178
4419	Silk Screen Making and Printing	14
4602	Blocking and Bracing	291
4845	Orthopedic Appliance Repairing	2
4848	Mechanical Parts Repairing	77
4850	Bearing Reconditioning	75
5205	Gas and Radiation Detecting	62
5384	Gas Dynamic Facility Installing and Repairing	11
5402	Boiler Plant Operating	1,316
5403	Incinerator Operating	18
5406	Utility Systems Operating	395
5407	Electric Power Controlling	509
5408	Wastewater Treatment Plant Operating	405
5409	Water Treatment Plant Operating	434
5413	Fuel Distribution System Operating	1,020
5415	Air Conditioning Equipment Operating	78
5419	Stationary-Engine Operating	21
5433	Gas Generating Plant Operating	5
5486	Swimming Pool Operating	11
6968	Aircraft Freight Loading	141
7002	Packing	1,839

26 Medical Service and Medical Care Technicians

MOC	MOC Title	Personnel
404	Biological Science Technician Series	292

603	Physician's Assistant Series	203
621	Nursing Assistant Series	755
622	Medical Supply Aide and Technician Series	155
625	Autopsy Assistant Series	5
642	Nuclear Medicine Technician Series	41
644	Medical Technologist Series	903
645	Medical Technician Series	585
646	Pathology Technician Series	125
647	Diagnostic Radiologic Technologist Series	527
648	Therapeutic Radiologic Technologist Series	25
649	Medical Instrument Technician Series	336
704	Animal Health Technician Series	4
3511	Laboratory Working	17
3515	Laboratory Support Working	1

27 Musicians and Media Directors

MOC	MOC Title	Personnel
1051	Music Specialist Series	12
1071	Audiovisual Production Series	551

28 Nondestructive Testers

MOC	MOC Title	Personnel
3705	Nondestructive Testing	867
5439	Testing Equipment Operating	57

29 Ordnance Specialists

MOC	MOC Title	Personnel
6502	Explosives Operating	735
6505	Munitions Destroying	77
6511	Missile/Toxic Materials Handling	283
6517	Explosives Test Operating	84
6641	Ordnance Equipment Mechanic	1,039
6652	Aircraft Ordnance Systems Mechanic	1,409

30 Nurses and Physical Therapists

MOC	MOC Title	Personnel
188	Recreation Specialist Series	1,314
189	Recreation Aide and Assistant Series	2,310
610	Nurse Series	4,025
620	Practical Nurse Series	1,594
631	Occupational Therapist Series	47
633	Physical Therapist Series	51
636	Rehabilitation Therapy Assistant Series	41
638	Recreation/Creative Arts Therapist Series	13
651	Respiratory Therapist Series	145
664	Restoration Technician Series	1
667	Orthotist and Prosthetist Series	41

32 Photographic and Audiovisual Specialists

MOC	MOC Title	Personnel
1008	Interior Design Series	81
1020	Illustrating Series	381
1054	Theater Specialist Series	8
1056	Art Specialist Series	96
1060	Photography Series	596
1386	Photographic Technology Series	14
3910	Motion Picture Projection	8
3911	Sound Recording Equipment Operating	5
3919	Television Equipment Operating	6
3940	Broadcasting Equipment Operating	9
3941	Public Address Equipment Operating	8
9003	Film Assembling and Repairing	5
9004	Motion Picture Developing/Printing Machine Operating	4

33 Physicians, Surgeons, Optometrists

MOC	MOC Title	Personnel
602	Medical Officer Series	734
662	Optometrist Series	22
668	Podiatrist Series	12

34 Pilots and Ship/Submarine Operators

MOC	MOC Title	Personnel
1815	Air Safety Investigating Series	8
1825	Aviation Safety Series	2
2181	Aircraft Operation Series	2,019
5782	Ship Operating	104
5784	Riverboat Operating	113
5786	Small Craft Operating	152

36 Precision Equipment Repairers

MOC	MOC Title	Personnel
856	Electronics Technician Series	6,622
1910	Quality Assurance Series	7,847
2502	Telecommunications Mechanic	549
2504	Wire Communications Cable Splicing	118
2508	Communications Line Installing and Repairing	18
2602	Electronic Measurement Equipment Mechanic	1,353
2604	Electronics Mechanic	7,141
2606	Electronic Industrial Controls Mechanic	840
2608	Electronic Digital Computer Mechanic	600
2610	Electronic Integrated Systems Mechanic	4,097
3314	Instrument Making	28
3359	Instrument Mechanic	825
3736	Circuit Board Making	21
4157	Instrument Dial Painting	1

4804	Locksmithing	213
4807	Chemical Equipment Repairing	20
6605	Artillery Repairing	361
6606	Artillery Testing	38
6610	Small Arms Repairing	353
6656	Special Weapons Systems Mechanic	28

37 Preventive Maintenance Analysts

MOC	MOC Title	Personnel
3306	Optical Instrument Repairing	300
3364	Projection Equipment Repairing	7
4839	Film Processing Equipment Repairing	5

38 Public Information Managers and Journalists

MOC	MOC Title	Personnel
20	Community Planning Series	239
23	Outdoor Recreation Planning Series	64
130	Foreign Affairs Series	152
131	International Relations Series	77
170	History Series	359
1001	General Arts and Information Series	630
1010	Exhibits Specialist Series	122
1015	Museum Curator Series	110
1016	Museum Specialist and Technician Series	146
1035	Public Affairs Series	1,642
1082	Writing and Editing Series	591
1083	Technical Writing and Editing Series	742
1084	Visual Information Series	989
1087	Editorial Assistance Series	459
1654	Printing Management Series	236

39 Radar and Sonar Operators

MOC	MOC Title	Personnel
5235	Test Range Tracking	14

41 Scientists and Engineers

MOC	MOC Title	Personnel
18	Safety and Occupational Health Management Series	2,365
28	Environmental Protection Specialist Series	2,377
688	Sanitarian Series	7
690	Industrial Hygiene Series	622
803	Safety Engineering Series	308
804	Fire Protection Engineering Series	68
806	Materials Engineering Series	723
807	Landscape Architecture Series	130
808	Architecture Series	936
809	Construction Control Series	1,757

MOC	MOC Title	Personnel
810	Civil Engineering Series	7,360
819	Environmental Engineering Series	2,950
828	Construction Analyst Series	1
830	Mechanical Engineering Series	8,461
840	Nuclear Engineering Series	1,338
850	Electrical Engineering Series	2,232
854	Computer Engineering Series	1,307
855	Electronics Engineering Series	19,094
858	Biomedical Engineering Series	45
861	Aerospace Engineering Series	3,513
871	Naval Architecture Series	738
873	Ship Surveying Series	72
881	Petroleum Engineering Series	4
892	Ceramic Engineering Series	17
893	Chemical Engineering Series	664
894	Welding Engineering Series	43
896	Industrial Engineering Series	1,346
1150	Industrial Specialist Series	1,383
1310	Physics Series	1,974
1313	Geophysics Series	100
1315	Hydrology Series	65
1320	Chemistry Series	1,623
1321	Metallurgy Series	87
1330	Astronomy and Space Science Series	138
1360	Oceanography Series	339
1515	Operations Research Series	2,767
1520	Mathematics Series	1,164
1529	Mathematical Statistician Series	74
1531	Statistical Assistant Series	124

42 Ship Engineers and Air Crew Members

MOC	MOC Title	Personnel
2185	Air Crew Technician Series	1001

43 Surveyors and Mappers

MOC	MOC Title	Personnel
150	Geography Series	70
817	Surveying Technician Series	255
818	Engineering Drafting Series	202
1021	Office Drafting Series	2
1361	Navigational Information Series	16
1370	Cartography Series	64
1371	Cartographic Technician Series	116
1372	Geodesy Series	8
1373	Land Surveying Series	23
1374	Geodetic Technician Series	17

44 Transportation Specialists

MOC	MOC Title	Personnel
2101	Transportation Specialist Series	855
2102	Transportation Clerk and Assistant Series	3,811
2131	Freight Rate Series	532
2135	Transportation Loss and Damage Claims Examining Series	136
2151	Dispatching Series	388
5736	Braking-Switching and Conducting	94

45 Vehicle Drivers

MOC	MOC Title	Personnel
5703	Motor Vehicle Operating	4,412
5705	Tractor Operating	557
5706	Road Sweeper Operating	25

46 Weather Personnel

MOC	MOC Title	Personnel
1340	Meteorology Series	274
1341	Meteorological Technician Series	246

INDEX OF MILITARY/CIVILIAN SERVICE OCCUPATIONAL CODES AND RAND OCCUPATIONAL CLUSTERS

This appendix provides cross-reference tables for the military and defense civil service occupations and occupational clusters we constructed for this study. The sequence of the index is Army, Navy, Air Force, Marine Corps, and civil service. The first entry in each pair is the military or civil service occupation code and the second entry is the code for the corresponding RAND occupational cluster. This index can be used in conjunction with Appendices F through J to find the cluster containing a specific occupation.

Table K.1

Army Occupational Codes and RAND Occupational Clusters

00B	12	02T	27	12Z	9	14D	10
00Z	40	02U	27	131A	21	14D	10
02B	27	02Z	27	13A	10	14E	10
02C	27	11A	10	13B	10	14E	10
02D	27	11B	10	13C	10	14J	10
02E	27	11C	10	13E	10	14M	10
02F	27	11H	10	13F	10	14R	10
02G	27	11M	10	13M	10	14S	10
02H	27	11X	10	13P	10	14T	36
02J	27	11Z	10	13R	39	14Z	36
02K	27	12A	10	13Z	10	151A	18
02L	27	12B	9	140A	41	152B	34
02M	27	12B	10	140E	36	152C	34
02N	27	12C	9	14A	10	152D	34
02S	27	12C	10	14B	10	152F	34

Code	Value	Code	Value	Code	Value	Code	Value
152G	34	31P	36	42E	25	55A	20
153B	34	31R	36	43M	9	55B	2
153D	34	31S	36	44A	15	55B	20
154C	34	31T	36	44B	3	55D	29
155A	34	31U	7	44E	25	56A	20
155D	34	31W	7	45A	15	56D	20
155E	34	31Z	36	45B	36	57E	2
15A	34	350B	21	45D	36	60B	33
15B	34	350D	21	45E	36	60C	33
15C	34	350L	38	45G	36	60D	33
15D	18	351B	21	45K	36	60F	33
180A	1	351E	21	45N	36	60G	33
18A	1	352C	21	45T	36	60H	33
18B	1	352D	21	46A	38	60J	33
18C	9	352G	21	46B	27	60K	33
18D	26	352H	21	46Q	38	60L	33
18E	7	352J	21	46R	38	60M	33
18F	1	352K	21	46Z	38	60N	33
18Z	1	353A	21	47A	20	60P	33
19D	10	35B	21	48A	38	60Q	33
19K	10	35B	36	48B	38	60R	33
19Z	10	35C	36	48C	38	60S	33
210A	41	35C	43	48D	38	60T	33
215D	43	35D	21	48E	38	60U	33
21A	41	35E	21	48F	38	60V	33
21B	41	35E	36	49A	41	60W	33
21C	43	35F	21	49B	18	61A	33
21D	41	35F	36	49C	41	61B	33
251A	8	35G	21	49D	41	61C	33
25A	21	35H	36	49E	41	61D	33
25B	8	35J	36	51A	41	61E	20
25C	6	35M	36	51H	9	61F	33
25D	41	35N	36	51K	9	61G	33
25E	41	35Q	36	51R	3	61H	33
25M	32	35W	36	51T	43	61J	33
25R	36	35Y	36	51Z	9	61K	33
25V	32	35Z	36	52A	41	61L	33
25Z	32	37F	21	52B	41	61M	33
27E	36	38A	38	52C	3	61N	33
27M	36	39A	38	52D	3	61P	33
27T	36	39B	36	52E	3	61Q	33
27X	36	39B	38	52G	36	61R	33
27Z	36	39C	38	52X	3	61U	33
311A	18	420A	18	53A	8	61W	33
31A	18	420C	27	53B	8	61Z	33
31C	36	42A	18	53C	8	62A	33
31F	7	42B	18	54B	13	62B	3
31L	36	42C	27	550A	23	62B	33

62E	9	67E	20	76J	2	91K	26
62F	9	67F	33	77F	25	91M	18
62G	9	67G	3	77L	13	91P	26
62H	9	67G	33	77W	25	91Q	11
62J	9	67J	34	79R	40	91R	14
62N	9	67N	3	79S	40	91S	14
63A	11	67R	3	81L	25	91T	26
63B	3	67S	3	81T	43	91V	26
63B	11	67T	3	81Z	43	920A	18
63D	3	67U	3	82C	43	920B	18
63D	11	67V	3	82D	43	921A	1
63E	3	67Y	3	880A	34	922A	18
63E	11	67Z	3	881A	42	92A	2
63F	11	68B	3	88A	18	92A	18
63G	3	68D	3	88B	18	92B	18
63H	3	68F	3	88C	18	92D	18
63H	11	68G	3	88D	18	92F	18
63J	36	68H	3	88H	25	92G	18
63K	11	68J	36	88K	34	92M	2
63M	11	68K	3	88L	3	92R	25
63N	3	68N	36	88M	44	92Y	2
63N	11	68X	3	88N	44	92Z	2
63P	11	70A	20	88Z	44	93C	4
63S	3	70B	20	90A	18	93F	46
63T	3	70H	38	910A	18	93P	2
63W	3	71D	23	912A	41	95B	22
63Y	3	71G	2	913A	10	95C	22
63Z	3	71L	2	914A	18	95D	22
640A	18	71M	2	915A	18	96B	21
64A	24	72D	41	915D	18	96D	21
65A	30	72E	41	915E	18	96H	21
65B	30	73B	20	916A	41	96R	21
65C	20	73C	2	917A	41	96U	21
65D	26	73D	2	918A	41	96Z	20
66A	30	73Z	2	918B	41	97B	21
66C	30	74A	41	919A	41	97E	20
66E	30	74B	37	91A	18	97Z	21
66F	30	74B	41	91A	36	98C	21
66H	30	74C	7	91B	18	98G	20
66J	30	74C	18	91B	26	98H	7
670A	36	74G	36	91C	26	98J	21
67A	20	74Z	8	91D	18	98K	7
67B	24	75A	24	91D	26	98X	20
67C	33	75B	2	91E	11	98Z	20
67D	20	75F	8	91E	38		

Table K.2

Navy Occupational Codes and RAND Occupational Clusters

0002	20	0249	33	0429	36	0808	20
0005	20	0254	33	0430	36	0812	20
0020	20	0259	33	0436	36	0814	18
0026	20	0264	33	0438	36	0820	20
0028	20	0269	33	0439	36	0822	20
0030	20	0302	39	0443	36	0840	24
0031	20	0303	13	0445	39	0841	24
0049	20	0304	39	0450	21	0845	41
0055	20	0310	13	0455	36	0847	41
0101	33	0311	39	0457	36	0848	24
0102	33	0318	39	0466	36	0849	24
0104	33	0319	39	0488	39	0851	20
0105	33	0321	39	0490	36	0852	20
0106	33	0322	39	0495	36	0854	20
0107	9	0324	39	0501	39	0860	41
0107	33	0325	39	0505	39	0861	41
0108	33	0332	10	0506	36	0862	41
0109	20	0334	39	0507	39	0866	41
0110	9	0335	11	0510	11	0868	20
0110	33	0336	8	0525	11	0871	20
0111	33	0340	11	0530	11	0873	30
0113	26	0342	7	0535	11	0874	30
0115	33	0343	34	0545	11	0876	20
0118	33	0344	7	0550	11	0877	36
0121	33	0401	39	0560	11	0878	36
0131	33	0402	36	0569	11	0879	36
0135	33	0404	36	0575	11	0880	33
0140	33	0405	36	0579	11	0887	20
0150	33	0406	36	0580	11	0892	33
0160	33	0407	36	0612	39	0904	30
0160	34	0410	36	0614	39	0925	30
0161	34	0411	36	0619	39	0932	30
0163	33	0412	36	0624	36	0935	30
0164	9	0413	36	0625	36	0944	30
0166	33	0414	36	0626	36	0944	30
0167	34	0415	36	0628	36	0952	30
0169	34	0416	21	0746	36	0963	30
0170	42	0417	21	0747	36	0981	36
0214	33	0418	36	0749	29	0982	3
0215	34	0419	36	0750	29	0983	3
0224	33	0421	36	0751	29	0989	36
0229	33	0422	36	0800	20	0991	36
0234	33	0424	36	0801	20	1005	15
0244	33	0425	36	0801	29	1015	15

1025	15	1194	3	1456	36	1530	18
1026	29	1196	36	1458	36	1568	36
1045	15	1202	29	1460	36	1570	36
1045	15	1204	36	1461	36	1571	36
1050	15	1205	18	1464	36	1572	36
1101	36	1205	18	1465	36	1573	7
1102	36	1205	36	1468	36	1574	36
1103	3	1215	18	1471	36	1576	36
1104	3	1242	18	1473	36	1578	36
1105	3	1245	18	1476	18	1579	36
1105	18	1272	18	1479	36	1580	36
1105	18	1272	18	1480	18	1589	36
1106	36	1295	18	1480	36	1590	36
1107	36	1302	18	1485	18	1613	36
1108	36	1302	18	1486	36	1615	36
1110	36	1306	18	1491	36	1622	36
1112	18	1312	36	1493	36	1623	36
1112	18	1313	36	1494	36	1624	36
1114	36	1315	36	1495	36	1633	36
1115	36	1320	36	14CM	36	1646	36
1117	36	1321	36	14EB	36	1647	36
1118	36	1322	36	14EP	36	1654	36
1119	36	1323	3	14ET	36	1656	36
1120	36	1324	3	14FA	36	1657	36
1121	36	1327	36	14HB	36	1658	36
1127	36	1332	3	14IC	36	1664	36
1130	18	1333	3	14NM	36	1671	36
1130	18	1345	18	14NO	39	1672	36
1130	36	1370	18	14QM	36	1673	36
1138	36	1370	18	14RD	36	1674	36
1140	36	1401	36	14RM	36	1676	36
1141	36	1412	36	14RO	7	1677	36
1142	36	1413	36	14SF	36	1681	36
1143	36	1415	36	14TG	36	1682	36
1144	36	1416	36	14TM	7	1684	36
1145	36	1419	36	14TO	7	1685	36
1147	36	1420	36	14ZA	36	1733	7
1149	36	1421	36	1502	36	1734	7
1157	3	1424	36	1503	36	1736	36
1158	3	1425	36	1504	36	1737	7
1159	3	1427	36	1507	36	1738	36
1160	36	1428	36	1510	36	1743	7
1167	36	1429	36	1511	36	1781	7
1169	36	1430	36	1515	18	1808	36
1170	36	1447	7	1516	36	1809	36
1174	36	1450	36	1522	36	1820	36
1175	36	1452	36	1523	36	1913	18
1179	36	1454	36	1530	18	1918	18

1918	18	2181	41	2558	20	2905	2
1918	36	2186	40	2591	20	3015	40
1920	18	2190	41	2592	20	3015	40
1933	18	2192	41	2605	18	3020	40
1935	18	2240	21	2605	18	3020	40
1935	18	2301	7	2610	18	3035	40
1940	18	2306	8	2612	2	3111	2
1946	18	2306	41	2612	18	3115	2
1946	18	2310	41	2612	18	3120	18
1955	18	2318	36	2614	18	3122	2
1955	18	2319	36	2615	18	3125	18
1976	18	2321	7	2615	18	3125	18
1978	18	2323	41	2617	35	3126	18
1978	18	2332	46	2642	18	3127	18
1984	18	2350	7	2670	18	3127	18
1984	18	2354	7	2690	38	3154	2
1990	18	2358	7	2708	8	3215	20
1990	18	2363	36	2709	8	3215	20
1991	18	2365	41	2715	38	3217	20
1991	18	2375	7	2720	8	3219	20
2002	22	2376	7	2730	8	3219	20
2005	22	2378	7	2735	8	3220	20
2006	26	23EY	36	2739	8	3221	38
2008	22	23JH	36	2740	41	3230	20
2050	41	23MZ	36	2740	41	3236	20
2060	41	23NJ	36	2743	8	3236	20
2070	41	23TA	36	2748	18	3240	20
2071	41	23TM	36	2748	18	3242	20
2085	41	2410	38	2750	8	3242	20
2098	41	2412	38	2750	18	3245	20
2105	41	2412	38	2750	18	3245	20
2145	41	2415	38	2755	8	3250	20
2153	43	2430	38	2756	8	3250	20
2155	41	2445	27	2757	8	3251	20
2160	41	2505	20	2771	18	3251	20
2161	41	2510	20	2775	18	3251	38
2162	41	2514	2	2775	18	3254	20
2163	18	2515	20	2776	8	3255	20
2164	15	2517	20	2777	8	3260	20
2165	41	2518	20	2778	8	3260	20
2166	41	2520	20	2813	2	3262	20
2167	41	2525	20	2814	2	3265	20
2168	41	2529	20	2815	2	3270	20
2170	41	2530	20	2819	44	3270	20
2170	41	2535	20	2820	2	3274	20
2175	41	2554	20	2821	44	3277	20
2176	41	2556	20	2824	2	3283	20
2180	41	2557	20	2825	2	3283	20

3290	20	3527	18	4125	3	4316	3
3290	20	3529	18	4126	3	4324	3
3298	20	3535	18	4128	3	4330	41
3298	20	3538	18	4129	3	4330	41
3305	36	3601	25	4131	3	4333	3
3307	36	3701	20	4133	3	4340	41
3310	36	3740	20	4135	3	4340	41
3311	36	3745	20	4136	3	4355	3
3317	36	3750	20	4204	3	4361	3
3319	36	3801	27	4205	41	4366	3
3320	18	3802	27	4206	3	4382	25
3323	36	3803	27	4210	41	4398	25
3324	36	3804	27	4210	41	4402	25
3327	36	3805	27	4215	41	4403	25
3328	36	3806	27	4220	41	4404	25
3330	18	3807	27	4225	41	4502	25
3349	36	3808	27	4230	3	4503	25
3350	20	3809	27	4230	41	4505	25
3351	25	3811	27	4230	41	4513	36
3353	25	3812	27	4231	3	4533	36
3354	3	3813	27	4232	3	4615	3
3355	3	3814	27	4233	3	4621	3
3356	25	3815	27	4240	41	4626	3
3359	25	3825	27	4245	3	4632	3
3363	25	3851	27	4246	3	4666	3
3364	25	3901	21	4250	41	4668	3
3365	25	3905	21	4252	25	4671	3
3366	25	3907	21	4255	41	4672	3
3373	25	3910	18	4260	41	4673	3
3377	25	3910	18	4265	18	4703	36
3383	25	3910	21	4265	18	4709	3
3384	3	3912	21	4270	41	4711	36
3385	3	3923	21	4275	41	4712	36
3386	3	3924	21	4275	41	4716	36
3389	25	3925	18	4283	25	4718	36
3393	25	3925	21	4291	3	4720	36
3394	25	3943	18	4295	3	4721	36
3395	25	3943	18	4296	3	4723	36
3396	25	3950	18	4302	3	4727	36
3397	36	3965	18	4303	3	4728	36
3412	18	3965	18	4305	41	4731	3
3415	18	3970	18	4308	3	4737	36
3420	18	3980	18	4310	3	4738	36
3421	18	3981	18	4310	41	4743	3
3422	18	3981	18	4313	3	4745	36
3520	27	3985	18	4314	3	4746	36
3525	18	4123	3	4315	41	4747	36
3525	20	4124	3	4315	41	4749	36

4752	3	5707	9	6417	3	6647	36
4755	3	5708	9	6418	3	6648	36
4756	3	5710	9	6419	3	6649	36
4757	3	5712	9	6420	3	6650	36
4758	3	5761	18	6421	3	6653	36
4775	3	5805	3	6422	3	6658	36
4776	3	5904	41	6423	3	6659	36
4777	3	5904	41	6424	3	6660	36
4805	14	5907	9	6426	3	6663	36
4811	14	5908	3	6428	3	6664	36
4935	28	5913	41	6457	10	6668	36
4942	28	5915	9	6470	10	6669	36
4943	28	5917	41	6472	10	6673	36
4944	28	5925	41	6503	10	6677	37
4946	28	5925	41	6516	10	6680	36
4947	28	5927	41	6516	10	6684	36
4954	25	5930	41	6522	36	6686	36
4955	25	5931	12	6526	36	6688	36
4956	25	5932	12	6527	36	6689	36
5311	12	5960	41	6529	36	6694	36
5320	12	5961	41	6534	36	6695	36
5323	1	5965	41	6537	10	6701	36
5326	1	5970	41	6537	10	6702	18
5330	12	5977	41	6556	36	6702	36
5332	1	5977	41	6582	10	6704	10
5333	1	5980	41	6582	36	6704	10
5334	12	5996	41	6605	36	6704	36
5335	12	5996	41	6606	36	6705	36
5336	12	6010	9	6607	36	6708	18
5337	12	6021	9	6608	36	6710	36
5341	12	6083	18	6609	36	6713	36
5342	12	6083	18	6611	36	6714	36
5343	12	6090	10	6612	36	6715	10
5344	12	6104	3	6613	36	6715	10
5345	12	6105	25	6614	36	6715	36
5346	12	6275	41	6615	36	6716	36
5348	20	6280	41	6618	36	6716	41
5350	1	6281	41	6619	36	6717	10
5351	1	6282	41	6621	36	6717	36
5352	1	6301	37	6622	36	6718	36
5375	12	6313	37	6628	36	6719	36
5501	9	6314	8	6631	36	6721	36
5503	43	6315	8	6633	36	6801	36
5601	3	6380	10	6634	7	6802	36
5633	3	6403	13	6635	36	6803	29
5635	3	6410	3	6639	36	6810	36
5642	36	6415	3	6640	36	6901	4
5644	36	6416	3	6641	36	6902	4

6903	4	7232	3	7874	39	8018	41
6914	18	7241	41	7876	39	8026	41
6920	10	7241	41	7877	39	8026	41
6930	41	7245	41	7905	41	8035	41
6936	10	7249	41	7905	41	8050	41
6940	10	7249	41	7910	41	8050	41
6942	10	7251	41	7927	41	8074	18
6942	10	7251	41	7930	41	8076	41
6948	10	7273	41	7930	41	8112	18
6960	10	7273	41	7931	41	8115	18
6960	10	7285	34	7936	41	8116	18
6962	18	7352	20	7937	41	8116	18
6966	18	7353	9	7937	41	8118	18
6968	41	7356	9	7938	41	8125	18
6968	41	7412	46	7939	41	8126	32
6974	18	7420	41	7939	41	8133	37
6978	10	7420	41	7953	36	8141	18
6978	10	7435	41	7955	36	8143	32
6980	18	7435	41	7958	36	8144	32
6982	10	7445	41	7959	36	8147	32
6990	10	7450	41	7959	41	8148	32
6999	10	7450	41	7964	36	8152	18
7004	19	7601	25	7966	41	8175	18
7005	19	7603	3	7968	41	8175	18
7006	19	7606	3	7970	36	8176	18
7011	16	7607	3	7970	41	8176	18
7022	25	7609	19	7971	36	8177	18
7105	3	7610	3	7974	41	8177	18
7120	41	7612	3	7976	41	8180	18
7131	3	7613	3	7976	41	8189	18
7133	3	7614	3	7978	36	8189	18
7136	3	7615	3	7984	36	8190	18
7137	3	7616	3	7984	41	8190	18
7140	41	7617	3	7984	41	8361	3
7144	3	7618	3	7988	36	8362	3
7165	41	7815	42	7989	36	8375	3
7165	41	7821	39	7991	36	8376	3
7173	3	7825	39	7992	36	8377	3
7174	3	7827	39	7996	41	8378	3
7175	3	7834	39	7997	41	8379	3
7182	3	7835	36	7998	34	8380	3
7184	3	7836	36	7998	34	8391	3
7187	41	7841	39	7999	41	8401	26
7197	3	7846	39	8002	41	8402	26
7212	3	7851	39	8004	41	8403	26
7213	3	7861	39	8012	2	8404	26
7222	25	7872	39	8013	8	8406	26
7225	28	7873	39	8015	41	8407	26

8408	26	8614	34	8847	3	9067	38
8409	26	8614	34	8853	27	9068	38
8416	26	8618	18	8853	27	9069	38
8424	2	8620	18	8877	3	9069	38
8425	26	8621	4	8878	3	9070	38
8427	26	8625	18	8891	3	9071	38
8432	14	8638	18	8925	18	9071	38
8434	26	8638	18	8925	18	9072	38
8445	26	8644	4	8950	41	9072	38
8446	26	8647	4	8960	4	9073	38
8451	26	8653	18	8972	4	9074	38
8452	26	8653	18	8976	4	9074	38
8454	26	8654	18	8976	4	9075	38
8463	25	8656	38	8995	41	9076	38
8466	30	8658	4	9005	34	9077	38
8467	30	8660	18	9006	34	9078	38
8472	32	8662	4	9009	34	9079	38
8478	36	8668	18	9015	34	9080	10
8479	36	8670	18	9016	34	9080	10
8482	11	8672	18	9018	34	9082	35
8483	26	8673	1	9019	34	9084	34
8485	26	8675	18	9021	34	9085	41
8486	26	8680	18	9025	34	9086	41
8489	26	8680	18	9034	18	9087	41
8491	26	8685	18	9034	18	9102	21
8492	26	8687	18	9038	34	9103	21
8493	26	8694	41	9040	34	9104	21
8494	26	8696	20	9042	34	9105	21
8495	26	8703	11	9044	34	9116	21
8496	2	8707	11	9045	34	9124	21
8501	34	8708	11	9045	34	9125	21
8503	26	8732	36	9046	10	9126	21
8505	26	8752	25	9050	18	9131	21
8506	21	8753	25	9051	18	9132	21
8506	26	8765	25	9051	18	9133	7
8541	26	8783	11	9052	15	9134	21
8543	34	8803	3	9053	10	9135	21
8583	41	8804	27	9059	38	9137	21
8585	41	8805	3	9059	38	9138	21
8588	34	8806	3	9060	38	9141	21
8591	20	8815	27	9062	1	9147	21
8592	20	8815	27	9063	34	9149	21
8593	20	8819	3	9063	34	9158	21
8594	20	8832	3	9064	10	9160	21
8606	21	8835	3	9065	38	9166	21
8606	21	8842	3	9065	38	9169	21
8608	38	8843	3	9066	10	9170	8
8608	38	8845	3	9067	38	9174	8

9176	8	9238	10	9289	10	9345	42
9177	7	9238	10	9289	36	9345	42
9178	7	9238	36	9290	34	9348	42
9185	7	9242	34	9291	1	9348	42
9188	7	9242	34	9291	1	9353	42
9190	2	9244	36	9292	10	9353	42
9192	20	9245	36	9292	10	9362	42
9193	20	9246	34	9293	1	9362	42
9194	20	9247	10	9293	1	9363	42
9195	20	9249	36	9294	1	9363	42
9197	20	9250	10	9295	36	9364	42
9201	20	9250	10	9296	10	9364	42
9202	10	9251	36	9296	10	9369	42
9202	10	9252	34	9296	36	9370	42
9202	20	9252	34	9297	36	9371	42
9203	20	9252	36	9299	41	9371	42
9204	20	9253	34	9301	8	9372	42
9206	34	9254	34	9302	8	9372	42
9207	20	9254	34	9302	42	9373	42
9209	20	9255	34	9302	42	9374	42
9209	34	9256	36	9303	8	9374	42
9211	20	9257	36	9304	8	9375	42
9212	20	9258	34	9305	42	9378	42
9212	34	9258	34	9305	42	9378	42
9212	34	9258	36	9306	42	9384	42
9213	20	9259	34	9308	42	9384	42
9214	34	9259	36	9308	42	9390	42
9215	20	9261	34	9311	20	9390	42
9216	20	9261	34	9312	20	9392	42
9216	34	9266	34	9312	41	9393	42
9216	34	9267	36	9312	41	9393	42
9217	34	9268	34	9313	20	9394	42
9217	34	9272	10	9313	34	9394	42
9222	34	9273	34	9313	34	9395	42
9225	34	9274	34	9314	20	9401	7
9225	34	9275	34	9314	41	9402	36
9226	36	9278	34	9314	41	9403	7
9227	34	9278	34	9315	20	9404	41
9228	34	9279	34	9315	41	9405	18
9228	36	9282	34	9315	41	9405	18
9230	10	9283	34	9322	42	9420	18
9230	10	9283	34	9336	42	9420	18
9231	1	9283	36	9337	42	9421	18
9233	34	9284	34	9341	42	9422	18
9234	34	9285	36	9341	42	9424	18
9235	34	9286	34	9342	42	9425	43
9236	34	9286	34	9343	42	9430	18
9237	34	9286	36	9343	42	9431	18

9436	18	9535	6	9608	36	9825	21
9442	41	9540	10	9610	36	9835	21
9442	41	9543	6	9611	36	9835	21
9450	41	9545	22	9616	21	9840	21
9456	18	9554	1	9617	21	9840	21
9462	38	9559	25	9620	21	9845	21
9464	42	9560	6	9620	21	9845	21
9464	42	9560	6	9635	38	9850	21
9465	42	9562	12	9640	21	9850	21
9465	42	9563	12	9640	21	9851	21
9466	18	9565	6	9650	21	9851	21
9466	18	9565	6	9650	21	9852	21
9467	18	9566	44	9651	21	9852	21
9470	18	9567	6	9660	21	9853	21
9471	18	9567	6	9660	21	9853	21
9476	18	9570	25	9670	21	9860	21
9476	18	9571	22	9680	21	9860	21
9480	1	9573	22	9680	21	9865	21
9486	18	9575	6	9682	21	9905	41
9497	18	9575	6	9683	21	9920	41
9502	20	9575	22	9683	21	9930	18
9503	36	9579	34	9684	21	9935	18
9504	20	9580	2	9686	21	9940	38
9505	20	9580	18	9705	8	9942	38
9508	20	9580	18	9705	8	9950	18
9509	36	9581	25	9710	8	9960	18
9510	6	9582	6	9710	8	9960	18
9510	6	9582	6	9715	8	9965	18
9512	6	9583	3	9715	8	9965	18
9512	8	9585	6	9720	8	9967	41
9515	6	9585	40	9720	8	9970	18
9515	6	9586	40	9730	8	9980	18
9515	20	9588	40	9735	8	9981	18
9516	20	9590	2	9735	8	9990	18
9517	6	9590	6	9740	8	9992	18
9517	6	9590	6	9740	8	10C0	18
9517	8	9594	3	9745	8	10C0P	34
9518	20	9595	6	9745	8	10C0S	34
9519	20	9595	6	9750	8	10C0U	34
9520	20	9595	14	9755	8	10C0W	34
9522	20	9597	13	9755	8	11A1A	34
9525	6	9598	13	9781	8	11A1B	34
9525	6	9600	21	9781	8	11A1C	34
9526	36	9602	36	9810	21	11A1D	34
9527	36	9604	36	9815	21	11A1E	34
9530	21	9605	36	9815	21	11A1F	34
9533	34	9606	36	9817	21	11A1K	34
9534	34	9607	36	9825	21	11A1L	34

11A1M	34	11A4R	34	11F1F	34	11G4	34
11A1R	34	11A4T	34	11F1G	34	11H1B	34
11A1S	34	11A4U	34	11F1H	34	11H1C	34
11A1T	34	11A4V	34	11F1K	34	11H1D	34
11A1V	34	11A4W	34	11F1L	34	11H1E	34
11A1W	34	11A4Y	34	11F1M	34	11H1Y	34
11A1Y	34	11A4Z	34	11F1N	34	11H2A	34
11A1Z	34	11B1A	34	11F1Q	34	11H2B	34
11A2A	34	11B1B	34	11F1R	34	11H2C	34
11A2B	34	11B1C	34	11F1S	34	11H2E	34
11A2C	34	11B1N	34	11F1T	34	11H3A	34
11A2D	34	11B1S	34	11F1U	34	11H3C	34
11A2E	34	11B1Y	34	11F1Y	34	11H3D	34
11A2F	34	11B2A	34	11F1Z	34	11H3E	34
11A2H	34	11B2C	34	11F3B	34	11H3T	34
11A2J	34	11B3A	34	11F3C	34	11H3Y	34
11A2K	34	11B3B	34	11F3D	34	11H3Z	34
11A2L	34	11B3C	34	11F3E	34	11H4C	34
11A2M	34	11B3N	34	11F3F	34	11H4D	34
11A2N	34	11B3P	34	11F3G	34	11H4E	34
11A2Z	34	11B3R	34	11F3H	34	11H4Y	34
11A3A	34	11B3S	34	11F3K	34	11K1A	34
11A3B	34	11B3T	34	11F3L	34	11K1C	34
11A3C	34	11B3U	34	11F3M	34	11K1D	34
11A3D	34	11B3Y	34	11F3N	34	11K1Y	34
11A3E	34	11B3Z	34	11F3P	34	11K1Z	34
11A3F	34	11B4A	34	11F3Q	34	11K3A	34
11A3G	34	11B4B	34	11F3R	34	11K3B	34
11A3H	34	11B4C	34	11F3S	34	11K3C	34
11A3J	34	11B4S	34	11F3T	34	11K3D	34
11A3K	34	11B4U	34	11F3U	34	11K3N	34
11A3L	34	11B4Y	34	11F3Y	34	11K3Y	34
11A3M	34	11E1A	34	11F3Z	34	11K3Z	34
11A3N	34	11E1B	34	11F4B	34	11K4C	34
11A3P	34	11E1Z	34	11F4C	34	11K4D	34
11A3R	34	11E3A	34	11F4E	34	11K4U	34
11A3S	34	11E3B	34	11F4F	34	11K4Y	34
11A3T	34	11E3C	34	11F4G	34	11R1A	34
11A3U	34	11E3Q	34	11F4H	34	11R1B	34
11A3V	34	11E3Z	34	11F4K	34	11R1C	34
11A3W	34	11E4A	34	11F4L	34	11R1D	34
11A3Y	34	11E4B	34	11F4M	34	11R1G	34
11A3Z	34	11E4C	34	11F4N	34	11R1H	34
11A4A	34	11F1A	34	11F4Q	34	11R1J	34
11A4D	34	11F1B	34	11F4U	34	11R1Y	34
11A4F	34	11F1C	34	11F4Y	34	11R2A	34
11A4K	34	11F1D	34	11F4Z	34	11R2C	34
11A4M	34	11F1E	34	11G3	34	11R2D	34

11R2F	34	11S3T	34	12A3E	5	12E1Z	5
11R2G	34	11S3V	1	12A3T	5	12E3A	5
11R2H	34	11S3W	34	12A3U	5	12E3B	5
11R3A	34	11S3Y	34	12A3V	5	12E3Z	5
11R3B	34	11S4A	1	12A3Y	5	12E4A	5
11R3C	34	11S4B	1	12A3Z	5	12E4Z	5
11R3D	34	11S4E	34	12A4A	5	12F1A	5
11R3F	34	11S4G	1	12A4C	5	12F1C	5
11R3G	34	11S4U	34	12A4D	5	12F1D	5
11R3H	34	11S4V	1	12A4E	5	12F1F	5
11R3J	34	11S4W	34	12A4U	5	12F1H	5
11R3L	34	11S4Y	34	12A4V	5	12F1K	5
11R3P	34	11T1A	34	12A4W	5	12F1T	5
11R3R	34	11T1B	34	12A4Y	5	12F1U	5
11R3S	34	11T1L	34	12B1A	5	12F1W	5
11R3T	34	11T1R	34	12B1B	5	12F1Y	5
11R3Y	34	11T1S	34	12B1C	5	12F1Z	5
11R3Z	34	11T1T	34	12B1D	5	12F3A	5
11R4A	34	11T1Y	34	12B1E	5	12F3B	5
11R4D	34	11T1Z	34	12B1S	5	12F3C	5
11R4G	34	11T2A	34	12B1W	5	12F3D	5
11R4J	34	11T2B	34	12B1Y	5	12F3F	5
11R4T	34	11T2Z	34	12B1Z	5	12F3G	5
11R4Y	34	11T3A	34	12B2A	5	12F3H	5
11R4Z	34	11T3B	34	12B2C	5	12F3K	5
11S1A	1	11T3L	34	12B2D	5	12F3S	5
11S1B	1	11T3N	34	12B2E	5	12F3T	5
11S1C	34	11T3P	34	12B3A	5	12F3U	5
11S1D	34	11T3R	34	12B3B	5	12F3W	5
11S1E	34	11T3S	34	12B3C	5	12F3Y	5
11S1F	34	11T3T	34	12B3D	5	12F3Z	5
11S1G	1	11T3Y	34	12B3E	5	12F4A	5
11S1Y	34	11T3Z	34	12B3S	5	12F4C	5
11S2A	1	11T4A	34	12B3T	5	12F4D	5
11S2B	1	11T4B	34	12B3U	5	12F4F	5
11S2C	34	11T4Y	34	12B3W	5	12F4H	5
11S2D	34	12A1A	5	12B3Y	5	12F4K	5
11S2E	34	12A1C	5	12B3Z	5	12F4U	5
11S2F	34	12A1D	5	12B4A	5	12F4W	5
11S2G	1	12A1E	5	12B4B	5	12F4Y	5
11S3A	1	12A1T	5	12B4C	5	12F4Z	5
11S3B	1	12A1U	5	12B4D	5	12G3	5
11S3C	34	12A1W	5	12B4E	5	12G4	5
11S3D	34	12A1Y	5	12B4U	5	12K1A	5
11S3E	34	12A3A	5	12B4W	5	12K1B	5
11S3F	34	12A3B	5	12B4Y	5	12K3A	5
11S3G	1	12A3C	5	12E1A	5	12K3B	5
11S3S	34	12A3D	5	12E1B	5	12K3Z	5

Code	Value	Code	Value	Code	Value	Code	Value
12K4Y	5	12S1K	5	13B3D	6	1A011	42
12R1A	5	12S1L	5	13B3F	18	1A031	42
12R1C	5	12S1T	5	13B3J	4	1A051	42
12R1D	5	12S1W	5	13B3K	4	1A071	42
12R1E	5	12S1Y	5	13B3L	4	1A091	42
12R1G	5	12S3A	5	13B4B	4	1A100	17
12R1H	5	12S3B	5	13B4C	4	1A111B	42
12R1J	5	12S3C	5	13B4D	6	1A131B	42
12R1K	5	12S3D	5	13B4F	18	1A131C	17
12R1T	5	12S3E	5	13B4K	4	1A151B	42
12R1Y	5	12S3F	5	13D1	4	1A151C	17
12R1Z	5	12S3G	5	13D3	4	1A171B	42
12R3A	5	12S3H	5	13D4	4	1A171C	17
12R3B	5	12S3J	5	13M1	4	1A190	17
12R3C	5	12S3K	5	13M3	4	1A200	17
12R3D	5	12S3L	5	13M4	4	1A211	25
12R3E	5	12S3S	5	13S1A	41	1A231	25
12R3G	5	12S3U	5	13S1B	41	1A251	25
12R3H	5	12S3W	5	13S1C	41	1A271	25
12R3J	5	12S3Y	5	13S1D	41	1A291	25
12R3K	5	12S4A	5	13S1E	41	1A300	7
12R3L	34	12S4B	5	13S1S	41	1A311	7
12R3S	5	12S4C	5	13S2C	41	1A331	7
12R3T	5	12S4G	5	13S3A	41	1A351	7
12R3W	5	12S4H	5	13S3B	41	1A371	7
12R3Y	5	12S4J	5	13S3C	41	1A391	7
12R3Z	5	12S4L	5	13S3D	41	1A400	7
12R4A	5	12S4W	5	13S3E	41	1A411	7
12R4B	5	12S4Y	5	13S4	41	1A431	7
12R4C	5	12T1A	5	14N4	21	1A451	7
12R4D	5	12T1Y	5	15W1A	46	1A451D	7
12R4E	5	12T3A	5	15W3A	46	1A471	7
12R4G	5	12T3T	5	15W4	46	1A471D	7
12R4H	5	12T3Y	5	16A1	38	1A491	7
12R4J	5	12T3Z	5	16A4	38	1A500	36
12R4U	5	12T4A	5	16A4W	38	1A511	8
12R4W	5	12T4Y	5	16G1	18	1A531	8
12R4Y	5	13A3W	41	16G3	18	1A551	8
12S1A	5	13B1B	4	16G4	18	1A571	8
12S1B	5	13B1C	4	16P1	38	1A591	8
12S1C	5	13B1D	6	16P3	38	1C000	2
12S1D	5	13B1F	18	16P4	38	1C011	2
12S1F	5	13B1J	4	16R1	18	1C012	2
12S1G	5	13B1K	4	16R3	18	1C031	2
12S1H	5	13B3B	4	16R4	18	1C032	2
12S1J	5	13B3C	4	1A000	42	1C051	2

Table K.3

Air Force Occupational Codes and RAND Occupational Clusters

1C052	2	1C691	36	1N333K	20	1N373J	20
1C071	2	1N000	21	1N334A	20	1N374A	20
1C072	2	1N011	21	1N334B	20	1N374B	20
1C091	2	1N031	21	1N334C	20	1N374C	20
1C092	2	1N051	21	1N334D	20	1N374D	20
1C100	4	1N071	21	1N334E	20	1N374G	20
1C111	4	1N091	21	1N334G	20	1N374J	20
1C131	4	1N111	21	1N335A	20	1N375A	20
1C151	4	1N131	21	1N335C	20	1N375C	20
1C171	4	1N151	21	1N335D	20	1N375D	20
1C191	4	1N171	21	1N335E	20	1N375E	20
1C200	4	1N191	21	1N335F	20	1N390	20
1C211	4	1N200	7	1N351A	20	1N411	21
1C231	4	1N211	7	1N352A	20	1N431	21
1C251	4	1N231	7	1N352B	20	1N451	21
1C271	4	1N251	7	1N352C	20	1N471	21
1C291	4	1N271	7	1N352E	20	1N491	21
1C300	7	1N291	7	1N353A	20	1N500	7
1C311	7	1N312A	20	1N353D	20	1N511	7
1C331	7	1N312C	20	1N353E	20	1N531	7
1C351	7	1N312E	20	1N353F	20	1N551	7
1C371	7	1N313A	20	1N353J	20	1N571	7
1C391	7	1N313D	20	1N354A	20	1N591	7
1C400	7	1N313E	20	1N354B	20	1N600	7
1C411	7	1N313K	20	1N354C	20	1N611	21
1C431	7	1N313L	20	1N354D	20	1N631	21
1C451	7	1N314A	20	1N354E	20	1N651	21
1C471	7	1N314B	20	1N354G	20	1N671	21
1C491	7	1N314C	20	1N354J	20	1N691	21
1C500	7	1N314D	20	1N355A	20	1S000	22
1C511A	39	1N314E	20	1N355C	20	1S011	22
1C511C	39	1N314G	20	1N355D	20	1S031	22
1C531A	39	1N314J	20	1N355E	20	1S051	22
1C531B	39	1N315A	20	1N371A	20	1S071	22
1C531C	39	1N315C	20	1N372A	20	1S091	22
1C551	7	1N315D	20	1N372B	20	1T000	20
1C551D	7	1N315E	20	1N372C	20	1T011	20
1C571D	39	1N332A	20	1N372E	20	1T031	20
1C591	39	1N332B	20	1N373A	20	1T051	20
1C600	36	1N332F	20	1N373B	20	1T071	20
1C611	36	1N333A	20	1N373C	20	1T091	20
1C631	36	1N333D	20	1N373D	20	1T100	9
1C651	36	1N333F	20	1N373E	20	1T111	9
1C671	36	1N333J	20	1N373F	20	1T131	9

1T151	9	2A051A	36	2A351B	36	2A551L	37
1T171	9	2A051B	36	2A351C	36	2A552	3
1T191	9	2A071A	36	2A352A	36	2A553A	36
1T200	26	2A071B	36	2A352B	36	2A553B	36
1T211	26	2A090	36	2A352C	36	2A553C	36
1T231	26	2A111	3	2A353A	36	2A571	3
1T251	26	2A112	3	2A353B	3	2A572	3
1T271	26	2A113	36	2A353J	3	2A573A	36
1T291	26	2A114	36	2A371	36	2A573B	36
1W000	46	2A117	36	2A372	36	2A573C	36
1W011	46	2A131	3	2A373A	36	2A590	36
1W031	46	2A132	3	2A373B	3	2A600	3
1W031A	46	2A133	36	2A373J	3	2A611B	3
1W051	46	2A134	36	2A390	36	2A611C	3
1W051A	46	2A137	36	2A411	36	2A611D	3
1W071A	46	2A151	3	2A412	36	2A611E	3
1W091	46	2A152	3	2A413	7	2A612	3
20C0	18	2A153	36	2A431	36	2A613	3
20C0W	18	2A154	36	2A432	36	2A614	3
21A1	18	2A157	36	2A433	7	2A615	3
21A1A	18	2A171	3	2A451	36	2A616	3
21A3	18	2A172	3	2A452	36	2A631B	3
21A3A	18	2A173	36	2A453	7	2A631C	3
21A4	18	2A174	36	2A471	36	2A631D	3
21G1	18	2A177	36	2A472	36	2A631E	3
21G3	18	2A190	36	2A473	7	2A632	3
21G4	18	2A300	36	2A490	36	2A633	3
21L1	18	2A311A	36	2A512A	3	2A634	3
21L3	18	2A311B	36	2A512B	3	2A635	3
21L3W	18	2A311C	36	2A513A	36	2A636	3
21L4	18	2A312A	36	2A513B	36	2A651A	3
21M1A	41	2A312B	36	2A513C	36	2A651B	3
21M1B	41	2A312C	36	2A531A	37	2A652	3
21M3	41	2A313A	36	2A531B	37	2A653	3
21M3A	41	2A313B	3	2A531C	37	2A654	3
21M3B	41	2A313E	3	2A531D	37	2A655	3
21M4	41	2A313H	3	2A531E	37	2A656	3
21S1	18	2A331A	36	2A531F	37	2A671A	3
21S3	18	2A331B	36	2A531G	37	2A671B	3
21S4	18	2A331C	36	2A531H	37	2A672	3
21T1	18	2A332A	36	2A532A	3	2A673	3
21T3	18	2A332B	36	2A532B	3	2A674	3
21T4	18	2A332C	36	2A532C	3	2A675	3
2A000	36	2A333A	36	2A533A	36	2A676	3
2A011A	36	2A333B	3	2A533B	36	2A690	3
2A011B	36	2A333C	3	2A533C	36	2A691	3
2A031A	36	2A333H	3	2A551J	37	2A692	3
2A031B	36	2A351A	36	2A551K	37	2A711	25

Code	Value	Code	Value	Code	Value	Code	Value
2A712	28	2E251A	36	2M011B	36	2T031	2
2A713	3	2E251B	36	2M012A	36	2T051	2
2A714	9	2E251C	36	2M013	36	2T071	2
2A731	25	2E271	36	2M013A	36	2T091	2
2A732	28	2E291	36	2M031	36	2T100	45
2A733	3	2E311	36	2M031A	36	2T111	37
2A734	9	2E331	36	2M031B	36	2T131	37
2A751	25	2E351	36	2M032	36	2T151	37
2A752	28	2E371	36	2M032A	36	2T171	37
2A753	3	2E391	36	2M033	36	2T191	37
2A754	9	2E411	36	2M033A	36	2T200	2
2A771	25	2E431	36	2M051	36	2T211	2
2A772	28	2E451	36	2M052	36	2T231	2
2A773	3	2E471	36	2M053	36	2T251	2
2A774	9	2E491	36	2M071	36	2T271	2
2A790	25	2E611	36	2M072	36	2T291	2
2E000	7	2E612	36	2M073	36	2T300	3
2E011	36	2E613	36	2M090	36	2T311	3
2E031	36	2E631	36	2P000	36	2T312A	3
2E051	36	2E632	36	2P011	36	2T312B	3
2E071	36	2E633	36	2P031	36	2T331	3
2E091	36	2E651	36	2P051	36	2T332A	3
2E111	36	2E652	36	2P071	36	2T332B	3
2E112	36	2E653	36	2P091	36	2T351	3
2E113	36	2E671	36	2R000	37	2T352A	3
2E114	36	2E672	36	2R011	37	2T352B	3
2E131	36	2E673	36	2R031	37	2T370	3
2E132	36	2E690	7	2R051	37	2T390	3
2E133	36	2E800	36	2R071	37	2W000	36
2E134	36	2E811	36	2R091	37	2W011	36
2E151	36	2E831	36	2R100	37	2W031	36
2E152	36	2E851	36	2R111	37	2W051	36
2E153	36	2E871	36	2R131	37	2W071	36
2E154	36	2E891	36	2R151	37	2W091	36
2E171	36	2F000	25	2R171	37	2W100	36
2E172	36	2F011	25	2R191	37	2W111C	36
2E173	36	2F031	25	2S000	2	2W111E	36
2E174	36	2F051	25	2S011	2	2W111F	36
2E190	36	2F071	25	2S012	8	2W111K	36
2E211	36	2F091	25	2S031	2	2W111L	36
2E211A	36	2G000	2	2S032	8	2W111Z	36
2E211B	36	2G011	2	2S051	2	2W131C	36
2E211C	36	2G031	2	2S052	8	2W131E	36
2E231	36	2G051	2	2S071	2	2W131F	36
2E231A	36	2G071	2	2S072	8	2W131K	36
2E231B	36	2G091	2	2S090	2	2W131L	36
2E231C	36	2M000	36	2T000	2	2W131Z	36
2E251	36	2M011A	36	2T011	2	2W151	36

2W171	36	34M4	18	3C371	8	3E771	16
2W191	36	35B1	27	3C391	8	3E791	16
2W200	36	35B3	27	3E000	43	3E800	36
2W211	36	35B4	27	3E011	3	3E811	29
2W231	36	35P1	38	3E012	3	3E831	29
2W251	36	35P3	38	3E031	3	3E851	29
2W271	36	35P4	38	3E032	3	3E871	29
2W291	36	36M1	18	3E051	3	3E891	29
30C0	18	36M3	18	3E052	3	3E900	13
30C0W	18	36P1	18	3E071	3	3E911	13
31P1	18	36P3	18	3E072	3	3E931	13
31P3	18	36P4	18	3E090	3	3E951	13
31P4	18	36P4W	18	3E111	3	3E971	13
32E1A	41	38M1	18	3E131	3	3E991	13
32E1B	41	38M3	18	3E151	3	3H000	38
32E1C	41	38M4	18	3E171	3	3H031	38
32E1E	41	3A000	8	3E191	3	3H051	38
32E1F	41	3A011	2	3E211	9	3H071	38
32E1G	41	3A031	2	3E231	9	3H091	38
32E1H	41	3A051	2	3E251	9	3M000	18
32E1J	41	3A071	2	3E271	9	3M011	18
32E1K	41	3A091	2	3E291	9	3M031	18
32E1V	41	3C000	8	3E411	25	3M051	18
32E1W	41	3C011	8	3E412	25	3M071	18
32E3A	41	3C012	8	3E413	14	3M091	18
32E3B	41	3C031	8	3E431	25	3N000	38
32E3C	41	3C032	8	3E432	25	3N090	38
32E3D	41	3C051	8	3E433	14	3N100	27
32E3E	41	3C052	8	3E451	25	3N131A	27
32E3F	41	3C071	8	3E452	25	3N131B	27
32E3G	41	3C072	8	3E453	14	3N131C	27
32E3H	41	3C090	8	3E471	25	3N131D	27
32E3J	41	3C111	7	3E472	25	3N131E	27
32E3K	41	3C131	7	3E473	14	3N131F	27
32E4	41	3C132	7	3E490	25	3N131G	27
33S1	8	3C151	7	3E511	43	3N131H	27
33S1A	8	3C171	7	3E531	43	3N131J	27
33S1B	8	3C172	7	3E551	43	3N131K	27
33S1C	8	3C191	7	3E571	43	3N131L	27
33S3	8	3C192	7	3E591	43	3N131M	27
33S3A	8	3C211	8	3E611	37	3N131N	27
33S3B	8	3C231	8	3E631	37	3N131P	27
33S3C	8	3C251	8	3E671	37	3N131R	27
33S3W	8	3C271	8	3E691	37	3N131S	27
33S4	8	3C291	8	3E700	16	3N131V	27
33S4W	8	3C311	8	3E711	16	3N151A	27
34M1	18	3C331	8	3E731	16	3N151B	27
34M3	18	3C351	8	3E751	16	3N151C	27

3N151D	27	3S031	2	42E4	33	43P4	20
3N151E	27	3S032	2	42F1	33	43T1A	24
3N151F	27	3S051	2	42F3	33	43T1B	24
3N151G	27	3S052	2	42G1D	26	43T1E	24
3N151H	27	3S071	2	42G3	26	43T3A	24
3N151J	27	3S072	2	42G3A	26	43T3B	24
3N151K	27	3S090	2	42G3B	26	43T3C	41
3N151L	27	3S100	20	42G3C	26	43T3D	41
3N151M	27	3S131	2	42G3D	26	43T3E	24
3N151N	27	3S171	2	42N1A	20	43T3F	24
3N151P	27	3S191	2	42N3A	20	43T3G	24
3N151R	27	3S200	20	42N3B	20	43T4A	24
3N151S	27	3S211	20	42N4A	20	43T4B	24
3N151V	27	3S231	20	42P3	20	43T4D	41
3N171A	27	3S251	20	42P3A	20	43V3E	24
3N171B	27	3S271	20	42S1	20	43Y3A	33
3N171C	27	3S291	40	42S3	20	43Y4A	33
3N171D	27	3U000	2	42S4	20	44A1	33
3N171E	27	3U031	2	42T1	30	44A3	33
3N171F	27	3U071	2	42T3	30	44D1B	33
3N171G	27	3U091	2	43A1	24	44D3A	33
3N171H	27	3V000	32	43A3	24	44D3B	33
3N171J	27	3V011	32	43A4	24	44D3C	33
3N171K	27	3V012	32	43D1	20	44D3D	33
3N171L	27	3V013	32	43D3	20	44D3F	33
3N171M	27	3V031	32	43E1A	41	44D3G	33
3N171N	27	3V032	32	43E1B	41	44D3H	33
3N171P	27	3V033	32	43E1D	41	44D3K	33
3N171R	27	3V051	32	43E1E	41	44E1A	33
3N171S	27	3V052	32	43E1F	41	44E3A	33
3N171V	27	3V053	32	43E3A	41	44E4A	33
3N190	27	3V071	32	43E3B	41	44F1	33
3N200	27	3V072	32	43E3C	41	44F3	33
3N231	27	3V073	32	43E3D	41	44F4	33
3N271	27	3V090	32	43E3E	41	44G1	33
3N291	27	40C0A	20	43E3F	41	44G3	33
3P000	22	40C0B	24	43E3G	41	44H3	33
3P011	22	40C0C	20	43E4A	41	44H4	33
3P031	22	40C0D	11	43E4C	41	44K1C	33
3P051	22	40C0E	30	43E4E	41	44K1E	33
3P071	22	41A1	20	43E4F	41	44K3	33
3R000	25	41A3	20	43H1	41	44K3A	33
3R031	25	41A4	20	43H3	41	44K3B	33
3R051	25	42B1	30	43H4	41	44K3C	33
3R071	25	42B3	30	43M1	24	44K3D	33
3R091	25	42B4	30	43M3	24	44K3E	33
3S000	2	42E1	33	43P1	20	44K3F	33
3S011	2	42E3	33	43P3	20	44K3G	33

44K3H	33	45B3F	33	46N1C	30	48G3P	33
44K3J	33	45B3G	33	46N1D	30	48G3R	33
44K3K	33	45E3A	33	46N1E	30	48G4	33
44K3M	33	45E3B	33	46N1F	30	48P1	33
44K4F	33	45E3C	33	46N1G	30	48P3	33
44M1	33	45E3D	33	46N1H	30	48P4	33
44M1B	33	45E3E	33	46N3	30	4A000	2
44M1D	33	45E3G	33	46N3A	30	4A011	2
44M1E	33	45G1D	33	46N3B	30	4A031	2
44M1F	33	45G3	33	46N3C	30	4A051	2
44M1G	33	45G3A	33	46N3D	30	4A071	2
44M1H	33	45G3B	33	46N3E	30	4A091	2
44M1J	33	45G3C	33	46N3F	30	4A100	2
44M3	33	45G3D	33	46N3G	30	4A111	2
44M3A	33	45N1	33	46N3H	30	4A131	2
44M3B	33	45N3	33	46N4B	30	4A151	2
44M3C	33	45P3	33	46P3A	30	4A171	2
44M3D	33	45S1	33	46S1	30	4A191	2
44M3E	33	45S1A	33	46S3	30	4A200	36
44M3F	33	45S1C	33	47B1	11	4A211	36
44M3G	33	45S1F	33	47B3	11	4A231	36
44M3H	33	45S1G	33	47D3	11	4A251	36
44M3J	33	45S1H	33	47E3	11	4A271	36
44N1	33	45S3	33	47G1A	11	4A291	36
44N3	33	45S3A	33	47G1C	11	4B000	41
44N4	33	45S3B	33	47G3A	11	4B011	14
44P1A	33	45S3C	33	47G3B	11	4B031	14
44P3A	33	45S3D	33	47G3C	11	4B051	14
44R1A	33	45S3E	33	47G4A	11	4B071	14
44R3	33	45S3F	33	47G4B	11	4B091	14
44R3A	33	45S3G	33	47H1	11	4C000	20
44R3B	33	45S3H	33	47H3	11	4C011	20
44R3E	33	45S3J	33	47K3	11	4C031	20
44S3A	33	45U3A	33	47P1	11	4C051	20
44S3B	33	45U3B	33	47P3	11	4C071	20
44T1	33	46A1	30	47S1	33	4C091	20
44T3	33	46A3	30	47S3	33	4D000	18
44Y3A	33	46A4	30	47S4	33	4D011	18
44Z1	33	46F1	30	48A1	33	4D031	18
44Z3	33	46F3	30	48A3	33	4D051	18
44Z4	33	46F4	30	48A4	33	4D071	18
45A1	33	46G3	30	48E3	33	4D091	18
45A3	33	46M1	30	48E4	33	4E011	14
45B3	33	46M3	30	48F1	33	4E031	14
45B3A	33	46M4	30	48F3	33	4E051	14
45B3B	33	46N1	30	48F4	33	4E071	14
45B3D	33	46N1A	30	48G1	33	4E091	14
45B3E	33	46N1B	30	48G3	33	4F000	26

4F011	26	4P000	11	4Y032	25	62E3C	41
4F031	26	4P011	11	4Y051	11	62E3E	41
4F051	26	4P031	11	4Y052	25	62E3F	41
4F071	26	4P051	11	4Y071	11	62E3G	41
4F091	26	4P071	11	4Y072	25	62E3H	41
4H000	26	4P091	11	51J1	20	62E3P	41
4H011	26	4R000	26	51J3	20	62E3V	41
4H031	26	4R011	26	51J4	20	62E3W	41
4H051	26	4R031	26	52R3	20	62E4	41
4H071	26	4R031B	26	52R3A	20	62E4W	41
4H091	26	4R051	26	52R3C	20	63A1	18
4J000	30	4R051A	26	52R4	20	63A1W	18
4J011	30	4R051B	26	5J000	23	63A3	18
4J012	30	4R051C	26	5J031	23	63A3P	18
4J031	30	4R071	26	5J051	23	63A3R	18
4J032	30	4R071A	26	5J071	23	63A3U	18
4J051	30	4R071B	26	5J091	23	63A3V	18
4J052	30	4R071C	26	5R000	2	63A3W	18
4J071	30	4R090	26	5R011	2	63A4	18
4J072	30	4T000	26	5R031	2	63A4P	18
4J091	30	4T011	26	5R051	2	63A4R	18
4J092	30	4T012	26	5R071	2	63A4T	18
4M000	20	4T031	26	5R091	2	63A4U	18
4M011	20	4T032	26	60C0	18	63A4V	18
4M031	20	4T051	26	61S1A	41	63A4W	18
4M051	20	4T052	26	61S1B	24	64P1	18
4M071	20	4T053	26	61S1C	41	64P3	18
4M091	20	4T071	26	61S1D	41	64P4	18
4N000	26	4T072	26	61S1E	41	65A3	15
4N011	26	4T073	26	61S3A	41	65A4	15
4N031	26	4T090	26	61S3B	24	65F1	15
4N031A	26	4U011	26	61S3C	41	65F3	15
4N051	26	4U031	26	61S3D	41	65F4	15
4N051A	26	4U051	26	61S3E	41	65W1	15
4N051B	26	4U071	26	61S3W	41	65W3	15
4N071	26	4U091	26	61S4	41	65W4	15
4N091	26	4V000	31	61S4W	41	6C000	2
4N111	26	4V011	31	62E1A	41	6C011	2
4N131	26	4V031	31	62E1B	41	6C031	2
4N151	26	4V031A	31	62E1C	41	6C051	2
4N151B	26	4V051	31	62E1E	41	6C071	2
4N151C	26	4V051A	31	62E1F	41	6C091	2
4N151D	26	4V071	31	62E1G	41	6F000	2
4N171	26	4V071A	31	62E1H	41	6F011	2
4N171B	26	4V090	31	62E1P	41	6F031	2
4N171C	26	4Y000	11	62E1W	41	6F051	2
4N171D	26	4Y011	11	62E3A	41	6F111	2
4N191	26	4Y031	11	62E3B	41	6F131	2

6F151	2	81C0W	20	8A000	44	8S100	21
6F171	2	81T0	20	8B000	20	8T000	20
6F191	2	81T0U	20	8B100	20	91C0	18
71S1	18	81T0W	20	8C000	20	91C0W	18
71S3	18	82A0	20	8D000	20	91W0	18
71S4	18	82A0W	20	8F000	2	92J0	20
7S000	22	83R0	40	8G000	22	97E0	18
7S031	22	84H0	38	8J000	22	9D000	18
7S071	22	86M0	18	8M000	2	9E000	2
7S091	22	86P0	38	8P000	2	9G000	18
80C0	20	87G0	15	8P100	21	9L000	20
80C0W	20	88A0	18	8R000	40	0100	2
81C0	20	88P0	38	8S000	36		

Table K.4

Marine Corps Occupational Codes and RAND Occupational Clusters

0121	2	0842	39	2171	36	2823	36
0131	2	0844	10	2181	29	2826	36
0151	2	0847	46	2300	29	2831	36
0161	2	0848	10	2305	10	2832	36
0180	18	0861	10	2305	10	2834	36
0193	2	1100	25	2311	29	2841	36
0200	21	1120	41	2336	29	2861	36
0201	21	1141	3	2340	18	2871	36
0202	21	1142	3	2340	18	2874	36
0203	21	1161	3	2500	7	2881	36
0204	21	1169	25	2510	6	2885	36
0206	21	1171	9	2512	7	2887	36
0207	21	1181	9	2513	7	2889	36
0210	21	1300	9	2515	36	2891	36
0211	21	1301	41	2519	36	3000	2
0231	21	1302	41	2531	7	3001	18
0241	21	1310	41	2532	7	3002	18
0251	20	1316	25	2534	7	3010	18
0261	43	1341	3	2535	7	3043	2
0291	21	1345	9	2536	7	3044	2
0300	10	1349	3	2537	7	3051	2
0301	10	1361	43	2542	7	3052	2
0302	10	1371	9	2549	7	3100	44
0311	10	1390	18	2591	7	3102	18
0313	10	1391	25	2600	21	3102	18
0321	10	1800	10	2602	21	3112	44
0331	10	1801	10	2621	7	3300	18
0341	10	1801	10	2629	7	3302	18
0351	10	1802	10	2631	7	3302	18
0352	10	1803	10	2651	21	3361	2
0369	10	1812	10	2671	20	3381	18
0400	2	2100	29	2673	20	3400	2
0401	18	2102	18	2674	20	3401	15
0402	18	2110	41	2675	20	3404	15
0411	37	2111	36	2691	21	3410	15
0430	18	2120	10	2800	36	3410	15
0431	2	2125	41	2802	6	3441	2
0451	2	2131	29	2805	6	3451	2
0481	2	2141	3	2810	6	3500	45
0491	44	2146	3	2811	36	3501	18
0800	10	2147	3	2813	36	3502	18
0801	10	2147	3	2818	36	3510	18
0802	10	2149	3	2821	36	3513	3
0811	10	2161	25	2822	36	3521	3

Code	Cluster	Code	Cluster	Code	Cluster	Code	Cluster
3523	3	5548	27	6031	17	6333	3
3529	3	5563	27	6032	17	6335	3
3531	45	5565	27	6035	3	6336	3
3533	45	5566	27	6042	2	6337	3
3537	45	5700	13	6046	37	6386	36
4000	8	5702	38	6047	37	6391	36
4010	8	5711	13	6051	3	6411	37
4010	8	5800	22	6053	3	6412	36
4066	8	5801	18	6055	3	6413	36
4067	8	5803	18	6056	3	6414	37
4099	8	5804	18	6057	3	6423	36
4100	2	5805	18	6060	9	6431	3
4130	18	5811	22	6071	3	6432	3
4133	2	5821	22	6072	3	6433	3
4300	38	5831	22	6073	3	6434	3
4301	38	5900	36	6075	25	6462	36
4302	38	5902	41	6081	3	6463	36
4341	38	5910	41	6083	3	6464	36
4400	23	5942	36	6085	3	6465	36
4401	20	5948	36	6086	3	6466	36
4402	20	5950	4	6087	3	6467	36
4421	23	5952	36	6091	3	6468	36
4429	23	5953	36	6092	3	6469	36
4430	20	5954	36	6094	3	6482	36
4600	32	5959	36	6112	3	6483	36
4602	27	5962	36	6113	3	6484	36
4602	27	5963	36	6114	3	6485	36
4611	32	5970	8	6122	3	6491	36
4615	25	5974	36	6123	3	6492	36
4641	32	5979	36	6124	3	6493	36
4671	32	5993	36	6152	3	6494	36
4691	32	6000	3	6153	3	6500	29
5500	27	6001	18	6154	3	6502	41
5502	27	6002	18	6172	17	6502	41
5519	27	6004	18	6173	17	6511	29
5519	27	6004	18	6300	36	6531	29
5521	27	6011	3	6302	18	6541	29
5523	27	6013	3	6302	18	6591	29
5526	27	6014	3	6311	36	6600	2
5528	27	6015	3	6313	36	6601	18
5534	27	6016	3	6314	36	6602	18
5536	27	6017	3	6315	36	6604	18
5537	27	6019	3	6316	36	6604	18
5541	27	6022	3	6317	36	6672	2
5543	27	6025	3	6322	36	6673	8
5544	27	6026	3	6323	36	6800	46
5546	27	6027	3	6324	36	6802	46
5547	27	6030	17	6331	3	6802	46

6802	46	7252	4	7545	34	7588	5
6802	46	7253	4	7556	34	7598	34
6821	46	7291	4	7557	34	7599	34
6842	46	7300	2	7558	34	8412	40
7000	42	7314	17	7560	34	9802	27
7002	38	7372	42	7561	34	9803	27
7041	2	7380	5	7562	34	9803	27
7051	16	7381	7	7563	34	9805	27
7200	10	7382	42	7564	34	9805	27
7201	10	7501	34	7565	34	9811	27
7201	10	7507	34	7566	34	9812	27
7204	10	7509	34	7567	34	9901	10
7208	34	7521	34	7568	34	9904	18
7210	34	7522	34	7574	5	9906	10
7212	10	7523	34	7580	5	9907	5
7234	39	7524	5	7582	5	9914	20
7236	39	7525	5	7583	5	9925	20
7242	39	7541	34	7585	5	9991	2
7251	4	7543	34	7587	5	9999	2

Table K.5

Civil Service Occupational Codes and RAND Occupational Clusters

18	41	230	18	413	24	644	26
19	22	233	18	414	24	645	26
20	38	235	18	415	24	646	26
21	2	246	18	430	24	647	26
23	38	260	18	435	24	648	26
25	18	299	2	437	24	649	26
28	41	302	2	454	24	651	30
29	14	303	2	455	24	660	20
60	20	304	2	457	24	661	11
80	18	305	2	458	13	662	33
81	16	309	2	460	24	664	30
83	22	312	2	462	24	665	20
85	22	313	2	470	24	667	30
86	22	318	2	471	24	668	33
101	20	319	2	480	24	669	2
102	20	322	2	482	24	670	20
105	18	326	2	486	24	671	20
110	15	332	8	487	24	673	20
119	2	334	8	501	15	675	2
130	38	335	8	503	2	679	2
131	38	340	18	505	15	680	11
132	21	341	18	510	15	681	11
134	21	342	2	511	15	682	11
142	18	343	18	525	2	683	11
150	43	344	2	530	2	688	41
160	20	346	18	540	2	690	41
170	38	350	2	544	2	698	14
180	20	351	25	545	2	701	24
181	20	356	2	560	15	704	26
184	20	357	2	561	2	803	41
185	20	359	2	602	33	804	41
186	20	360	18	603	26	806	41
187	20	361	2	610	30	807	41
188	30	382	7	620	30	808	41
189	30	390	7	621	26	809	41
190	20	391	6	622	26	810	41
201	18	392	7	625	26	817	43
203	2	394	7	630	20	818	43
204	2	401	24	631	30	819	41
205	18	403	24	633	30	828	41
212	18	404	26	636	30	830	41
221	18	405	20	638	30	840	41
222	18	408	24	640	14	850	41
223	18	410	24	642	26	854	41

855	41	1105	18	1601	3	2508	36
856	36	1106	2	1630	18	2602	36
858	41	1107	2	1640	18	2604	36
861	41	1130	18	1654	38	2606	36
871	41	1144	18	1658	18	2608	36
873	41	1150	41	1667	18	2610	36
881	41	1152	2	1670	2	2805	3
892	41	1160	15	1701	20	2810	3
893	41	1163	15	1702	20	2854	3
894	41	1170	18	1710	20	2892	3
895	14	1171	18	1712	20	3103	9
896	41	1173	18	1720	20	3105	9
904	20	1176	18	1740	20	3106	9
905	20	1202	23	1750	20	3111	9
945	23	1221	20	1801	22	3306	37
950	23	1222	20	1802	22	3314	36
962	23	1306	24	1810	22	3359	36
963	23	1310	41	1811	18	3364	37
967	23	1311	13	1812	22	3414	25
986	23	1313	41	1815	34	3416	25
990	23	1315	41	1825	34	3417	25
992	23	1320	41	1890	22	3422	9
995	23	1321	41	1897	22	3428	25
998	23	1330	41	1910	36	3431	25
999	23	1340	46	2001	2	3502	9
1001	38	1341	46	2003	18	3508	9
1008	32	1360	41	2005	2	3511	26
1010	38	1361	43	2010	2	3515	26
1015	38	1370	43	2030	18	3543	25
1016	38	1371	43	2032	2	3546	9
1020	32	1372	43	2050	2	3602	9
1021	43	1373	43	2091	2	3603	9
1035	38	1374	43	2101	44	3604	9
1040	20	1382	18	2102	44	3605	9
1046	20	1386	32	2130	18	3606	9
1051	27	1410	20	2131	44	3609	9
1054	32	1411	20	2135	44	3610	9
1056	32	1412	20	2144	25	3611	9
1060	32	1420	20	2150	18	3653	9
1071	27	1421	20	2151	44	3702	25
1082	38	1510	18	2152	4	3703	25
1083	38	1515	41	2154	4	3705	28
1084	38	1520	41	2161	25	3707	25
1087	38	1521	2	2181	34	3708	25
1101	2	1529	41	2183	5	3711	25
1102	18	1530	2	2185	42	3712	25
1103	18	1531	41	2502	36	3720	25
1104	18	1550	8	2504	36	3722	25

3725	3	4602	25	5330	3	6605	36
3727	25	4604	9	5334	3	6606	36
3735	25	4605	9	5335	3	6610	36
3736	36	4607	9	5350	3	6641	29
3741	25	4616	9	5352	3	6652	29
3769	25	4618	9	5364	3	6656	36
3802	25	4639	9	5365	3	6902	2
3806	25	4654	9	5378	3	6903	2
3807	25	4716	3	5384	25	6904	2
3808	25	4717	9	5402	25	6907	2
3809	25	4737	3	5403	25	6910	2
3816	25	4741	9	5406	25	6912	2
3818	25	4742	3	5407	25	6914	2
3819	25	4749	9	5408	25	6941	2
3820	25	4754	2	5409	25	6968	25
3830	25	4804	36	5413	25	7002	25
3858	25	4805	3	5415	25	7006	3
3869	25	4806	3	5419	25	7009	3
3872	9	4807	36	5423	9	7010	9
3910	32	4808	3	5427	13	7304	2
3911	32	4812	3	5433	25	7305	2
3919	32	4816	9	5439	28	7306	2
3940	32	4818	9	5454	13	7307	2
3941	32	4819	3	5486	25	7402	18
4005	25	4839	37	5703	45	7404	18
4010	25	4840	3	5704	9	7405	18
4102	9	4844	3	5705	45	7407	18
4103	9	4845	25	5706	45	7408	18
4104	9	4848	25	5716	9	7420	18
4157	36	4850	25	5725	9	7603	2
4204	9	4851	3	5729	9	7641	2
4206	9	4855	3	5736	44	8255	3
4255	25	5026	14	5738	9	8268	3
4351	9	5205	25	5767	9	8602	3
4352	9	5210	9	5782	34	8610	3
4360	9	5220	9	5784	34	8675	3
4361	9	5221	9	5786	34	8810	3
4371	3	5235	39	5788	9	8840	3
4402	25	5306	3	5803	3	8852	3
4405	25	5309	3	5806	3	8862	3
4406	25	5310	3	5823	3	8863	3
4413	25	5312	3	5876	3	9003	32
4414	25	5313	3	6502	29	9004	32
4416	25	5317	9	6505	29		
4417	25	5318	9	6511	29		
4419	25	5323	3	6517	29		

Century Foundation, *Corporate Investments in Workers*, Website document, Policy in Perspective, 1999.

Colihan, J., and G. K. Burger, "Constructing Job Families: An Analysis of Quantitative Techniques Used for Grouping Jobs," *Personnel Psychology*, Vol. 48, 1995, pp. 563–586.

Cohen, William S., *Defense Planning Guidance, FY 1999–2003*, Office of the Secretary of Defense, Washington, D.C., July 2, 1997.

Employment and Training Administration (ETA), *O*NET 98 Data Dictionary, Release 1.0*, U.S. Department of Labor, Washington, D.C., 1998.

Fortune, "Wanted: Liberal Arts Grads," May 12, 1997.

Hecker, D., "High-Technology Employment: A Broader View," *Monthly Labor Review*, June 1999.

Joint Chiefs of Staff, *Joint Vision 2010*, Washington, D.C., 1995.

Landis, J. R., and G. G. Koch, "The Measurement of Observer Agreement for Categorical Data," *Biometrics*, Vol. 33, 1977, pp. 159–174.

National Center for Education Statistics (NCES), *Education and the Economy: An Indicators Report*, U.S. Department of Education, Washington, D.C., 1997.

National Center for Education Statistics, *The Condition of Education, 1998*, U.S. Department of Education, Washington, D.C., 1998.

O*NET Final Technical Report, Utah Department of Workforce Services, Washington, D.C., 1997.

Peterson, Norman G., Michael D. Mumford, Walter C. Borman, P. Richard Jeanneret, and Edwin A. Fleishman, *O*NET Final Technical Report,* U.S. Department of Labor, Washington, D.C., 1996.

Urban Institute, "Upgrading Work Force Skills," *Policy and Research Report,* Washington, D.C., Spring 1996.

U.S. Department of Labor (DoL), *Futurework: Trends and Challenges for Work in the 21st Century,* U.S. Government Printing Office, Washington, D.C., 1999.